# THE

# TRAUMA

# TOOL KIT

# THE
# TRAUMA
# TOOL KIT

## HEALING **PTSD** FROM THE INSIDE OUT

SUSAN PEASE BANITT, LCSW

QUEST
BOOKS

Theosophical Publishing House
Wheaton, Illinois * Chennai, India

First Quest Edition 2012

Quest Books
Theosophical Publishing House
P. O. Box 270
Wheaton, IL 60187-0270

www.questbooks.net

The author and publisher specifically disclaim all responsibility for any liability, loss or risk, personal or otherwise, that happens via a consequence, directly or indirectly, of the use and application of any of the contents of this book. The ideas, procedures, and suggestions in the book are not a substitute for consultation with a medical or mental health professional.

Cover design by Mary Ann Smith
Typesetting by Prepress-Solutions.com

Library of Congress Cataloging-in-Publication Data

Pease Banitt, Susan.
The trauma tool kit: healing PTSD from the inside out / Susan Pease Banitt.—1st. Quest ed.
    p.    cm.
Includes bibliographical references and index.
ISBN 978-0-8356-0896-1
1. Mind and body therapies. 2. Post-traumatic stress disorder—Alternative treatment. I. Title.
RC489.M53P435 2012
616.85'21—dc23                                                    2011041574

5   4   3   2   1   *   12   13   14   15   16

Printed in the United States of America

*This book is gratefully dedicated to two pioneers whose loving and wise courage in the medium of television has facilitated the healing of millions. Phil Donahue and Oprah Winfrey brought the reality of domestic violence and child abuse front and center in American consciousness, despite risk to themselves and their careers, by making public what clinicians were just beginning to understand—that vast numbers of people suffer from traumatic stress. Without their work, it is unlikely I would have ever healed enough to write this book. Thank you, from the bottom of my heart.*

# Contents

# CONTENTS

# What to Do in Case of an Emergency

---

IF YOU ARE CURRENTLY experiencing any kind of psychological or spiritual crisis, whether it be related to suicidal or homicidal thoughts, alcohol or other substance use, sexual abuse, domestic violence, high anxiety, or any other intense traumatic feelings, please stop reading and take immediate steps to care for yourself.

Call 911, your therapist, or a local hotline that fits your situation. Hotlines are usually listed in the yellow pages; or, if you have internet access, you can easily find them in your area with a quick search on Google.

# Preface

In the current state of the art of Western medicine, stress is a subjective event. We cannot peer into the psyche of a human being the way a cardiologist can examine the stresses on a heart by injecting dyes and looking at vascular function. We cannot predict the effect of a traumatic event on a person the way we can predict the effect of a gunshot on tissue. Yet, stress and psychological trauma profoundly affect the health of the human body as well as the mental, social, and spiritual functioning of the human being. Until recently, treatments of post-traumatic stress disorder (PTSD) and stress-related disorders have been woefully inadequate and poorly understood. I know this from the inside out, both as someone who has provided services over the past thirty-five years for those with traumatic stress and as someone who has suffered from it herself.

When I trained as a psychotherapist in the Harvard medical system in the 1980s, I was blessed to have some of the best teachers and supervisors in the fields of social work and psychotherapy. Dr.

Sigmund Freud's granddaughter, Sophie Freud, Ph.D., taught at Simmons School of Social Work. She was brilliant, open-minded, and unconventional, teaching her students not to rest on their laurels but to forge ahead theoretically, always incorporating new knowledge. Well-known psychoanalysts trained all of my supervisors. I, like almost every other student of therapy in Boston, was engaged in my own psychodynamic psychotherapy with a highly trained and qualified therapist. The people I trained under and worked with were profoundly compassionate healers with a great deal of knowledge. Their interest and study, however, was confined, for the most part, to the psyche or mind. Other parts of the human organism, such as the body, were not given a great deal of attention, much less more esoteric ideas such as the yogic energy concept of *prana* or the Chinese medicine correlate of *qi*. Traditional therapists largely left the concept of a spiritual self untouched, considering it the purview of religion.

At the same time interest in yoga was burgeoning, greatly enhanced by two facilities on the East Coast: the Kripalu Center, a yogic ashram turned training center, and the cutting-edge Omega Institute for Holistic Studies, cofounded by Elizabeth Lesser, author of the recently popular book *Broken Open: How Difficult Times Can Help Us Grow*. These centers focus on deeper and broader aspects of human nature, guided by the philosophy that healing is holistic in essence. They draw heavily on Eastern spirituality and philosophy for their workshops. I, along with tens of thousands of healers, attended courses at these and other facilities each year. We went to broaden our understanding of healing and, more importantly, to seek our own. Inevitably, what we learned at these holistic workshops seeped into our clinical practices up and down the East Coast, creating a surprisingly progressive atmosphere among the bastions of traditional psychotherapy.

David Eisenberg, MD, convened the first complementary therapies committee at Beth Israel Hospital in Boston in the early 1990s and began investigating mind-body medicine, following up on Dr. Herbert Benson's pioneering 1970s work on the connection between stress and disease in the human body. As an intern with a known interest in alternative medicine, I was thrilled to be invited to attend these early committee meetings. The surprisingly broadminded approach to medicine in the Harvard medical system left an indelible progressive mark on my work. Dr. Eisenberg went on to do research with the National Institutes of Health, conducting the 1993 landmark research survey that shocked the medical community, showing that US citizens were spending *billions* of dollars of their own money for alternative therapies treating a variety of medical conditions. Why, the experts wondered? The medical community was dumbfounded. The psychological community was skeptical but intrigued. Clearly there was a disconnect between what providers thought was helpful and what patients experienced as healing.

The last two decades have seen more research than ever on the connection of stress to illness, mind states to body results. Several recent studies have linked PTSD to heart disease, diabetes, and other prevalent and difficult-to-treat conditions. The National Institutes of Health and even the Pentagon have conducted studies into therapies as diverse as acupuncture, aromatherapy, and biofeedback. This openness heralds a new way of thinking in modern medicine and psychology, yet, for a variety of reasons, there is much resistance in mainstream medicine to researching these areas and getting the information out to the public or even to physicians. One of the obstacles to alternative care is that we in the West lack pathways of explanation for these modalities.

Eastern thought and philosophy has started to inform Western theories and practices of healing in the psychological community, largely thanks to the Dalai Lama, Thich Nhat Hanh, Pema Chödrön, and Jack Kornfield, along with many other prominent teachers. Scientists have even been researching the brains of Buddhist monks in meditation, trying to determine why the monks are so happy and seemingly stress free. Deepak Chopra and Ken Wilber have introduced ancient wisdom teachings of India, such as the philosophies of Advaita Vedanta, to the West. It is an exciting time, when so many wisdom teachers of all traditions have stepped forward to contribute to the alleviation of world suffering!

While some American researchers and academicians are just starting to give attention to these ancient systems of thought, others might note that Indian philosophy has long influenced thinkers and leaders in the United States. In *American Veda*, Philip Goldberg traces the profound influence that Indian spirituality has had on the American soul, starting with Ralph Waldo Emerson, through Thoreau and Whitman, and into the twentieth century via the Beatles, the cultural revolution of the 1960s, and the recent explosion of yogic teachings all over the country. I was amused recently to see that even my neighborhood Christian church was offering yoga classes in the mornings, something that would have been unthinkable a decade ago.

I separate my own clinical practice into two parts, before PTSD and after PTSD. From the beginning of my career I worked with highly stressed and difficult populations, including severely autistic teens, runaway youth, psychotic and violent clients, people diagnosed with life-threatening medical diagnoses, and victims of sexual abuse. Over the years I worked with adults and children in both inpatient and outpatient settings, in crisis and over the long term, in groups and individually. I thought I was compassionate and had a good understanding of traumatic stress. I kept up to date on the latest emerging information, which, in Boston's Longwood medical area, was a fairly easy thing to do. I purchased the best supervision money could buy (supervision is usually a weekly meeting with a more experienced clinician who guides one through the complex tasks of being a therapist) and completed my own therapy. I thought I understood PTSD and traumatic stress. I was wrong.

In my forties, I was shaken to the core with an eruption of PTSD from the bowels of my being. Nothing could have prepared me for it. The details are unimportant and possibly triggering to readers, so suffice it to say that family abuse issues were, in my case, the root cause. What I did not know, what I had not been trained for and could not know until I experienced it, was how all-encompassing, how *physical* the experience of PTSD is, and how long it takes to heal from it. The healing of one moment's realization took several years of intensive work on body, mind, and spirit. I now understood, in a visceral way, what the terms "nervous exhaustion," "mental breakdown," and "meltdown" actually meant.

I was blessed with the presence of amazing healers in my life. I was willing to do anything and everything to heal. Not only did I survive this PTSD volcano, but I have healed and thrived. I tentatively started recommending that some of my patients get acupuncture and naturopathic treatment and was surprised at how this smoothed out their therapy. I smudged, soaked, chanted, and sweated and then shared my knowledge about these modalities with clients. Like-minded patients started to seek me out. Together we laughed, cried, and moved them out of their PTSD with surprising speed. It was obvious that this hidden knowledge needed to be shared, now more than ever. One hour per week just doesn't cut it when you are in the middle of massive trauma! With the tools to use between sessions, people were healing faster than I had thought possible.

When I began this book, my mission was to provide a framework that allowed for the introduction of techniques and treatments that are outside the comfort zone of the Western mind, but nonetheless are potent and effective modalities for treating traumatic stress. I started to understand that we didn't have enough intellectual hooks to hang our hats on. We had no framework with which to understand, for example, energy medicines or wisdom practices as medicine because our view of the human vehicle was too restricted, too materialistically focused on the body. Mind, for most of us, is a vague notion of thinking, one we have not examined very deeply because we are all too busy. In our culture we are encouraged to use our minds for production, looking outward, but to heal in therapy we need to turn our minds inward, a task we are little equipped for, in part due to Western educational methods that teach us to look outward for answers instead of inside ourselves. Even our spiritual traditions have been suspicious of too much contemplation, as evidenced by the saying "Idleness is the devil's workshop" or referring to meditators as "navel gazers." We, as a culture, are often suspicious of stillness, of peacefulness, yet our frantic lives are stressing us out. Over time, as I delved into methods to heal myself and my clients, it became obvious that we needed a more complete, multidimensional description of the human being. Little did I know that it had already been done, hundreds, if not thousands, of years ago.

Over the years I have been part of medical teams that wondered what role secondary gain plays in people's complaints about traumatic stress, if there wasn't just a lot of drama and attention seeking going on. In the hospitals, especially, doctors, nurses, and even social workers were skeptical about the amount of distress some people seemed to experience around their diagnoses and treatment. Many times, too often, these patients were labeled in a negative way. They were seen as obstacles to the smooth functioning of the system due to their "excessive demands," and their complaints just seemed overblown. As I healed, I slowly began to realize that we don't understand. PTSD is not all in your head. It is a multisystem event. Just as you can't be severely physically injured without having mental and emotional consequences, you can't be severely mentally and emotionally injured without having physical consequences. Trauma runs both ways. The mind-body connection isn't just a nice, feel-good, New Age idea. It is a literal reality.

PTSD is a whole-body tragedy, an integral human event of enormous proportions with massive repercussions. We cannot patch it up in twelve weeks of counseling or with a pill or with surgery. Left untreated, it grows and morphs into a destructive beast that erodes the very fabric of wellness in the human being. It has the unique power to unravel body, mind, and spirit. From there, the erosion spreads into the relationships, families, and the very fabric of society itself, affecting whole cultures for generations to come.

I am writing this book to offer what I know, what I have learned (and am still learning) in my years as both a provider and a consumer of human services, as both healer and healed, in order to finally address the comprehensive needs in healing from PTSD and traumatic stress of all kinds. It is intended to be a reference guide, companion, and comforter in the process of healing. May it serve you well.

Blessings on your journey of healing,
Susan Pease Banitt, LCSW

*That which begins like poison, ends up like nectar;*
*and that which at first seems like nectar ends up as poison.*

—Bhagavad Gita

# Introduction

# The User's Manual

---

How is a human being like an appliance? Both need to be grounded to work. Although this sounds like a joke, it is not; it is a necessary truth in healing from traumatic stress. The human being is an amazingly intricate electromagnetic composite. Our brains emit different frequencies of electrical energy depending on the state we are in (alert, excited, meditative, etc.). Our hearts have a measurable electrical rhythm upon which our lives depend. Each of our organ systems emits its own signature frequency.

If we become too anxious, angry, dissociated, or spaced out, nothing we read or do will help us because our processing centers are "shorted out" and shut down. Our judgment may become impaired, leading to poor decisions. Yet, this state is the very one we might find ourselves in when seeking relief from trauma. If it describes you or someone you care about, please do not worry. This manual is here to help you calm down, get safely grounded, and maximize your ability to use the tools in your toolbox. (If at any time you become overloaded and need immediate

1

help, please turn to the "Tips and Troubleshooting" section at the end of this introduction for helpful safety information.)

Grounding, for humans, refers to the extent that we are "in" our bodies, calmly present, aware, and ready to respond. The more grounded people are, the more they can feel their own bodies, own their own thoughts, and have control over their actions. People who are grounded have an effective interface between their own internal world of thoughts and external reality. *Groundedness is not a value judgment. You are not a better or worse person if you are grounded.* Some endeavors require that we let go of the "ground." Healers, high creatives, and artists are examples of people who regularly enter ungrounded states. But in order to heal the body from traumatic states we need to get and stay grounded, especially because the experience of trauma encourages people to move their awareness away from or even out of their bodies altogether.

How can you tell if you are grounded? The best way I've found is to plant your feet flat on the floor in a seated or standing position. Can you feel the bottom of your feet? If you can't, you are probably not all the way in your body. Bring your attention up your body, scanning for sensation and awareness. If you have traumatic stress, chances are you will find an area that feels fuzzy or difficult to sense. If you have PTSD you may have large areas that are numbed out and dissociated. If you lose time, lack memories, or have discontinuity of thoughts, those symptoms can also indicate a lack of grounding due to dissociation. If your symptoms are severe, you may need to seek immediate professional help. In any case, if you know you have large amounts of trauma, take it easy with this exercise because coming into the body can also produce trauma symptoms.

To utilize this book well, and for your own safety, it is important that you remain as grounded in your body as possible. The first-aid chapter (chapter 2) has an extensive grounding section, but here are some quick ways to ground while reading this book:

1. Go outside and find a large rock, tree, or patch of earth. Sit on it, making a conscious intention to feel fully what you are sitting on.

2. Put a hand over your heart and a hand over your belly and breathe deeply, feeling the connections of your hands with your body.

3. Walk, allowing yourself to feel your feet on the earth, to feel the earth supporting you. If you can, picture the center of your feet opening like the shutters of a camera and send roots deeply down into the earth. If it is difficult to feel the connection by walking, try stomping (but don't hurt yourself!).

4. Pray. Ask for divine guidance, grounding, and strength. Have others pray for you. Be specific. Ask for the qualities and resources you need to come through.

5. Eat something, but not sugar or caffeine; those can have the opposite effect. Some people report that meat, salt, or root vegetables are particularly grounding foods.

6. Wash your hands or take a shower, being very focused on the sensation of water.

7. Look around you. Let your visual senses firmly anchor where you are. If you are in a flashback, affirm to yourself the objects around you that were not there at the time of your traumatic event(s). Stay present!

8. If you have access to safe animals, be with them. Physically be in touch with your pets. Horses can be particularly grounding.

9. Physical contact with another human being who is safe for you may be helpful. Sometimes human contact can be ungrounding if the source of your trauma is through some kind of touch. Otherwise, safe touch, like hugging, holding hands, or sitting closely while the other person is grounded can help you find that place of connection.

10. Aromatherapy. Find a pleasant, fairly strong essential oil that you can put in a diffuser or even just on a cotton ball under your nose. Historically, noxious smelling salts were used for this purpose. I imagine they are quite effective, if unpleasant! Rosemary and eucalyptus essential oils are good candidates. Young Living Essential Oils even has a blend available for purchase called Grounding.

Now, you may already have some favorites that aren't on this list. Go ahead and make your own list. The first thing we lose when we get ungrounded is our ability to remember what helps us! Post the list somewhere you can access it easily—like your medicine chest, refrigerator, first-aid kit, or car.

## OPERATING INSTRUCTIONS

In the Adhara[1] system of Indian Vedanta, we have a kind of unified field theory for the human being. Why is this important for healing from trauma? Trauma is such an all-encompassing experience and such a universal one that most single interventions are inadequate to address it. Over the years I have watched patients bounce between practitioners, interventions fail, and therapists implode with guilt and frustration over their inability to help deeply traumatized children and adults alike. There is no one pill, one class of drugs, one therapy, or one technique that can begin to address the multifarious nature of trauma. The Adhara system provides a profound template for healing in four ways:

1. It is understood in this system that the core of the human being is indestructible, eternal, and divine. This provides profound hope and a basis for healing for whatever level of injury has been sustained.

2. The human being is "unpacked" in an easy-to-understand system of layers progressing from the densest (physical) to the subtlest (bliss).

3. Unlike Western philosophical systems that tend to pathologize or belittle experiences beyond our understanding, the Adhara system provides a positive means to understanding the full range of human suffering and healing.

4. The Adhara system clarifies, beyond the shadow of a doubt, the necessity of multidimensional, multimodal healing from trauma. In other words, all parts of the human need to be healed in order to recover fully from traumatic stress.

Using the Adhara system as a framework, *The Trauma Tool Kit* contains multidimensional keys to healing from traumatic stress. It deliberately packs a lot of information into a small space. To some readers it may feel dense, especially if the ideas are new. For others, the concepts may be quite familiar. I encourage you to *take your time.* This book has been designed to help you heal. In order to heal, you need to incorporate new ideas. To incorporate these ideas, you will need to change your mind about some concepts of reality. As your mind changes, your body (including your brain) needs to change along with it. Because trauma takes us into some of the most difficult territory known to humankind, these changes can present some challenges along the way. In order to fully digest this material, adequate time, and rest between readings, is an absolute requirement.

Years ago I started reading the sacred text *Vasistha Yoga* and was surprised to find a warning in the beginning cautioning the reader to go slowly and not read too much at any given time. The reader was advised to read only one to two pages per sitting! As a typical Western blow-through-any-book reader, I found this advice a little shocking, and, honestly, in the beginning I ignored it. But as I paid attention to my mind I found that I could, in fact, only absorb a couple of pages in one sitting. More than that, and my mind would "fall out"; in other words, I would become sleepy, distracted, or overloaded.

Although this book is not in the same class as *Vasistha Yoga*, the principle is the same. Working in deep mind structures takes a lot of focus and integration. Before I wrote this book I recognized that the needs of people with traumatic stress were going to far outstrip the resources available to deal with trauma. There are not enough therapists to go around! So I designed a book that would not only put therapeutic tools in the hands of those who need them but also *act as a change agent in and of itself.*

The advantage of having an actual therapist is that part of the therapist's job is to regulate the pace of healing. We therapists push (gently and appropriately, of course) when people are stuck or moving slowly; we hold back and contain when people are racing ahead at an unhealthy pace. Obviously, this book cannot do that for you, so monitoring your own pace while reading is an important task. How can you do this? Well, start by paying attention to these factors while you read:

- How does your body feel before you read? After? Check in frequently with yourself. You could even keep a notebook or write in the margins (I won't mind!) to keep track of where you are in the process of reading. If you start to feel any symptoms of being triggered (headache, stomachache, dizziness, etc.) or ungrounded, *stop immediately!* Your body is signaling that something is "up" that needs to be dealt with. Figure out what it is, and then you can proceed. You may even need to stop and look up interventions to deal with what has been triggered.

- Is the material connecting with your actual experiences in day-to-day life? Ideally, this book will not remain an idea in your head but become embodied in the process of your healing. Intellectualization is a risk of any book. If you understand the ideas but nothing changes in your life or body, you may need to seek a healer in addition to the book.

- Notice when it is time to stop. You will know if you become sleepy, overwhelmed, confused, or have some kind of big reaction. A joyful feeling of "aha" is just as important as a feeling of irritation as a signal to stop and process. Both extremes and the range of affect in between need to be felt, integrated, and understood. The effects of what you have read will continue long after you close the book.

- Take one exercise at a time as you go. There are many exercises in the book. It is best not to rush through them. In therapy, we might dwell on one of these exercises for several weeks. Alternatively, read through a section and save an exercise for the end of your reading period or another time when you can give it your complete and fully embodied attention. You might get the most out of the exercises if you tape the descriptions, perhaps with lovely background music, and then play them to yourself when you are ready. It is hard to read and relax at the same time!

Most people feel they need to sit down and read a book from start to finish, cover to cover. This is not that book. As with any tool kit, you will want to look over the contents to find the right tool for the job. You may want to read the book in order, and it is designed with a certain structure that builds on itself for that purpose. Or you may want to comb through the detailed table of contents to find help with the particular issue you are working on in the moment. Or you can read it back to front, or start anywhere in the middle and work your way out! Even reading just one section might be helpful and plenty to digest.

## LETTING GO OF "SHOULD"

It would be easy to mistake exercises and instructions in this book for another list of things you have to do when you are already feeling overwhelmed. My intent is not to be burdensome but to ease your suffering! There is no "have to" here. Choose what works for you, but if the "woulda, coulda, shoulda's" keep coming up you might want to consider the following.

People often substitute "I should" for "I want." I call this the beginning of internal civil war. The minute you say, "I should," you have created division within yourself. "I should" always comes from others. Parents, rules, religious teachings, and cultural norms give us our shoulds. Not that this is necessarily bad. We do need to learn how to function in society in a helpful way. At some point along the road to adulthood, though, we need to internalize those ideals or discard them for good. If you say "I should," it means some part of you doesn't want to. Honor those parts! They have precious information for you. Let them speak to you fully, like a good council. Hear everyone's opinion, and then make your singular decision.

If you can say "I want," then you are coming from a more integrated place inside yourself. Try it for a moment: "I should clean the kitchen." Doesn't that just tighten your stomach and make you feel as though you don't want to? Now say "I want to clean the kitchen!" How does that feel different? When we say "I want to," we are taking complete ownership of our situation. No excuses, no resistance, no blame.

Sometimes "I should" is a habit of resistance to going forward. Many people say "I should" automatically to every task they undertake, while at the same time being resentful. This is like driving with one foot on the brakes. If your energy is tied up in inner conflict, you will have less impetus to accomplish your tasks and will reinforce the sense of being a victim. Lots of patients ask me, "Should I do such and such?" My reply is always the same: "What do you want to do?" When you know what you want, you know what to do!

## DISCLAIMER

Although this book is full of ideas on healing, *it is not prescriptive*. It presents a smorgasbord of healing techniques and tools for your perusal and personal choice. These tools are meant to help. *But there is no "one size fits all" for healing for anyone.* What is lifesavingly wonderful for one reader might make someone else feel much worse.

Let me give you a personal example. I had a meditation practice for years that was working well for me, until it wasn't. One day I sat down on the cushion and just felt like crying. From that point on, every time I started to get ready for meditation I would just cry. This went on for weeks. I felt that I "should" keep going and move through it, but, you know, I just couldn't. What I know now that I didn't know then is that this experience was the beginning of a deeper level of healing for me. I actually had to go away from my established meditation practice for a while in order to rediscover it, and this led to many vital realizations about myself and my history.

In other words, *do not force yourself!* If some modality scares you or doesn't work for you, don't do it! Or find a teacher or guide that can lead you to it in a different way. The answer for my meditation practice eventually came in a new teacher and a new mantra. *You have to empower yourself to find your own answers.* You, and only you, are the expert on you! Everything else is merely a suggestion, hopefully a helpful suggestion, but a suggestion all the same.

## TIPS AND TROUBLESHOOTING

Many different feelings and thoughts could arise during the reading of this book. If you are deeply engaged in your own healing, these feelings could become quite intense. Intense and intolerable feelings can become hazardous to your health (as some of you may already know quite well). Below, you can find a quick user's guide to possible urgent situations that might arise in this process. The key here is to *recognize and act on your symptoms.* Give yourself permission to get help as needed!

| Issue | Solution |
|---|---|
| Suicidal or Homicidal Thoughts | • Stop reading, breathe, assess for safety.<br>• If feeling persists, call 911, your local county crisis line,[2] your therapist, or a local suicide hotline.<br>• Tell someone: a spouse, friend, or family member you trust.<br>• Go to your local emergency room.<br>• *These feelings should always be taken seriously!* |
| Panic Attack or High Anxiety | • Put one hand on heart and one hand on belly below navel and breathe deeply.<br>• Turn to first-aid chapter (2) and follow directions for "Clearing."<br>• If feeling persists or escalates, seek immediate help as outlined above. |
| Urge to Self-Mutilate or Other Form of Nonlethal Self-Harm | • These feelings are actually quite common during intensive trauma work. Contact your therapist or a (preidentified) safe friend to stop from acting out.<br>• If you are practiced and confident of control, stop what you are doing and focus on self-care.<br>• Breathe, refrain from harm, and refocus on an activity that will nurture you and/or safely express your feelings.<br>• If feelings persist, feel uncontrollable, or escalate, seek emergency help as outlined above. |
| Dizziness, Spaciness, Vertigo, or Feeling as if You Are in a Vortex | • Sit or lie down.<br>• Drink some water or eat something.<br>• Turn to first-aid chapter (2) and follow directions for "Grounding."<br>• Resume reading only when fully grounded. |
| Intense Feelings Such as Anger, Sadness, Despair, or Grief | • Stop reading and give your feelings full attention.<br>• Create a safe space where you can ride the feeling to its peak, at which point it will begin to subside.<br>• Refrain from acting out on the feeling (i.e., this is *not* the time to confront your perpetrator).<br>• Allow yourself the time to express your feelings safely and with containment.<br>• Safely begin to release your feelings. If they feel endless, set a timer, and then do something else. |

11

| Urge to Use Substances or Engage in Addictive Practices | • Stop what you are doing. Pause and breathe.<br>• Become aware of your choice to use or not to use. *Think through consequences of each option.*<br>• Call your sponsor or therapist, if you have one, or a safe nonusing friend or family member.<br>• Identify what is driving the urge to use (anxiety, thoughts of self-harm, upwelling memories, and/or sensations), and then take action in the category as noted above.<br>• Read through the first-aid chapter (2), and apply what is most helpful in the moment. |
|---|---|
| Feelings of Toxic Shame and/or Self-Loathing | • Assess what percentage belongs to you and how much belongs to your perpetrator(s).<br>• Send the portion that is not yours back to its original owner or somewhere else (burn in fire, send into tree or to Spirit/God, etc.)<br>• Call a safe person. Isolation is not your friend here.<br>• Turn your attention to self-forgiveness.<br>• This state can be a kind of spiritual emergency. Call your chaplain, priest, or spiritual guide.<br>• Pray.<br>• Read scripture of whatever religion speaks to you or inspiring literature/poetry.<br>• If feelings escalate to suicidal and/or self-harming thoughts, take action as outlined above. |

## IMPLEMENTING CHANGE

Let's face it. Healing from trauma stinks (clinically speaking). But not healing from trauma can last a lifetime, and that stinks worse. When you are suffering from traumatic stress you are, by definition, stuck between a rock and a hard place. That is why I put the quote from the Bhagavad Gita at the beginning of this chapter. Avoidance is natural and can feel good . . . until it doesn't. The poisons of awareness and the pain of the healing process transmute to the delicious nectars of wisdom, peace, and freedom from traumatic stress. Isn't that worth a try?

So sit down with this book. Read it and then read it again, all, of course, in the doses you can manage. Your persistence will pay off. Keep your eyes on the prize of a healed life. You won't be the same as you were before your traumatic events happened, but who of us stay the same through a life anyway? Allow yourself to harvest the bounty of your experiences and live, as Oprah would say, your best life!

*Frodo: I wish the ring had never come to me.*
*I wish none of this had happened.*
*Gandalf: So do all who live to see such times,*
*but that is not for them to decide. All we have to*
*decide is what to do with the time that is given us.*
—*The Fellowship of the Ring* (film)

# Tool 1

# Road Map for Healing from Trauma

---

TRAUMA ARRIVES UNWANTED in all shapes and sizes. It can appear early in life or late. It can be as large as a country or as small as an individual. It can be sudden or cumulative, or both. Trauma knows no rules, no ethnic identity or age. It does not know when to say when. You can be at the breaking point, and still more trauma will come. Why? Maybe the answer is ultimately unknowable, but if we have encountered trauma we want answers. Many of the world's greatest texts, scriptures, and works of art owe their origin to struggles around this very question. Here's what is knowable about trauma and traumatic stress: (a) trauma is a universal human experience; (b) there is an endpoint to all forms of trauma; and (c) it is possible to recover fully from traumatic stress.

Post-traumatic stress disorder has been increasingly featured in the media, and it may be the disorder of our time. Legions of returning soldiers and hundreds of thousands of child-abuse survivors compose just a few of the ranks of those with PTSD. But, *you don't have to be*

15

*diagnosed with PTSD to be dealing with traumatic stress.* You might be in the first several weeks of recovering from a traumatic event such as a natural disaster, accident, sudden life change, or medical diagnosis. You may have been running beyond your capacities in a high-pressure job or lifestyle for years, and the effects are now catching up to you. Or you may have some symptoms of traumatic stress but not enough to qualify for a full-fledged psychiatric diagnosis. If you are reading this book, chances are you have come looking for some help with traumatic stress, either for yourself or for a loved one. What I would like to say to you, then, is congratulations. Congratulations for surviving and being alive, for reaching out for help and picking up this book. Whether you have PTSD or are struggling with chronic overwhelming stress, no matter how dire your life may be or may have been, it is possible to lead a healed, vibrant, and joyful life.

Traumatic stress entails a great deal of confusion, as if we were dropped in a perilous foreign land with no familiar landmarks and no map, all the while experiencing tremendous pain. Because of my own deep journey through trauma as well as my role as healer with traumatized people, the terrain of trauma has become very familiar, with reliable guideposts, paths, and stages. These stages are your roadmap through the experience of trauma. You can use these developmental steps to assess where you are and where you are headed or need to go. Depending on your progress, some of these may seem easier or harder, obvious or puzzling. You may feel overwhelmed at the length of the journey or resist certain steps (e.g., why should I have to be the one to forgive?). Not to worry. Do not fight your natural feelings; just notice them, and *keep moving forward.* When you look at a map, what is the first point you look for? Where you are going? Nope. You look for that You Are Here arrow. Once you know where you are and where you want to go, only then can you make your journey safely and without a lot of unnecessary detours.

Healing from trauma has a developmental path all its own with distinct stages of healing. Like other models of healing, these stages are not necessarily linear, progressing from one to another in order. In psychology we think of time moving upwards in a spiral rather than in the usual straight line. True healing consists in forward and apparently backward directions in healing called *regressions*. Regressions can feel like out-of-control backsliding, but they are really loops in the spiral that end up moving forward again and are universal to human development. For example, when a baby learns to walk, often sleep patterns that have been well established for months become chaotic for a couple of weeks. This behavior does not mean the baby has gone backwards in its development, even though regression looks and feels like that to the new parents. The baby brain is busy incorporating a new ability, walking. When the skill is consolidated, the baby will continue to progress in its development.

As you look at the stages in healing from trauma, know that, like that baby, you may need to go backwards (regress) occasionally to a previous stage in order to go forward again. Some stages may take a few months, while others can take years. Some manifest according to age and development. Certain stages may loop or overlap simultaneously. Healing from trauma is very individual. There is no one-size-fits-all approach to how people traverse this terrain. Because trauma involves the wounding of multiple dimensions within the human being, the stages of healing from trauma are also multidimensional. So, use what follows as a guideline. Nothing as complex as the human mind can be completely outlined. This roadmap is not supposed to be dogma. As you go through these steps, if they fit for you, great; if not, temporarily put them aside and focus on healing where you are.

The seven stages of healing from traumatic stress are, in the usual chronological order, trauma shock, rebooting, acceptance, feeling and releasing, integration, restoration, and forgiveness. These are not merely psychological stages but whole-body processes that unfold as one moves through the journey of healing from trauma.

## TRAUMA SHOCK

Trauma literally stuns the mind. When the mind can't accept what it sees, or when the amount of information about reality becomes too big to process, people go into psychological shock. Broca's area, the center of language in the brain, may shut down, rendering victims temporarily mute. You may have seen this phenomenon if you have ever come upon the scene of an accident. The victims are often staring off into space, unsure of where they are or what has just happened to them. They might be wandering aimlessly or sitting on the ground with their heads in their hands.

Trauma shock occurs in the immediate aftermath of a traumatic or horrifying event. Signs of trauma shock can include a fixed stare; a racing heart rate; a feeling of spaciness, dizziness or lightheadedness; incongruence between words and tone of voice (e.g., speaking in a monotone when describing the trauma); a feeling of being out of one's body; muteness; rigid bodily posture; and a deceptive calmness that belies the seriousness of the event. Trauma shock is not to be confused with the medical term "traumatic shock," shock that results from a physical injury. Trauma shock is a purely psychological mechanism that kicks in automatically, much as physical traumatic shock does. In a situation in which physical injury may have occurred, it is important not to confuse the two. Medical personnel can help rule out any physical traumatic shock to the body that can look like this first stage of trauma. Of course, physical shock should always be treated first.

It is easy to think that someone in trauma shock is all right. To the untrained eye, the victim can look calm, like someone in control of the situation, when nothing could be further from the truth. People in trauma shock have an almost locked-in feeling; they seem to have disconnected their internal world from their outer expression and being. They sometimes describe later how they were "screaming on the inside." People can also experience trauma shock as being numb, dissociated, or ungrounded. Trauma shock is like a system freeze or crash in a computer; one is overwhelmed with too much emotional data to process all at once.

Trauma shock is not well understood in our society yet. Recently, in Portland, Oregon, a suicidal man was shot because he did not answer a policeman quickly enough in the heat of crisis. To many psychiatric professionals it seemed obvious that the man, whose brother had just died suddenly, did not answer because he was in a state of deep trauma, but the police assumed he did not answer out of a dangerous resistance to orders, so he was fatally shot, a tragic outcome for all involved. Had the police had a better understanding of the mechanisms of trauma and how trauma shock affects the speech centers of the brain to the point of muteness or delayed speech, they would not have confused a traumatized suicidal man with a dangerous sociopathic one.

Ideally, trauma shock would last just long enough for one to get help and pass quickly. In some cases, though, I have seen people who were in mild to severe states of trauma shock for weeks, months, or even years. Trauma shock can occur at the time of the event but also in the future, whenever the trauma is retriggered. Many of the people who cannot move through the stages of healing from trauma keep getting stuck in trauma shock, a helpless and uncomfortable state of frozen numbness. The first step in releasing trauma shock is recognizing it. Just knowing you are dealing with shock will help to move you forward in healing, along with some techniques described later in this book.

## REBOOTING

If trauma shock is like a computer system freeze or crash, then the next stage involves rebooting our brain and functioning. Now there still might be some bugs in the system, but to carry on with our daily lives we need to get our brains up and running. How easily we do this depends both on the severity of the trauma endured and the number of previous traumas we have lived through.

In rebooting, we get grounded in our bodies and engaged in our lives again. We reenter relationships, but everything has changed. This time of reentry is delicate and fraught with hazards. Others wish to support us, but they have no clue what we have been through unless they are trauma survivors themselves. We often feel as if we are moving through an alien landscape even though externally nothing has changed. Our internal landscape has shifted so profoundly that we can have a sense of disorientation at this stage. It's as if someone has put an invisible 150-pound backpack on us and then encouraged us to move about freely. Easier said than done.

This changed landscape itself is traumatizing. Rebooting finds us in territory where we have the potential to feel challenged, alienated, and abandoned at every turn. We want to share our experience, but we don't want to see the look on peoples' faces when they hear our story. Some stories are so horrendous that those suffering from traumatic stress feel they can never tell them to anybody. We naturally want company (the human being is a social animal, after all), but feel it's hopeless. This feeling creates for many a secondary level of trauma, the trauma of disengagement, lack of functioning, and abandonment, sometimes perceived and sometimes real. It is not unusual for previously healthy relationships to fall apart at this stage or for people to lose their jobs or marriages.

When these secondary traumas kick in, sometimes trauma shock returns. I have seen many people who have been caught in a repeating loop of trauma shock and rebooting for years. If you find yourself in this situation, I want you to know that healing is possible. The way out is to move forward into the third stage.

## ACCEPTANCE

Acceptance is the most crucial and also the most challenging stage in the journey of healing from trauma. To understand acceptance we need to look at its opposite. What is the opposite of acceptance? Denial. What is denial? Simply put, *denial is the automatic and unconscious response of our defensive systems to protect us from information that would destroy our sense of the world and ourselves.* To fully accept what has happened to us, to embrace the trauma, means that structures of our self and our world need to go utterly away, possibly never to return. Denial protects us from unbearable loss, confusion, and intolerable anxiety, but it also puts us in prison and tosses away the key.

The process of acceptance can include recovering previously repressed memories, but it doesn't have to. For example, a victim of date rape might define her event as "having done something stupid," or an earthquake survivor might rationalize, "So many people had it so much worse than I did." This altering of reality, which can range from minimization to outright fantasy, is quite common in survivors of traumatic events. To come fully into reality and acceptance in order to heal trauma, a person might have to admit that a "funny uncle" was a pedophile, that a bomb dropped actually did kill innocent people, or that acceptable child-rearing practices never involve floggings. Acceptance always entails a shift in the current reality to one that is more horrible, if more real, than the reality of denial. No wonder it is so very difficult. Yet, without this acknowledgment and acceptance no healing is possible. Those unacknowledged traumas then remain locked within the body-mind, creating dysfunction and disease.

The horrors to which people are subjected and to which they subject others are literally endless. Humans are capable of every kind of barbarity and cruelty, and there is no era of history in which these acts have not been performed. When I used to work on an after-hours child-abuse hotline, every report of abuse in the entire state was funneled into our little room each night and weekend. Every time I thought I had heard it all, I assure you I hadn't. A person couldn't make those things up. Hearing twenty to forty stories of child abuse per night for four years, I did get to a place in which I wasn't outright shocked any more, but I could still be surprised at horrible variations on a theme. I do understand why you might not want to accept your story or tell someone else, but it is so important that you do so for your own healing.

Acceptance is particularly challenging when part or all of a memory has been repressed. What is a repressed memory? A repressed memory is simply a memory that has yet to be acknowledged in full consciousness. Cognitive psychologist Jennifer Freyd has been researching the phenomenon of repressed memories for decades at the University of Oregon. Her research shows that a memory is more likely to be fully repressed or dissociated when the victims were traumatized by someone who was supposed to be caring for them. She calls this type of trauma betrayal trauma. If you have been traumatized through abuse by a caregiver, especially if you were a child at the time, the acceptance stage can be a lengthy one. Be patient, and give yourself all the time you need without forcing the issue. Eventually you will know everything you need to know about your past; the developmental process of aging naturally aids in the recovery of memories. If your trauma stems from abuse by a caregiver, a therapist with extensive experience in betrayal trauma is highly recommended to help traverse this difficult terrain.

## FEELING AND RELEASING

Traumatic events, by definition, overwhelm our ability to cope. When the mind becomes flooded with emotion, a circuit breaker is thrown that allows us to survive the experience fairly intact, that is, without becoming psychotic or frying out one of the brain centers. The cost of this blown circuit is emotion frozen within the body. In other words, we often unconsciously stop feeling our trauma partway into it, like a movie that is still going after the sound has been turned off. We cannot heal until we move fully through that trauma, including all the feelings of the event.

If you are very young when trauma strikes, under seven years or so, the brain is still very plastic and malleable enough to divide and conquer. The visual image gets stored in one compartment, smell in another, the narrative of what happened in yet another, and so on. This separation is why it is so hard to piece together a memory from a young age or why it feels unreal. Patients will sometimes say that they see a snapshot of themselves in a traumatic situation they can't feel or that they are having flashes of intense negative feelings without any story or picture. In some cases children can completely dissociate from events in their history until years (perhaps decades) later, when memories tend to return. If you are older than seven years or so at the time of the event(s), the brain does not seem able to dissociate as easily. In that case it is very common for traumatized people to turn to substances (prescribed or not) for dissociation from unbearable memories and sensations. The result for both processes is the same: stuck memories that have never processed fully and safely through the body for release and integration.

The key to unfreezing, making sense of your history, and moving on in your healing is *feeling everything related to your traumatic event and letting the energy of that emotion leave your body forever.* Scary, isn't it? Many of us spend decades trying to avoid just that. The pain seems too intense to deal with. Some people feel they should be able to do this on their own, but I say, "Don't try this at home!" You wouldn't attempt a dangerous ascent on a glacier without assistance and instruction, would you? So why try to manage unmanageable feelings on your own?

Fortunately, society offers many resources to help us move through this difficult phase. *Although this phase can be extremely intense, it doesn't have to be lengthy.* What takes a really long time is *not* healing yourself; that feels like an eternity. Once you have fully experienced your trauma, it is as if the gates open and you are allowed to pass. Mission accomplished, lesson over. When you truly let your entire experience unfreeze and let the body go through the necessary releases, *you can never be traumatized by that memory again!* It becomes just another memory. I, and many others, have lived this truth. That is not to say this process is easy or for the faint of heart, but your efforts will be well rewarded.

Feelings to be processed include but are not limited to fear, sadness, horror, despair, guilt, and rage. For many people, rage may come last, when they finally know they are safe enough to endure that primal state without getting too unraveled. For others, and not to generalize too much, but often for men, sadness is the last emotion to be released.

Each feeling state deserves your full attention, and your body will accept nothing less. Even though the feeling-and-releasing process is often arduous and painful, *the relief afterward will be like nothing you have felt since the trauma occurred.* It is also not necessary to pull up every single memory from your past in order to release stuck emotions. As one friend put it, "You don't read every newspaper you recycle, do you?"

If you are determined to heal, life will provide you with the necessary support. A good therapist can be a great place to start in this feeling-and-releasing process, especially depth psychologists, who are highly trained. Other good resources for healing include chaplains and clergy (unless they are too triggering), depth workshops, shamanic practitioners, and bodyworkers. If you feel you cannot trust another person to help you just yet, this book is full of tools to help you in your healing process while you go solo. As a therapist and a client who has given and received much help, I am biased towards getting help in a relationship with a professional healer who specializes in recovering from traumatic stress.

## INTEGRATION

As you allow feelings to come up and move through your body, you may experience new aspects to existing memories or even memories you didn't remember having—the so-called repressed memories. Once the feelings of trauma lose their charge and hold on you, your next task is to integrate a new sense of your self, your community, and your life history based on your revised reality.

Sometimes I think the integration process can be even harder than releasing all of the old emotions of trauma (and those can be brutal). The integration period is often a time of intense grieving. I was struck by the comment of a colleague who said, "All trauma work is grief work," and while I do not totally agree, I get her point.

Nothing looks or feels the same after feeling and releasing trauma, after discovering your true self, your true history. This integration phase can feel devastating and disorienting, much as the original stage of trauma shock did. It can be one of those "relooping" points at which you could recycle through all the previous stages. If you do, remember you are in an upwardly moving spiral, and take heart! You will want to be careful not to get stuck in the stage of trauma shock and rebooting again during this phase, but to keep moving forward with integrating your experience(s) or, if necessary, processing again through all the preceding stages until you pull together all the pieces of your experiences into a whole narrative.

Sometimes, the integration phase demands action. It might be the time when you leave a job, file a lawsuit, leave abusive friends or family members behind, or take a new direction in life. You might press charges, start an organization, or write a book! Whatever you do in the integration phase, make sure you think it through carefully and honor the fact that you are still very much in the midst of a difficult and lengthy healing process. Be tender and patient with yourself, especially patient, for this stage takes some time. All this work has an enormous payoff: freedom from traumatic stress!

## RESTORATION

We are only now reaping the results of research that shows us what an unbelievable toll psychological trauma takes on the physical body (more about that in chapter 10). Incredibly, restoration is almost never talked about in psychological circles. The absence of this discussion may be a result of the mind-body split in modern health care. After completing the tasks of feeling and releasing as well as integration, the body itself needs healing.

Recent research has shown the profound effects of stress on what is called the hypothalamic-pituitary-adrenal (HPA) axis. The hypothalamus and pituitary glands sit within the brain; the adrenals rest upon our kidneys. Together these three glands are responsible for the state of our endocrine (hormonal) system. They mediate immune function, sleep, sexual desire, appetite, and overall stress response in the human body. Dysfunction in the HPA axis has been linked to such medical disorders as irritable bowel syndrome, insomnia, sexual dysfunction, obesity, alcoholism, chronic fatigue syndrome, and fibromyalgia. There is increasing evidence that heart disease also belongs on this list. Psychiatrically, HPA dysfunction is related to several major mental illnesses, including PTSD, bipolar illness, mood disorders, and some of the more troublesome personality disorders such as borderline personality disorder.

When the body has been subjected to prolonged periods of stress, recovery is required to restore function to the central nervous system and the HPA axis. After (and, if you can, during) processing through the first five stages in healing from trauma, it is time to turn to the body for healing. Many people manage to heal their emotional wounds but are unaware of the effects of lingering trauma within the body. With the rise of mind-body consciousness in medicine physicians are slowly becoming aware of this research.

Ironically, before we had such advanced pharmacology (drugs), people whose HPA axis gave way were diagnosed as having a "nervous breakdown," and they were sent to sanatoriums, beautiful and healthy places, to heal. They were sometimes given six months to a year or more to rest in a natural environment of extreme beauty and freshness, with all of their daily needs seen to by the staff. In our fast-paced culture, such a healing break seems almost unimaginable, but what if this is what the body requires? We cannot expect a nervous system that has been bombarded with corticosteroids from a stressed-out brain for years to recover and heal overnight.

Of course, very few people can afford to take a year off to heal, even without staff to bring meals and set out our lawn chairs. In lieu of such a setting, we still need to order our life in a way that acknowledges the depth of our healing. Just acknowledging that trauma is a *very physical phenomenon that affects the whole body* shapes our view of what is needed to heal. The body itself is a wondrous mechanism of self-healing. If we give it just a little nourishment and rest, it sets about repairing itself. Without the stage of restoration, our healing from traumatic stress will remain incomplete and set the stage for unwanted disease processes as we age. A substantial later portion of this book is given to restoration techniques.

## FORGIVENESS

Forgiveness is not so much an act of will as it is *the natural outcome of depth healing and safety*. Without safety, forgiveness is impossible and undesirable. Premature forgiveness can be a very dangerous situation indeed, leaving one open to possible revictimization. If you have not processed all your memories and feelings around the trauma you have endured, forgiveness is premature, like signing a contract without reading it. Indeed, if I may act as devil's advocate for a moment, holding a grudge may be the very thing that keeps people safe until they are able to complete their process of healing and recovery. But everything has its time and season; holding onto bitterness past its sell-by date will prevent you from moving forward in your life and experiencing all the joy and beauty life has to offer.

In clinical psychology terms, forgiveness has some notable differences from the concept of forgiveness in religions. In the Christian religions in particular, forgiveness can equate to absolution, the releasing of sins from the perpetrator. This understanding of forgiveness does not necessarily require the abuser to be remorseful or to make reparations. For people who have been severely injured, especially in betrayal traumas, this forced forgiveness is an obstacle to healing. Most people who have been severely injured want only one thing; they want their perpetrator to really "get it," and if getting it involves suffering, then so be it. The urge to punish is often the urge to make the other feel what we have been through. Underneath vengeful feelings, what we often want is validation, remorse, and empathy for our own experience from the offender, the one who created that experience.

Most victims of trauma via abuse want their perpetrator(s) to be held accountable. This natural desire holds great social value. Many positive changes have come about in society by people holding perpetrators' feet to the fire. Whether it is Nazis at the Nuremberg trials, cigarette companies that cost taxpayers millions in health care costs, or a neglectful governmental response to a disaster, providing meaningful and stinging consequences to perpetrators insures a greater level of safety for those who follow and benefits society as a whole.

Forgiveness embodies the final release of trauma. It does not preclude pressing charges or lawsuits, but insists on a fair resolution to utter horror and pain. Once healing has occurred and the scales of justice are balanced, however that happens for each survivor, then, and only then, is the time ripe for forgiveness. Although a natural process, forgiveness work often brings up the last bits of trauma that have not yet been fully given their due. If survivors cannot forgive, their work is not yet done. It does not mean they are bad or immoral people. Likewise, if some survivors forgive early on in the healing process, it does not mean they are saints. Occasionally very mature souls manage to do this, but in my experience, early forgiveness is more often an unconscious attempt to circumvent some of the more painful steps of healing. Can you see how tricky this can be?

What forgiveness looks like in the final stages of healing is a complete release of the traumatic event, the emotional effects of the event, and any need to punish the abuser(s). It is not necessary to wish them harm or well but merely to release them on their journey without any emotional charge. If you are a religious person this can look like turning them over into God's hands. If you are not religious, it is merely letting them drift away into their own destiny, one that probably does not have you in it.

Occasionally, a true reconciliation can take place in a process that is different from one-sided forgiveness. In reconciliation, the offending party recognizes what he or she did as wrong, understands the effect of those actions, and wants to make amends. *Reconciliation is not required for true forgiveness to occur.* When you are convinced that your offender is truly sorry and has healed his or her own wounds and you *want* to stay in a relationship that has the possibility of being safe and healthy, then reconciliation is a wonderful bonus to the process of forgiveness. Almost everyone wishes for reconciliation deep down, but sadly this is often not possible or desirable. It says nothing about you if you or the offending party do not want to or cannot move toward reconciliation. Do not take it personally; many people and institutions are too limited to move towards true healing. *And remember, reconciliation is not necessary for you to complete your healing through forgiveness.*

One of the things that causes many victims the greatest pain and shame is their love for their abuser, be it parent, lover, sergeant, country, or whomever. Every single traumatized client I have ever seen has struggled profoundly with this shame at some point in his or her recovery. This shame often interferes with the process of forgiveness, as if the psyche says, "How can I respect myself if I forgive that so and so!" It took years of deep work for me to realize that the way out of this dilemma lies within. We don't love our abusers because they deserve our love, trust, or respect. In many cases they do not. *We love our abusers because we **are** love and our love for them is inevitable.* We cannot help but love certain figures in our life whether they have earned it or not. This is nothing to be ashamed of but something to celebrate! When we realize that our love really has nothing to do with them but only with us, to accept our feelings and then let go or start from a new place becomes much easier. *We do not ever need our perpetrators to validate our feelings; we only need to embrace fully our own loving essence.* Acknowledging this fundamental love does not mean, however, that we necessarily return to a potentially dangerous relationship foolishly or prematurely. As a wise saint once said, "God is indeed in everything, but salute the tiger from a distance."

---

Now, go back over these stages. Where do you see yourself in the process of healing? Remember, you can be in two or more phases at the same time. Do not judge yourself about where you are on your journey. Adopting a nonjudgmental stance will help you immensely in the healing tasks ahead. Like Frodo in the epic *Lord of the Rings* series, many of us wish with all our hearts that our evil fate had never come to us, but what a fantastic story of survival and courage we would have missed if Frodo had not accepted his fate! The burden of our very real doom has arrived, and it is now up to us to choose how to respond. There is no neutral position in healing from trauma. We are either engaged in moving forward in healing or stuck in despair and dysfunction. Will we check out, give up, and suffer the consequences, or will we become the hero of our own journey and, like Frodo, cast that ring back into the fire? The choice lies before us.

*Something in me, dark and sticky,*
*All the time it's getting strong*
*No way of dealing with this feeling,*
*Can't go on like this too long*
　　　　—Peter Gabriel, "Digging in the Dirt"

# Tool 2

# First Aid for Psychological Trauma and Shock

In the first chapter we covered the roadmap for traumatic terrain in the body-mind, the developmental stages of healing from trauma. But, what if you or someone you know is in the middle of something big—immediate and terrifying? There is no time to call anyone, or help may be on the way, but your help is needed right now. What do you do? What can you do? Practical interventions for trauma shock fall into four categories: grounding, clearing, restoring, and altering/suppression. Some of the interventions below will be expanded in subsequent chapters. Use this chapter as the first-aid kit it is meant to be, providing ways to deal safely with overwhelming trauma and stress in the moment, when time is of the essence.

## GROUNDING

When the mind is assaulted by overwhelming events that threaten our feeling of well-being and safety, the body tends to go into lockdown mode automatically and becomes filled with overwhelming tension and adrenaline. The breath is held or becomes very shallow and rapid, which can lead to a feeling of light-headedness. These automatic reactions are part of the "fight/flight/freeze" response and are unconscious and largely out of our control—at first. If this breathing pattern persists past a couple of minutes, it causes a negative cascade of events in the body—one being the perpetuation of stress and tension. If prolonged for months to years, it can start to affect the entire circulatory system adversely.

Let us focus on breathing because you always have your breath with you. There are several breathing exercises that are immediately helpful to unlock the body's response of extreme tension and facilitate regulation back to a normal state.

## Circular Breath Technique

The beautiful part of this exercise is that it can be done anywhere and anytime:

*Sit in a comfortable upright position on the floor or on a chair or sofa: if on the floor, cross your legs or, if you are a yoga practitioner, place them in a half-lotus position. If you are seated on a chair or a sofa, place your feet flat on the floor. Gently and without force, inhale naturally and count the seconds or "beats" of your inhale. Most people can count six to eight beats, but more or less is fine. At the top of your inhale, the point when you want to exhale, hold the breath for the same number of beats as the inhale. This may feel a little strange or even uncomfortable, but it is an important part of the exercise. Gently exhale, again for the same number of beats. Do not force air out or blow vigorously; just allow the breath to exit naturally from your lungs. At the end of the beats, even if all the air is not released, hold the breath again for the same number of beats. I highly recommend counting to yourself throughout the exercise so you can maintain the evenness of the flow of breath. You may say to yourself: Inhale, 2, 3, 4, 5, 6, 7, 8, hold, 2, 3, 4, 5, 6, 7, 8, exhale slowly, 2, 3, 4, 5, 6, 7, 8, hold, 2, 3, 4, 5, 6, 7, 8 . . .*

This breathing exercise acts like a reset button for the nervous system. I have been with people in full-blown traumatic reactions and have watched them come right down out of trauma shock in seconds to minutes using this technique. The reason this exercise initially feels uncomfortable is that you are actively going against the physiology of your body in the moment to change the trauma pattern. At first the body will resist you, but you must persist to gain the calmer state. If the count pattern is too short or too long, alter it after *one full cycle*. The most important thing is to keep the counts even for all four parts of the breath. Continue until you begin to feel calmer.

## Belly Breathing

This exercise is designed to move from shallow (apical) breathing to deep breathing. If you ever watch a puppy or a baby sleep deeply, you can easily observe the rhythmic deep breath moving in the belly. We lose this natural state of relaxation as we mature and live more in the mind and less naturally in the body.

This breath has three distinct stages. You are going to imagine filling up the body with air the way you would fill a glass of water— from the bottom up—and then expanding the glass with air sideways, and then finally emptying the breath from the top down as if you are emptying the glass. It might be helpful to first practice each stage separately and then string them together.

35

*The first stage is to inhale into the lowest part of the belly. Of course air will not go into your actual stomach (at least not this way) but when the diaphragm, which sits under the lungs, expands, it feels as if it is pushing air into the belly. Ideally you would begin filling about two inches below the belly button. If you are a Tai Chi practitioner you will know this area as the* tan tien. *Most people have trouble sensing this area of the body, so begin by placing your hand lightly on your stomach directly over your belly button. Through your hand you can feel the movement of the belly. Now breathe deeply and intentionally into this space. If you are breathing deeply and correctly, you will feel your hand rise with the inhale and fall with the exhale. Possibly you are one of the many people who actually breathe in the opposite way: sucking in your belly as you breathe in and forcing it out as you breathe out. If you are, just notice it, pause, and try again to push your hand out gently with the inbreath.*

*The second stage is breathing the rib cage. Your lungs are, of course, surrounded by this marvelous bone structure, and in between and around the ribs are sets of muscles that move, expanding and relaxing with each breath. To get a sense of how this system works, sit with your back against a wall or solid surface. Some people breathe up and down, raising their shoulders with each breath (and creating a lot of tension in the process). You will want to get a feeling for breathing "sideways," expanding the ribs horizontally and relaxing with each exhalation.*

*The final stage is apical breathing, breathing at the top of the chest and lungs. It is the breath we automatically use when we are stressed or in pain and every breath hurts. We also use this breath to repress and manage intense feelings. The muscles of the chest and neck, rather than the diaphragm, are used to breathe in and out shallowly. Using this breath after the first two is like topping off. The three stages complete a full inbreath. Breathing out we empty the glass by pouring out the air at the top from the upper lungs, releasing held air in the lower lungs with the rib cage, and finally expelling the last bits of carbon dioxide–ladened air using the deep belly exhalation.*

This breath has the effect of replenishing fresh air in the lungs, getting us out of stuck breathing patterns created by stress, and forcing a relaxation response in the body. When this breath is used in the face of traumatic shock, it often has the effect of unsticking the emotional logjam. It is not unusual to weep, shout, or feel rage as the breath frees up emotions we have been deliberately or unconsciously holding in. Allow your emotions to unfold safely. Keep breathing through any emotional release you may be having. As with any exercise in this book, use your own good judgment about when the time and place are right for you to use this breathing technique, and make sure you have enough support for you to do this work. You may feel more comfortable doing it alone, or you may prefer the support of a partner, close friend, or family member who can be with you or talk you through this exercise.

## Progressive Relaxation

If you have taken yoga or stress-management classes, chances are you have already done this type of relaxation exercise. In addition to releasing trauma shock, progressive relaxation works spectacularly well with chest pain of unknown etiology. I have had patients experience complete remission of symptoms in two weeks when doing this technique as recommended. It works with the breath and the parasympathetic nervous system to evoke a profound relaxation response. I recommend doing this exercise one to two times daily, in the morning and/or the evening before sleep. You can do this in ten minutes or forty-five or longer, depending on how slowly you move through each body part. It is extremely effective and has been well researched. Progressive relaxation can also be used sitting up in an office, in a waiting room, etc. *Please do not do this exercise when driving!*

*Begin by tensing the toes and releasing. Imagine your toes are relaxing and getting warm and heavy. They are fully relaxed now at the end of your feet. Next feel your feet; if it helps, you can tense up the muscles in the feet and then release. Your feet are getting warmer and heavier. The blood is circulating and relaxing your feet, which now want to sink deeper into the ground. Next your ankles are getting relaxed. You can imagine warm water or oil being poured over them, creating a feeling of deep relaxation. Keep this dialog going up the body with specific body parts: calves, shins, knees, thighs, hamstring muscles, pelvis, lower back, stomach, middle back, upper back, lungs, heart, chest, shoulders, upper arms, lower arms, hands, fingers, neck, throat, back of the head, face, forehead, scalp, and so on.*

You may end up falling asleep in this exercise, and that is perfectly okay. The idea here is to unwind and dismantle the trauma tension piece by piece. If you are very traumatized and in shock, it may be hard to feel certain parts of your body at first. That is fine; just visualizing the exercise in the mind will have a beneficial and measurable effect. For an even deeper effect, you may want to make a recording of this exercise with favorite background music.

## Dissociating and Reconnecting

A universal aspect of encountering an overwhelming event is a feeling of disconnecting from your own body, which can be additionally distressing. People describe this state by saying things such as "I felt weird," "I couldn't feel my body," "My body was numb," "I was beside myself." Some people even describe out-of-body experiences.

There can be a sense that everything has become surreal or that you are in somebody else's story or in a movie or even that you are floating up in the corner of the room! Another name for this disconnection is dissociation. It is important to understand the dissociation as negative space; it's what isn't there. I used to have a patient who dissociated every time he tried to remember the word "dissociation"; he would laugh and say, "What's that word again?" I would have to name it for him every single time. But dissociation is no laughing matter.

A state of being ungrounded or dissociated is *one of the least recognized and least understood symptoms of trauma.* It is very hard to spot with the untrained eye because it is an absence rather than a presence. In contrast, other states, like rage or panic, are very easy to detect. Disconnection and dissociation can actually look like calmness, and the victim may seem to be managing well. Physical signs of dissociation can include, but are not limited to, a fixed or inward gaze, pupils fixed in a dilated or constricted position, a flattened affect (nonexpressive emotionally), sighing, shallow breathing, physical rigidity, and noticeably decreased or increased motor activity, the latter more common in children. Cognitive signs present as a sudden inability to process information—forgetting what one was saying or not understanding concepts one usually understands, losing the ability to concentrate, "spacing out," changing the speech pattern, becoming mute, or talking overly rapidly.

When you are ungrounded your reality testing will become impaired. Accidents can happen more easily because the perceptual system is not fully online. Judgment can easily become faulty because to have good judgment your feelings have to be switched on. We can only feel our feelings if we are consciously connected up with our body. More importantly, we can only begin to release the traumatic dissociation by moving feelings through our bodies. To respond effectively in any crisis, one must keep one's attention connected to the body, but in trauma shock the circuits are thrown and the mind and body temporarily disconnect!

Fortunately, there are many good ways to get grounded quickly and reestablish contact with your body, perceptual system, and judgment. But first, how do you know if you've dissociated? My favorite technique is to do a quick check by putting your feet flat on the floor. Can you feel them and their points of contact with the floor? Quickly scan up the body. Is there any area of the body you cannot feel? Can you feel your heart beating and your breath moving in and out? Can you identify your emotions? Can you feel body temperature, what kind of surface you are sitting on? I've seen people so profoundly dissociated that most of their body was numb, but not due to a physical numbness. Sometimes this state is accompanied by a feeling of internal coldness that no amount of heating up will fix. Doing this assessment is a grounding exercise in and of itself, because it brings the attention (and prana, or life force) back into the body.

## CLEARING

In a trauma crisis the body is overwhelmed and feels taken over by what Peter Levine, in his remarkable book *Waking the Tiger: Healing Trauma* has called the trauma vortex. In an emergency people feel as though they are in the middle of a swirling, disorienting, disturbing energy field. Sometimes this energy is so intense it can cause dizziness, nausea, or severe headaches. We can conceptualize this vortex as a trauma storm: a release of intensity around an event or memory that threatens to completely overwhelm the mind and body. Often people just retreat or collapse under the weight of such intensity. Even therapists can end up feeling helpless or traumatized secondarily by this storm. Fortunately, there are some quick ways to reduce the intensity of the vortex or storm people find themselves in when they are processing trauma. Many of these techniques originate from indigenous cultures, some of which have been around on the earth for a very long time. Later in the book we will explore the origin and history of some of these methods and why they are so helpful.

## Smudging

Possibly the best quick clear is smudging with sage or sweetgrass. It is traditional to ask God or Spirit to bless the plant before using. Some offer it to the six directions: north, south, east, west, above, and below. Take a smudging stick or break off a piece of dried sage (white sage is particularly potent) or sweetgrass. Light it, blow out the flame so it is smoking, and wave the smoke completely around the whole body: front and back, over and under. (It might be helpful to place the smudge in a fireproof bowl to preserve your carpet and your toes.) Sensitive people, including children, will feel relief instantly. Most healers I know use smudging on a regular basis for themselves, their clients, and their offices. Another technique is to crumple up a dried sage leaf, hold it before your nose, and inhale deeply; this instantly grounds the body and mind, with the bonus that to most people it smells really good!

## Mineral/Epsom Salts

Salt baths are designed to pull toxins out of the body, and they help provide relief from intense trauma toxicity, relaxing both body and mind. I have found Dead Sea salts to be particularly effective, but any genuine mineral salts will do, and pharmacy-grade Epsom salts can also provide some relief. Fill the tub with hot water, and put at least one cup of salts in the water. Soak for ten to twenty minutes. Too long a soak may make you feel drained. Occasionally people feel threatened by the bath or are worried about the amount of release from immersing the whole body, or they may not even have a bathtub. In that case, a simple footbath can also provide relief. Adjust the amount of salts used proportionately. If you use the footbath, be sure to visualize energy running down through the soles of the feet as described above in the grounding section.

## Sprays and Essential Oils

Some products are available that provide essential oil blends in spray form. Sometimes people make their own blends. Use these sprays the way you would use the smudge stick, spraying all around the body and in your living area. Traditional healing fragrances include lavender and rose, but any fragrance that appeals to you can provide relief—just be sure it is not a triggering fragrance that reminds you of your trauma. Essential oils can be put in baths, on pillows, and directly onto the skin for aromatherapy. You can also use essential oils with a diffuser for longer-lasting aromatherapy.

## Homeopathic Remedies

In the process of writing this book I interviewed naturopathic healers all over the United States, several of whom had worked in New York with 9/11 victims. They all agreed on two items that should be in everybody's first-aid kit at home: arnica montana and aconitum. These are available in natural health or food stores and online. They are over-the-counter remedies. Arnica is indicated if there is a physical component to the trauma—burns, bumps, bruises, sprains, etc. Aconitum is the remedy to alleviate the sudden shock of the experience and is good in a wide variety of situations such as car accidents, abuse, falls, shocking news, etc. Use as directed on the label.

## Tea

Chamomile is the hands-down favorite for a drink that is calming to mind and body. It is fine in a mix with other tea blends as long as the other ingredients don't increase agitation (as caffeine does).

## Flower Essences

Many alternative-healing practitioners have familiarity with the Bach flower essences and especially the famous Rescue Remedy, a blend of several essences especially designed to work with stress and sudden shock. These essences are dripped in drops or dropperfuls under the tongue or taken with a small amount of liquid. Favorites for trauma shock are Rock Rose, Sweet Chestnut, and Star of Bethlehem, although many other remedies are also useful. When setting up your pharmacy at home, you can use intuition and kinesiology or the prescription of a naturopathic physician to discern which remedies are right for you. You cannot hurt yourself with the wrong remedy. They can be blended into one bottle for greater ease of use.

## Herbal Remedies

These are best used under the supervision of a physician, either naturopathic or allopathic. They are more potent than homeopathic remedies and do have contraindications. Having said that, two herbal remedies are outstanding for anxiety and overwhelming stress. These are valerian and kava,[1] which come in a variety of preparations, including tinctures. Use as directed.

## Incense

Your favorite incense can be a wonderful antidote to help clear the shock of a trauma. If you meditate regularly with it, the incense fragrance will act as a stimulus for the conditioned response of relaxation even if you cannot enter a meditative state in the moment. At the energetic level, incense acts like a smudging agent, removing stagnant and negative energies. Popular fragrances are sandalwood, rose, and jasmine, but stock your kit with whatever you find relaxing.

## Water

Water is one of the most healing substances we have access to for grounding and clearing. Water can be utilized as a quick clearing technique in many ways. Showering, washing your hands, splashing your face, and washing your hair are all quick methods of clearing negative feelings and energies around your space. If you have access to a sauna or whirlpool, the combination of heat and water is particularly relaxing, especially when your stress doesn't respond to other means. Do you live near a clean body of water: stream, river, ocean, hot pool? Go! If it is too cold, just wade ankle deep and let the traumatic feelings empty into the pure water around your feet. It is amazing how many resources we have around us that we do not use when we need to. I recommend putting a reminder note in your kit about the closest cleansing water resource in your area. Tell your friends or family to take you there when you are overwhelmed.

## Journaling

Write, write, write! Let your feelings flow out onto paper from the depths of your being. Do not intend to share this with anyone, so that you may feel perfectly free to express yourself however you need to. Poetry, letters, or diary entries are cathartic and provide you with a record of what you were going through in your darkest hours. Sometimes we can let go of our difficult feelings when we know they are safely stored somewhere "for the record." They can also be helpful if you are in counseling. When it is hard to speak the unspeakable, you can always bring in your writing.

## Art

The same guidelines and benefits apply with art as with writing, except that art goes underneath words and is sometimes easier to express in dark times. Have an art kit ready and waiting with your favorite materials. One of the more helpful exercises for releasing traumatic stress by using art as a calming meditation is mandala design. On a blank piece of paper draw a circle. Your circle becomes your inner world on paper, with boundaries, yet without limits to express your true feelings as only you can.

## Induced Emotional Release

This aid is the emotional version of syrup of ipecac found in many first-aid kits to induce vomiting and expel toxic substances. Sometimes we need a little help getting our feelings out. If you think about it, you probably have a piece of music, a book, a picture, or a movie guaranteed to bring on the tears. Holding in the terror, the pain, the grief, and the sadness is a form of suffering in and of itself. When you are ready, set a safe place and time to go into your feelings and release them with your aids. Sooner rather than later is best! I recommend setting a time limit for this catharsis to provide a safe container for your experience.

## The Talking Cure

Freud famously proclaimed that talking was the cure for traumas, hysterias, and neuroses. Now we have the research to show how true that is. For instance, we know that women secrete oxytocin, the relaxation hormone, even in nontraumatic discussion, when talking casually with friends. The brain continually organizes experience through verbalization. It is important to tell one's story many times until the experience is fully integrated and worked through. Some people have even made a career out of telling their tragic stories repeatedly. Find a friend, a beloved one, and/or a counselor to confide in. Make sure that person knows he or she doesn't have to "fix" you, just to be present and hear your story. Everyone I have met who has fully healed from trauma has had to process through talking for hours at some point. Now, if you are a sensitive person, you may be aware that telling your scary or overwhelming story might be scary or overwhelming to your listener, and you might not want to tell even your closest friends initially. If this is your case, hire someone professional—a licensed therapist or counselor—who is trained in this sort of listening and has support in place to handle hearing people's difficult stories. If you feel you cannot afford a counselor, there are many wonderful hotlines you can call to talk with people who are highly trained in crisis and stress management.

## RESTORING

The third category of the first-aid kit is restoring or energizing. It is not a category that we Americans are good at! We always want to do something about our problems, which is fine, but sometimes we need to do nothing and allow the healing processes in the mind and body to do their work. After grounding and clearing, restorative practice is especially beneficial to allow the body to recover and integrate from stressful experiences. As mentioned in chapter 1, in days gone by someone who had what used to be known as a nervous breakdown, neurasthenia, or a weakness of nerves, was sent to a sanatorium at a beach or on a mountain where fresh air and total rest were the cure. Due to the advent of modern medicine and pharmaceuticals and their associated costs, we no longer prescribe these health stays as part of medical treatment. We may have thrown out the baby with the bathwater here. Many of these treatments have been extraordinarily effective over time, as evidenced by the popularity of spa stays today.

First, when you are in the middle of your emergency, you need to give yourself permission to stop and drop everything possible. I have seen people in ungrounded states of traumatic stress try to push through their regular schedules with harmful results; I have done it myself. I once fell down a flight of stairs because I had not recognized how weak and ungrounded I had become. I didn't notice that I didn't feel my feet until I was lying on the garage floor (fortunately wounded only in my pride).

So, call in sick to work. Yes, I know mental health days aren't allowed. Too bad! Call in sick anyway; your health depends on it. I call it the emotional flu, and this is exactly how it feels. Your boss won't give you permission; you have to give yourself the validation and permission to deal with crisis. Flu knocks you involuntarily off your feet, and no matter what you do it has to run its course. Crisis or trauma has the same mechanism. It has to be metabolized in its own time, and, as you will see later, it is a very physical process indeed. When it comes to traumatic stress, a stitch in time really can save nine. Please don't let yourself become completely unraveled.

## Mauna

Yoga and other spiritual traditions have a practice to build power and life force that is used from a few days on retreat to several years, depending on the needs of the practitioner. That practice is silence, total silence, and it is called *mauna*. It is a commitment to refrain from speaking out loud. In a crisis mauna can be one of the most powerful restorative practices you could use.

How do you practice mauna in today's society? In a crisis, it could be part of your mental health day. Turn off your phone. Let everyone close to you know what you need, to not speak today. Wear a little badge if you need to as a reminder. At some retreat centers silent retreatants wear a badge that says something like "In Loving Silence." This does not have to be an unfriendly silence. It should not be punitive but peaceful. If you have to communicate, try writing instead. Of course there are situations in which one must talk in order to be kind; mauna is not an exercise for you, for example, if you are caring for little ones. If you need to remove yourself to maintain a friendly silence I strongly encourage you to do that.

What about texting, emails, etc.? As long as you do not use your voice you will get a certain amount of rest. If you restrain your outgoing communications of all types you will get even more. Maintaining silence is an exercise in conservation of energy and of personal power and strength. Even practicing it one day will bring noticeable results. You may find that as a result of crisis you do not even want to speak or feel capable of speaking. There are several famous cases of individuals losing their power to speak or choosing not to speak after trauma. Maya Angelou describes in her moving and beautiful book *I Know Why the Caged Bird Sings* how she did not speak as a child for several years after a traumatic incident. She emerged from her silence as one of the most brilliant writers and poets of our time. If you are caring for someone who has been through something traumatic, it would be good to let that person be in silence when silence is needed; this approach is counterintuitive for many healing practitioners.

## Retreat

What is the difference between a vacation and a retreat? Vacations can be splendid and exhausting affairs full of must-dos and excitement. I love vacations, but if the order of the day is restoration, I highly recommend a retreat. The word *retreat* means to withdraw, or alternately a quiet or secluded place to rest and relax. Retreats can be but do not have to be associated with a religious or spiritual group. They can mean going away or setting up a tent in your backyard. When you are facing overwhelming stress or trauma, give yourself permission to withdraw from the world for a time: a day, a week, a month, whatever you can manage. Go somewhere lovely and nurturing where you can tend to your needs and rest. Whatever amount of time you think you might need in terms of a break, double it to get closer to what you could benefit from the most.

## Sunbathing

Many, many of my clients over the years have touted the benefits of being in the sun when stressed. There is some speculation about the pituitary gland being activated and balanced in sunnier climates. I do not know about that, but I do know that cultures have used sunny, warm locations for vacations and healing retreats from time out of mind. If you go out in the sun, please use adequate sun protection and check with your dermatologist if you have any history of skin cancers in your family.

## Nutrition

When you are in immediate need of restoration after a trauma, what you take in becomes supremely important for restoring your physical strength and life force and potentially in helping balance neurotransmitters. Your body will benefit from easily digestible food loaded with nutrition and kindness—the proverbial chicken soup. After encounters with dementors (soul-sucking demons) in the Harry Potter series, young witches and wizards must eat chocolate. We Muggles also gravitate towards chocolate and other sugary things when feeling poorly. This is natural, but not always helpful. Juicing can be of great benefit, as can salads and soups. You may not feel like eating healthily, but few things are more restorative than good nutrition eaten with a beneficial attitude and supportive company!

**Water**

Water is the lifeblood of this planet. It is the only substance in two categories because it is so powerful and important. Drink plenty of water to restore and nourish yourself after a time of crisis. Pure, blessed, filtered water is best!

**Sleep**

Sleep is the ultimate restorative therapy, and according to recent studies none of us seem to be getting enough of it even in the best of times. Your body has had quite a shock with the stressful event(s) it has been through; it needs to rest. Give yourself permission to sleep during the day. If you can fit a cozy chair or sofa in your office, you could nap for ten to fifteen minutes at lunch instead of fitting in a couple more chores. Now more than ever, be sure to get to bed on time. If you are having trouble sleeping, see your therapist or a physician.

**Visualization**

Have you ever been somewhere beautiful? Can you remember a time when you felt perfectly safe, loved, or relaxed? Have you ever read about such a place or seen it in a movie or television show? If so, you can revisit this place time and again in your own mind. The body follows the mind. If the mind is engaging in relaxing thoughts, the body will relax. If the mind has tense thoughts, the body will tense up. When you are in a state of shock or crisis, imagining yourself in a better, more beautiful, and peaceful place can be helpful. Ask yourself questions: What does this place look like, smell like? What is the temperature, the weather? What do I want with me—humans, animals, plants? How does my body react to this place? What are the sounds around me? The more you can anchor the visualization with sensory imagination, the more profound the effect. Some people spontaneously visualize when they are stressed. Be careful not to dissociate when you do this exercise, and take care to make sure you are truly in a physically safe place before you unwind with visualization.

## Meditation and Prayer

There are many ways to meditate, many forms. Some people are afraid of meditation or think it is against their religion. Meditation should always be peaceful, never against your beliefs. Praying the rosary can be a kind of meditation, as can repeating the kaddish or any prayer. During a crisis is not usually a good time to begin your first meditations; on the other hand, maybe it is the perfect time! For those of you who want to learn to meditate, some instruction will be given later in the book. I highly recommend meditation as the best stress-busting tool there is; it is never too late to begin learning. If you are already a practitioner, there is no better friend in a crisis than your meditation skills. As one of my teachers used to tell me, "Don't forget to remember!" It is easy to forget our skills when we are in shock or trauma. Remind yourself that you have skills and now sit down and go deep within using whatever meditation practice feels best to you in the moment. You will be guided to exactly the right practice for you.

### Personal Time

Many people already have rituals of restoration: lunch with friends, a hot cup of tea, walks with their dogs, and so forth. In a crisis you may need to remind yourself about what it is you do to restore yourself. I recommend writing it down. You may not feel like engaging in normal activities or they may feel useless or trivial. Try to stick with them anyway. What has worked for you in the past will likely work for you now. You may not feel like yourself for a while, but you will benefit from this self-care. A note of caution here: some people engage in activities they think are restorative but are actually depleting. Really heavy workouts, parties, or too much of anything may be draining at the moment. You will know if you are in a draining or restorative activity by how you feel afterward: renewed or depleted. Honor where you are; rejuvenate yourself slowly, and you will be able to again take life at your own pace.

## ALTERING AND SUPPRESSING

Even though altering and suppression are usually what people (and often practitioners) want to do first, I have put them here, last. Grounding, clearing, and restorative practices all work directly with the trauma and healing energies in the body to facilitate a more natural and complete healing, especially in the early stages. When you are having trouble functioning in spite of these practices you may want to turn to activities or substances to bring relief of your very intense suffering. Some of these interventions can be very helpful (and legal), others not so much. Just as aspirin makes the headache go away but not the cause (e.g., low blood sugar, tension), these activities or substances provide temporary relief but do not work with healing trauma directly; you will still be left with the work of healing after your symptoms are ameliorated.

## Television

The first place people are likely to go to restore themselves is in front of their television sets. Television is not restorative; it is entertainment or information. What it does help us do is to interrupt our thoughts (which can be stressing us very much) and put our brains in a slightly hypnotic state, one that makes us more suggestible than normal. Watching television is not restful for the brain and nervous system. In a crisis state, though, there can be something very soothing about it. Of course, some programming is more helpful than others. Watching *Planet Earth* has a much different effect on the central nervous system than does watching *CSI: Crime Scene Investigation*; watching ballet is different than watching basketball (especially if your team is losing!).

Watching television is a lot like dreaming. If you are watching an exciting show, your nervous system is getting stressed whether you are enjoying yourself (and your show) or not. Your body believes your brain to a certain extent. Recent research from the aftermath of 9/11 suggests that you are adding to your stress if you watch coverage of disasters or calamities continually. (A few minutes seem not to have much effect.) After several hours you will be processing these images in the dream state, which reflects additional stress to the body-mind. You can't choose your dreams, but you can choose what you "dream" on television or even on the Internet. If you feel you need the distraction of media, choose a good dream for yourself, one that will make you feel better and uplifted as opposed to more scared and depressed. Laughter is always good as long as it is not triggering.

## Herb-Seeking Behavior

When animals are sick or stressed they naturally seek relief. We have all observed cats, dogs, horses, or other animals eating unusual foods, presumably to help them feel better. It is natural for us to do that too. Unfortunately the readily available "herbs" or substances we have at hand are often not the best choices for our fragile constitutions. At best there is temporary relief; at worst we can really mess up our regulatory systems and create an additional problem of addiction.

I work in Portland, Oregon. Unlike my colleagues' experiences in other states, my experience has been that very few of my clients here wish to be on medication, that is, legal medication. A rather large number of people are using marijuana to self-medicate out of anxiety and trauma states, and there seems to be a widespread belief that pot is safer and more natural than "big pharma" medications. Pot certainly is cheaper and more readily available than other medications for people who may not have health insurance. The problem with using pot for stress management is that so far the latest meager research shows that marijuana ends up making people feel more anxious and paranoid rather than less over the long term (much to the disappointment of the researchers). There is, of course, also the problem of its illegality.

Having said that, I'd also like to share that in my clinical practice, and anecdotally across the country, many people report a high degree of relief of PTSD symptoms from marijuana without the troubling side effects of other pharmaceuticals. In some states it is possible to get a medical prescription for using marijuana to treat PTSD. We simply do not have conclusive research on the efficacy of marijuana. At the time of this book going to press, many studies that will do just that are being proposed and evaluated. Stay tuned.

Alcohol, on the other hand, is legal. It is also cheap and plentiful and does not require a prescription. Getting drunk or "taking the edge off" will at best bring a temporary dulling relief, but it has its price. Alcohol is a depressant and disrupts the sleep cycle. There is the risk of misuse and addiction, and when you sober up you still have all your problems staring you in the face. *Alcohol is not the drug of choice for extreme stress or trauma.*

Caffeine is popular here in the Northwest and elsewhere. If you have experienced overwhelming stress, your adrenal glands have already been put into hyperdrive. Fueling yourself with caffeine is going to exhaust your adrenals further, leading to cycles of lower and lower energy. Use sparingly if at all! Ditto for sugar.

## Pharmaceutical Relief

If you are really overwrought and in that place where your system cannot wind down without help, please know there are safe options. Effective interventional medications need a prescription from a licensed physician. Sooner is better than later. As with pain management, you don't want to wait until you are way over your threshold or what you can cope with. Extreme stress can be well managed by medication until you are in a more advanced stage of healing. Do not hesitate to use the emergency room or your local crisis team as needed. Otherwise you can go to your primary care physician, psychiatrist, or licensed nurse-practitioner to get a medication evaluation and prescription. Your physician is likely to prescribe beta-blockers, a form of relaxant or antianxiety medication, an SSRI (selective serotonin reuptake inhibitor) antidepressant, sleep medication, or some combination of the above.

As with the above therapies, cultivate awareness of how these substances make you feel—whether they are helpful or not, whether you feel you need to reduce or increase the dose, whether you experience unusual or unpleasant side effects—and communicate any concerns to the physician right away. Most people have an excellent sense of how they respond to medication. Your feedback is the single most important diagnostic tool your doctor has when it comes to antianxiety medication. Please resist the temptation to borrow someone else's medication. Besides being illegal, this is a very dangerous practice that can result in addiction, coma, or death.

**Exercise**

Exercise has an altering effect on our brain and central nervous system. Most of the time this effect is very beneficial, helping us to oxygenate our blood, release stress in our muscles, and release endorphins in our brain that contribute to a feeling of well being. After a significant amount of stress or trauma, there may be physiological changes in the body that make our systems respond differently to exercise. In working with post-traumatic stress disorder, I have seen some people who previously liked exercise develop a sudden intolerance to it. Perhaps this reaction manifests because exercise can stimulate the fight/flight/freeze response, revving up a system already on high alert. I know of at least one case in which a panic attack was induced through strenuous exercise. My recommendation in the early stages of coping with trauma shock is to take it easy. Do not push yourself. Gentle, consistent exercise—activities such as walking, yoga, and swimming—can be very helpful and help the body regulate itself. Intense and/or competitive sports should be engaged in cautiously if at all until you are past the crisis phase of the event.

-------

If this information is familiar or evokes the "duh" response, it is because, yes, much of this first aid is common sense or forgotten folklore. Depending on your age and cultural history, some of this information may be very new to you. In our fast-paced culture we often do not give ourselves the permission we need to take good care of ourselves, even when we know what works. The tendency, heightened by American cultural values, is to be stoic, to minimize what we have been through, or to rationalize it. Rarely do I see people who overemphasize the horrendous incidents they have lived through. This tendency of minimization is not helpful to our minds, our bodies, or those around us. I encourage you to give your experience its full due. Be fully present with your suffering and with what you need to do to take care of it, thus minimizing the harm to yourself emotionally and physically. And keep your first-aid kit fully stocked in a prominent location.

*Fire cannot burn it, water cannot wet it,*
*wind cannot dry it, weapons cannot shatter it.*
*Eternal, unborn, it cannot die.*

—Bhagavad Gita

# Tool 3

# The Treasure
# at the Core

---

YEARS AGO A YOUNG WOMAN found her way into my practice. She had a tremendous abuse history, first discovered at age two when she was found wandering the streets and was placed in foster care. For the rest of her childhood she bounced between home with her heroin-addicted prostitute mother and sociopathically violent, unimaginably abusive father, foster homes, and, eventually, residential group care. In addition to suffering from every form of child abuse, she had her integrity and safety repeatedly violated by the institutions that were supposed to help her. As a teen she had a very serious suicide attempt that would have completed if she had not been found in time. She was referred to me as a last-ditch attempt to keep her out of prison. As I slowly got to know her history, I was amazed that she was still alive. In those fragile first years of therapy, she sometimes missed as many appointments as she kept. I often did not know if she would show up or even if she was alive, due to her very risky lifestyle. Early on, I had to prepare myself that this was a patient I might lose. Everywhere we went in therapy seemed to be dangerous. Every topic was laden with trauma. I had never encountered so many roadblocks with a patient. It was clear that she was nowhere close to being ready to do trauma work or even regular psychotherapy work; there was nowhere safe to land, no topic that was not dangerous. Except one deep place.

This client, despite her horrendous childhood and the extreme abuse she suffered, had a keen interest in spirituality. She felt the numinous and essential goodness of creation in stark contrast to her personal history. Whenever we discussed spiritual matters, she would relax, her eyes would brighten, and she came alive. Although raised Christian, she did not have a rigid set of beliefs. In that first year, she came in one day with the book *The Tao of Pooh*. In an unorthodox move, we decided to let go of anything resembling traditional therapy and plunge into spiritual exploration together. We discussed everything from Buddhism to Vedanta, the Tao Te Ching to Christianity. She would go to her local bookstores and copy pages of mantras (spiritual chants) from different texts, which she would paste all over her room along with affirmations. She built an altar, a living focus for her spirituality that sustained and nourished her soul. Although she had only a high school education, she read voraciously about chakras, crystals, Buddhism, the Hindu gods and goddesses, intuition, and reincarnation, as well as the works of Nietzsche. She had a great love for Jesus.

One black, rainy Portland evening, on her way to therapy, my patient became uncharacteristically lost. After driving around, she found herself back at her old residential school in front of a statue of Jesus. She stood in the dark and pouring rain, crying and connecting. Shortly afterward, she came in and showed me her new ink. Tattooed over her suicidal wrist scars were the Hebrew words for "the blood of Christ." This creative act of affirmation marked a turning point in her healing. She now felt ready to embark on the road of more traditional therapy. From that moment she was able to begin to tackle her trauma and her dysfunction. Slowly, she began to work her way towards a life she wanted.

What this patient began to realize was that there was a place inside her that was whole, a place that was never hurt or raped or wounded, a place that exists through and outside of space and time. Together we found that place over and over again, the core beneath the core. In standing upon and identifying with this spiritual place of depth, she grew the ability to work with the level of her personality, *because it was not her only identity.* When I sat with her, I saw her as the undying eternal Being of light that she is, that we all are. Nothing, no person and no experience, could take that away from her. Since then, this client has done much hard work, as we all must do to move on from trauma. In her worst moments she has been able to come back to the touchstone of her deepest whole self, her spirit, and draw sustenance from that connection to continue her journey.

## THE DEEPEST WOUND

Trauma wounds us in our deepest sense of self. Trauma victims often feel that they have lost an essential part of themselves, that they are wounded to the core and fully broken. The sense of devastation is so extreme at this stage that people can feel life is no longer worth living or, conversely, that others' lives are meaningless and worthless. Some have described traumatic states as not so much a wound of the soul as a loss of soul, a fragmentation or destruction of self so complete that it is as if essential parts of the personality die or go into permanent hiding.

The language of trauma reflects this feeling. Some common phrases people use to describe themselves after a horrible event include:

*I feel like an empty shell.*
*I'm shattered.*
*I'll never be the same.*

In many ways the experience of psychological trauma is ineffable. For those who have been traumatically broken, no words are necessary to communicate the experience. For those who have not experienced trauma, no words are sufficient. Many survivors of traumatic experiences turn to art or poetry to communicate their feelings. Prose addresses the mind, but art addresses the soul.

But, what is this soul that we so vitally need to express in times of trial, this deep self we look for or feel that we have lost? In his remarkable book *Mindsight*, Daniel Siegel, a psychiatrist and neurobiologist, describes a brain-injured patient whose injury prevented her from feeling her essential sense of self, which in turn had a profound effect on her family. Trying to describe how her traumatic brain injury had disabled her in a car accident, she finally said, "I suppose I'd say that I've lost my soul."[1]

In this moment, Dr. Siegel had an epiphany about the role of the brain in self-development and self-recognition. He recognized that this patient had been damaged in her middle prefrontal cortex and that this damage correlated with her lost sense of soulfulness, the loss of her sense of self. According to Siegel, this part of the brain serves nine important functions: regulation of body functions, modulation of emotions, attunement to others, the ability to respond with flexibility to our environment, modulation of fearful responses, insight, intuition, morality, and empathy. He came to the awareness that these nine functions are soulful functions, functions that all religions and spiritual practices seek to address.

Yet, as profound as these insights are, some of us may be uncomfortable with the reduction of soul to a section of the brain. We may wonder if there isn't an even deeper, subtler structure, one that fundamentally persists even in the face of severe brain damage, disability, or even coma. After all, the woman Dr. Siegel describes is still essentially herself under duress, even if she can't feel herself as herself, even if she behaves in profoundly different ways. She is still there. Her personality has changed but perhaps her "suchness," as the Buddhists might call it, hasn't. Who is the subject in that patient that is able to observe and report on her own personality changes? What is the essence of that person? What is the core beneath the core? Is it our soul, our self, or something else?

## The Core beneath the Core

The idea of a core beneath the core has been given many names in many times and cultures. Recently in Western thinking, Freud conceptualized an "observing ego," the part of the mind that is a nonparticipatory observer. He considered the development of this awareness a key to healing from psychological stress and dysfunction. Western yoga practitioners have an almost identical counterpart they call witness consciousness. For millennia India has called this witness consciousness the *atman*, the indestructible, eternal center of the human being. Christian and Jewish references to an immortal soul or even to a conscience infer an existence deeper than personality, a part or substratum of our being rooted in absolute truth. Some people seem to be more naturally aware than others of a part of the self that is unchanging, nonparticipatory, and full of peace. I consider this aspect of our being to be the treasure at the core.

After you read this next paragraph, sit back for a moment, with your eyes open or closed. See if you can remember a time when you were very happy or very upset (do not choose a triggering or heavy memory). Can you notice that at that time you did not feel like one but two? There was the you having the big reaction, and then there was the you that was strangely detached, observing, just witnessing with awareness and not acting at all. Perhaps this detachment felt reassuring or disturbing. Which part did you identify as you? Can you shift your consciousness back and forth between the two yous of that memory, into the implacable eternal observer, then into the excited reactive feeling self, and then back to the awareness of the observer? Haven't you ever wondered what or who (for it certainly is not an object) that observer self is?

The part that only is aware, present to what is happening, is what I mean by the core beneath the core. It sees all and knows your whole history throughout time and space. Dr. Brian Weiss and others such as Dr. Roger Woolger who have pioneered past-life-regression therapies affirm through their extensive research that there is a part of our consciousness that indeed is never born, never dies, exists outside of three-dimensional reality, and *can never be hurt or wounded in any way.* Unfortunately, for most of us mortals our consciousness resides most of the time inside our limited, fragile human existence that is very subject to pain and trauma. When you start to be aware of the treasure at the very center of your existence, this pain changes subtly and profoundly, forever losing the intense death grip it once held on your mind. It is not even necessary to believe in reincarnation to access this deep place. Freud was essentially an atheist, yet he still grasped the importance of the immutable depth aspect of the human psyche.

Interestingly, this sense of a larger timeless self that not only observes the personality but holds answers to its history can be found in the literature of those who have studied and worked with patients suffering from what used to be called multiple personality disorder, now officially called dissociative identity disorder. Many therapists have engaged a timeless, knowledgeable part, or "alter," to help protect, heal, and integrate the personality systems of fragmented clients, a part they have termed the internal self-helper. The internal self-helper is less a spiritual construct than an observation based on therapy and hypnotherapy, but it does reflect the fractal concept that underneath shattered personality shards lies intactness that can be utilized in profound healing.

## SPIRITUAL DIVERSITY

In 2009 I had the privilege of hearing Captain Mark Smith speak at an international trauma conference. At the time he held the position of Coast Guard Pacific Area Chaplain and Force Readiness Command Chaplain, and administered the Coast Guard's religious programs, providing supervision to seventeen chaplains as well as to lay leaders and clergy volunteers. This highly educated, bright, soft-spoken man has been deployed in areas as diverse as the Desert Storm and Desert Shield operations, as well as Operation Deep Freeze at McMurdo and South Pole stations, Antarctica. Captain Smith has a deep interest in the connection between trauma and spirituality and has published research in these areas. The Department of Defense has included him in the development of modern operational stress programs. His latest initiative at the time I saw him was to train all military chaplains in the various manifestations of post-traumatic stress disorder.

In one of his first slides he challenged the stereotype that there are no atheists in foxholes, stating that foxholes were sometimes the very places where people painfully lost their faith in and connection to

God or, conversely, they experienced their current view of God as too limiting and went on to develop a deeper and more comprehensive theology. The military is a microcosm of American society, a veritable melting pot of beliefs and ideologies, with its share of atheists and agnostics, as well as religious people. The task of a military chaplain is to counsel all those in spiritual distress, whether they are church-going Christians, contemplative Buddhists, or ironclad atheists.

For many people the idea of spirituality is relegated to religion and belief in God only. Some atheists consider it nonsense to talk about any kind of spiritual realm, but I have also met atheists who considered every single day a sacred gift to be lived to the fullest because, in their belief system, the end of life is the end of consciousness, and nothing is more important than living a good life. Captain Smith defines spirituality as "the expression of the *human spirit* in thoughts, actions and relationships. The *human spirit* is the set of attributes that makes us unique among living creatures—the attributes humans more fully embody."[2] This human spirit *is* the treasure at the core. Spirituality, then, becomes an inseparable part of the human experience, manifesting through many forms. Smith divides these forms roughly into the Abrahamic faiths (Jewish, Muslim, Christian),[3] Hindu/Buddhism (which could also include Taoism), and nontheistic spirituality. At his talk he presented, in a beautiful slide, these categories nestled inside a "world tree." In the table below I have added a fourth category of world spirituality, that of indigenous, Earth-based spirituality.

Rudolf Steiner, founder of the philosophy of anthroposophy and the international Waldorf Schools, pointed out that nature is a child's first religion. It is also probably Earth's first religion. One could argue that all religion springs from an Earth-based spirituality (a lengthy argument I will save for another book, but here's a hint: what are the

Christmas *tree* and Easter *bunny* all about?). There is a certain irony in that as humanity "develops" it tries to stamp out indigenous cultures having an Earth-based sensibility. Yet, these spiritual forms, some more recent than others, are the ground from which we all spring. For me, as someone of Irish ancestry, tales of the faery realm, trees with spirits, uncanny intuition, banshees, prescient dreams, and the power of song and story resonate strongly in my cells. Intuition springs powerfully from the Irish genetic composition, as it does from many other cultures. As I say to my patients, "If you are born Irish you are missing a couple of veils." Oddly enough, they all know what I mean by that!

| Spirituality[4] | Abrahamic | Hindu/Buddhist | Nontheist | Indigenous |
|---|---|---|---|---|
| Meanings and Beliefs | Faith<br>Hope<br>Good vs. Evil<br>Divine Determination<br>Forgiveness<br>Salvation<br>Sanctification | Samsara<br>Impermanence<br>Detachment<br>Compassion<br>Karma<br>Moksha | Rational Authority<br>Self-determination<br>Sanctity of Nature<br>Limited Existence<br>Humanism | Earth as Mother<br>Highest Good of the Group<br>Harmony<br>Nonordinary Reality<br>Cocreation |
| Practices | Prayer<br>Bible Study<br>Worship<br>Charity<br>Music<br>Service<br>Fasting<br>Pilgrimage | Right Views, Intent, Speech, Conduct, Livelihood, Mindfulness<br>Work without Attachment<br>Devotion<br>Psychophysical exercise<br>Wisdom Teachings | Environmentalism<br>Social Activism<br>Work<br>Education<br>Exercise<br>Self-help<br>Ethics | Storytelling<br>Vision Quest<br>Divining<br>Initiation<br>Ceremony<br>Purification<br>Walking in Beauty |
| Connections to the Transcendent, Others, and Self | Prayer<br>Silence<br>Awe<br>Spiritual Direction<br>Community | Meditation<br>Yoga<br>Samadhi, "Emptiness"<br>Nirvana | Observation<br>Rational Deduction<br>Community Support | Journeying<br>Visions<br>Dreaming<br>Councils<br>Intuition |

# FINDING YOUR COSMOLOGY

If trauma strikes at the core of personality, it also strikes a blow to a person's core spiritual beliefs. Many times, severe trauma just has no place in a person's cosmology or theology. Beliefs are severely challenged by thoughts such as, *How could a loving God allow such horrible things to happen? Why wasn't I saved/spared? What is the meaning of so much pain?*

The problem of suffering has long been discussed in Western and Eastern forms of spirituality, with differing conclusions reached by each. In Judeo-Christian religions we have the story of Job, who suffered the loss of his children, the loss of his home, and the loss of his health, eventually having a complete breakdown. When he confronts God with the perennial question, "Why me?" God in essence pulls trump, saying, in sum, "Because I said so." Actually, the text is much more beautiful and poetic than that, implying that the finite mind cannot possibly hope to understand the workings of the infinite mind, but, in the end, Old Testament God leaves it at that, a black God-shaped box of mystery. For many people of faith, that is a good enough answer—because God said so. With that level of acceptance, suffering can cease immediately. For many others, though, that is not a good enough answer, giving rise to a horde of new questions leading eventually to a new theology and/or cosmology.

In Eastern religions, suffering is to be accepted and transcended by certain practices. Not only is suffering understood to be an inescapable fact of life, but it is the very reason that we have a world. In the philosophically radical movie *The Matrix*, beings are inextricably hooked up to a program designed by machines, unaware that they are living a virtual life of the mind. The original program design was too perfect and "crops" of humans were lost because their minds could not stay grounded in a perfect world. In like fashion, underpinning Eastern philosophies is the idea that without suffering, minds would become enlightened very quickly, seeing through the play of maya, and the entire world would transcend and vanish with our clarity. (Alternatively, we might all bring Heaven to Earth)!

Swami Vivekenanda, the first monk to bring yoga to America in the 1800s, was asked why we had so much suffering in the world. His answer: because it's a world. In Eastern religions, suffering is both a cause of our bondage and the motivation to liberation and freedom from all suffering, no matter what happens or does not happen to us. Suffering results from unsatisfied cravings and desires, but it is also the result of our past actions coming back to us (karma) and is especially the result of ignorance of our true nature. Some philosophies even go so far as to say that suffering is an illusion, like a bad dream we mistake for reality, and that when we wake up from the delusion all suffering evaporates.

Christianity has historically been enthralled with the idea of redemptive suffering, the idea that our suffering can purify us and lead us closer to God. Redemptive suffering also refers to the doctrine that Jesus suffered on the cross for the sake of humanity's sins. Growing up Catholic, when I was injured physically or emotionally I often received the advice to "offer it up to Jesus" or "to the cross." Sometimes it made me mad, sometimes it helped. Lately, it has reminded me of the yogic teachings on karma.

In human services it is not unusual to find Buddhist Jews, Hindu Christians, and other hybrid combinations of therapists and social workers. Those of us who choose to work in the realms of human pain for a living very quickly find ourselves confronted with the problem of suffering in our clients and in ourselves. This openness to alternative spiritual forms is a direct result of looking for philosophies and techniques that fit with the circumstances in which we find ourselves. It is a healthy response. In the end, unless we have direct spiritual experience (and while most of us do not, there are those who do), we choose our beliefs. We may not start out choosing, having been forced to be in religion classes and churches or not having been allowed to be involved in religion. As adults, though, we choose either consciously or unconsciously. Nothing forces the issue of what we believe quicker than trauma and suffering.

To be aware that one is choosing one's beliefs is empowering. It means that if your cosmology doesn't fit, if it is too dissonant with your current experience, you can choose again. And again. And again, until you find a belief system that is most helpful for you and your current level of awareness.

Dr. Daniel Siegel, whom we met earlier in the chapter, set out to define spirituality with a group of scientists. He realized he had never heard a definition that was universal for the purposes of writing and teaching, so he assembled a group to find a universal definition of spirituality that appealed to all believers and atheists alike. After much work, the definition everyone could agree on was this: *the awareness of the reality that we are part of an interconnected whole.* It is interesting that through a scientific process Siegel ended up with a definition that is very much an indigenous, Earth-based spiritual perspective.

———————

Whatever you do or do not believe about spirituality, whatever religion you may belong to, dive deep into the possibilities of your consciousness. Go deep into the fabric, not only of your mind, but of your being, and see if you can't find a resting place, a reprieve from trauma. If not, find someone who can hold that reality with and for you, whether that person is a clergy member, therapist, friend, or family. You are far more than your trauma and your brokenness.

This treasure is what it means to be fully human. There is no better model for the core beneath the core than in the Indian philosophies that have considered it for many millennia. The next chapter, your next tool, will lay out a concrete model for understanding this core as the Indian atman and look at how all the layers of the human being surround that core. This model does not conflict with any religion but is a philosophy of being that will help us in our journey of healing from trauma.

*Yoga teaches us to cure what need not be
endured and endure what cannot be cured.*

—B. K. S. Iyengar

# Tool 4

# A Yogic Model for Healing

NORMALLY WE THINK of air as empty. It looks clear; it feels clear. Sure it has smells, fragrances, yet outside we unconsciously equate air with spaciousness. But have you ever sat outside at sunset on a summer's eve watching the air as the sun slips to just above the horizon in front of you? Did you notice that the air was shockingly full, full of pollen, full of highways of hurrying insects, full of dust motes? Air is anything but empty. With every breath we take, we inhale countless organisms and particulates of matter. And we are designed to do so with our marvelous noses, airways, and lungs adroitly equipped for expelling matter. Likewise we think of space in the universe as empty. But what if space is not empty? What if space is full like the air we breathe? Consider, if you will, an ancient definition of space: *a sacred field of infinite potential full of consciousness.*

Most of us Westerners understand consciousness to be something that lies inside our skull. Quantum physicists are nibbling away at this idea with such concepts as the nonlocal mind, but their theoretical arguments mean little to the average person. Why should we care about the nature of consciousness? In order to heal from extreme stress and trauma, we need to know if consciousness is found merely in the brain or if it extends beyond the realms of what we can directly observe given our current technologies. This inquiry is especially relevant when looking at alternative medical and psychological treatments that were developed in different regions, eras, and belief systems.

## The Infinite Monkey Theorem

The infinite monkey theorem is a famous thought experiment that says if you place enough monkeys in a room with enough typewriters for enough years they will eventually type a work of Shakespeare—*Hamlet*, for some reason, is usually cited as the work of choice. This theorem implies that the universe, given a random start and enough random events, will eventually generate enlightened beings or at least intelligent life. It is a fair representation of what modern Western scientists believe and is sometimes used to describe evolution, but to be precise it describes evolution in a random and unconscious universe.

Here's the rub: when scientists in 2003 conducted their infinite-monkey-theorem experiment at Plymouth University and the Paignton Zoo in Devon, England, the monkeys, in fact, urinated and defecated all over the typewriters, when they weren't typing the letter *S*.

A *Simpsons* episode lampoons the theorem. In it, the scheming and nefarious Montgomery Burns says, "This is a thousand monkeys working at a thousand typewriters. Soon they'll have written the greatest novel known to man. Let's see. [*Reading*] 'It was the best of times, it was the "blurst" of times!' You stupid monkey!"[1] Why is this funny? Because at some level we know there is something deeply flawed about randomness generating consciousness. A bazillion monkeys in a bazillion years will never type Shakespeare (or Dickens, for that matter)!

Creationists agree. They then conclude there is a magical space god or creator god that in an instant creates an intelligent universe. This conclusion is the argument for intelligent design.

There is, however, a third position far more ancient (and elegant) than either Darwinism or creationism. Ancient seers in India pronounced that the whole universe of universes, the multiverse, was an emanation of something they termed *Brahman*. Other names for Brahman include the One without a Second and Sat-Chit-Ananda: truth-consciousness-bliss.

The name Brahman is akin to the nondualistic Hebrew version of YHWH; neither can be seen or truly spoken of. Although YHWH has many manifestations and descriptions, these well-accepted interpretations are listed in the BDB Theological Dictionary:

*The one who is;*
*The absolute and unchangeable one;*
*The existing, ever-living;*
*The one ever coming into manifestation.*[2]

This is also an apt description of the formless Brahman! This singular beingness is not an entity, not a person, but rather the consciousness behind consciousness, the intelligence behind intelligence, the substratum of all reality, beyond name and form. (Eyes have not seen, ears have not heard, etc.) In Indian cosmology consciousness permeates the universe, albeit in forms we neither see nor understand in our current state of awareness (strings, dark matter, anyone?). Interestingly, this cosmology does not preclude either Darwinism or creationism, but it does render Darwin's theory of evolution incomplete and creationism superfluous.

## LOCAL VERSUS NONLOCAL CONSCIOUSNESS

Wrapping our minds around the concept of a universe filled with consciousness can be difficult. One day, after listening to a fantastic talk by a well-known expert in the field of PTSD, I approached him to ask about the idea of consciousness being limited to the skull. Even though he vehemently (and almost irrationally) opposed the idea of nonlocal consciousness, several people behind me in line later affirmed to me their belief that consciousness is boundless and pervasive. Perhaps it was a coincidence that the people behind me were women and the presenter was a man. For some reason, ideas that explore and push the boundaries of consciousness are often more self-evident and/or relevant to modern women in Western countries than to men. The numerous workshops on alternative healing and consciousness that I have attended over the years have almost always been attended by a large majority of women (80 percent or higher). I am going to take a big (and almost certainly controversial) leap here and wonder if that is because these women tend to have more integration of right- and left-brain hemispheres, a fact noted years ago by neurologists who observed that women recovered functioning after strokes more quickly than men.

Now, don't get me wrong here. Men have many wonderful attributes and strengths, but for centuries here in the West they have been suspicious of intuition, women's ways of knowing, feelings, and other phenomena they consider "soft" as opposed to hard evidence. This attitude has not served any of us well. Men and women who heal from traumatic stress often find they need to negotiate a major paradigm shift in the healing process. This process is not one anybody can muscle through or tough out. In fact, many survivors often will find themselves having nonordinary experiences during and after the traumatic event and/or during the healing process.

Belief and biology affect each other. Research is showing that our brains' ability to adapt and heal go beyond anything we had previously expected and has potentials we have yet to explore, including the abilities to connect over time and space, beyond birth and death. The nonlocal is local. In fact, the whole multiverse is our neighbor and our friend if we can open ourselves to it!

## I Don't Think Therefore I Am . . . Blissful

One of the most remarkable books on consciousness to come out in recent times has a unique view of the brain's left hemisphere versus the right one. Jill Bolte Taylor's *My Stroke of Insight* has taken the world by storm. Taylor, a Harvard-trained neuroscientist, describes the phenomenon of her left hemisphere shutting down during a massive stroke. She was left conscious, though almost completely nonfunctional. But not only was she not suffering, she found herself in a state of unbroken bliss, feeling her oneness with everything in the universe. With the tasks of the rational mind suspended— no language, no thinking, no lists, no comprehension—she was free to enjoy the blissful unfettered nature of right-hemispheric consciousness: in her own words, "nirvana."

Her experience certainly flies in the face of Descartes's famous proclamation *Cogito, ergo sum*, "I think, therefore I am," the saying that transfigured Western philosophical thought. Apparently what disappears in the true absence of thought is the individual ego sense, not the person or the person's consciousness. In fact, it appears that the very nature of this unmodified consciousness is unalloyed bliss. This discovery looks very much like what Indian philosophers have been telling us for thousands of years.

## THE RISHIS

Thousands of years ago, before Buddha, before Lao-tzu, before Jesus of Nazareth, were the Indian rishis. The Sanskrit word *rishi* means "sage." In those distant times, five to ten thousand years ago,[3] there were whole cultures in India built upon the principles of self-realization, modernly called enlightenment. The rishis, many of them women, reached heights of meditation and awareness we can hardly comprehend today. They knew about the outer realms of the cosmos as well as the inner realms of the mind and body. Without benefit of electron microscopes or Hubble telescopes, they saw that all matter is vibration and that everything in the universe changes. They wanted to know what did not change, to pull back the curtain behind the universe and see Brahman. This quest led them to a deep spiritual awareness of concepts of oneness, or nonduality, the reality of universal transpersonal connection. Jesus' saying "I and my Father are one" is an example of a nondual teaching in which divine and human are ultimately considered one.

These ancient ones realized that the core of each human being was divine and inseparable from every other being, from the very nature of reality itself: *sat-chit-ananda*, or knowledge, consciousness, and bliss absolute. They concluded that our perceived separation in space and time was the root cause of suffering in all beings, but especially in humans. The divine core, they saw, never suffered nor changed in any way. As they said, "Fire cannot burn it, water cannot drown it; knives cannot cut it," etc. The Sanskrit word for this central core is *Atman*. It is considered not different from Brahman, in the way that water inside a cup is not different from water outside a cup. In the West we might say "soul," although soul, in the West, is a loosely defined term. The rishis felt that if people knew what they were not at their core, they would eventually realize who they are (knowledge, consciousness, bliss absolute). In that moment of self-realization, suffering would cease forever. They called this process *neti, neti*, "not this, not that."

## THE ADHARA SYSTEM

The rishis conceptualized the human being as a set of sheaths (in Sanskrit, *koshas*), or bodies, superimposed upon the central divine core of Atman. Imagine Russian nesting dolls sitting one inside of another. The koshas are like those dolls, only they interpenetrate and affect each other. They are the mechanisms that keep us separate from the divine in having our human experience. Without them we would be like the proverbial salt doll that walks into the ocean of Brahman. Game over.

In this system, the core is the same as God, Brahman, the All That Is, Great Spirit, Allah, or whatever name you apply to that ineffable supreme Beingness. Our koshas, wondrous though they are, keep us from experiencing our core, and thus we suffer. We "see through a glass darkly" thanks to the distracting and deluding power of the koshas. Not only that, but each sheath over time develops its own distortions, giving rise to illnesses and diseases of all kinds. This process is natural, given that everything in the manifest universe is subject to entropy and decay. It is also a huge clue to our healing!

Swami Vivekananda tells a wonderful story about the Deva Indra in his classic text *Raja Yoga*. In the Indian mythology there are gods and goddesses (*devas* and *devis*), though most Indians still consider themselves ultimately monotheists. The gods and goddesses are diverse and have mysterious powers, and they inhabit other realms of being that sometimes interact with our own. Indra is the lord of all this universe, the king of gods, as it were—almost like Zeus in Greek mythology. In this story, Lord Indra wants to find out about pig life, and he takes a pig body. He finds a pig wife and has pig babies and thinks himself very content rolling around in the muck, having forgotten completely about his life in the realm of the gods. After a while the other gods become concerned that he will never come back to himself. They try to remind him who he is, that he is the lord of all creation and king of all gods. He brushes them off, saying that while he has his pig family he does not care for his life in heaven. Tiring of waiting for him to come to his senses, which he shows no sign of doing, they decide to take away his pig wife and family. Even in his suffering he does not recognize himself. Finally they kill his pig body. Lord Indra emerges, laughing that he could have ever mistaken himself for a pig! If we are truly "spiritual beings having a human experience," then perhaps, like Indra, we have become so enchanted with our daily lives that we have almost completely forgotten who we are.

The Adhara system provides a unique way to understand the various modes of healing that have evolved over time in various cultures. It is also known to yogis and yoginis as the five sheaths or the five bodies. In the following chapters, interventions for traumatic stress are sorted into the relevant kosha, each of which has its own chapter.

## Physical Body Sheath (Annamayakosha)

The Sanskrit terms for the sheaths can be a little intimidating until we realize they are really three words in one. You will notice that all of the terms contain *maya* and *kosha*. *Maya* means "all of creation," or, as the Indians put it, "the illusion of relative existence."[4] *Kosha*, as mentioned earlier, means "sheath" or "body"—again, think of the nesting dolls. *Anna* means "of food." So the physical body here is literally identified as the body made of food appearing in maya. The body is made from food, is sustained by food, and eventually becomes food. It is not to be confused with your eternal self, the Atman.

We need to take care of our physical body! It is our "earth suit" while we are here in our lives. Western medicine has excelled at focusing on the body and its need for healing from various conditions. Many of the symptoms of overwhelming stress that bother us are the ones manifesting in the physical body. Stress, as we saw earlier, can also shorten the life in the body, so it is important to address the effects of trauma and stress at this level.

## The Energy Body (Pranamayakosha)

If you have ever seen the dead body of any animal or person it is perfectly obvious that the body has no inherent life in and of itself. The animating force of the body is called *prana*, a word that can also mean "breath" or "breath of life." We could refer to prana as the life force of bodies. It is similar and related to the concept of qi found in Chinese medicine and Taoist philosophy. Prana has no inherent intelligence of its own. It just is, like the laws of nature.

All over the world we can find healers whose practices are largely based in manipulation of prana or qi. To understand the relevance of prana in healing, we need to look at the chakras, a word you may have heard if you are involved in alternative healing of any kind. Another Sanskrit word, *chakra* means "wheel." Clairvoyants and medical intuitives can actually see the chakras spinning in the body. Chakras step down and qualify universal prana for use in the body, analogous to the way transformers work with electrical energy. Each chakra is connected with the functioning of an organ system and emotion. In the traditional Indian system there are seven chakras; in the Taoist, there are six (the second and third chakras are combined). The chakras spin off energy into the *nadis*, channels that conduct this life force throughout the body. In Chinese medicine, channels of energy or qi are called meridians.

The first chakra is located around the perineum. Also called the root chakra, it has the color red and is associated with the organs of evacuation—intestines, kidneys, and such. Our sense of material well-being and safety on the planet in our physical bodies correlates to this center, so it also governs the adrenals (the fight-or-flight glands, which sit on top of the kidneys). The name for it is *Muladhara*, which literally means "root support." The fundamental statement of the root chakra is "I live." The sacred Kundalini energy of the universe rests in this center.

Moving up to the center about two inches below the navel, we find the second chakra, whose color is orange. (The seven chakra colors correspond to the seven colors of the rainbow, ROY G BIV: red, orange, yellow, green, blue, indigo, and violet). It is associated with the organs of reproduction. At subtler levels this center has to do with the energy of every kind of creation, not just procreation, though that is one manifestation. Artists, poets, builders, and architects all work within the realm of this chakra, and the statement associated with it is "I create." In martial arts and the Chinese healing modality called qigong, this center is known as the *Dan Tien*, and in Japan it is called the *Hara*. It is considered to be the repository of one's internal energy.

The third chakra in the yogic system lies in the solar plexus area. Its corresponding color is yellow, and it is the energetic seat of the sense of self or, one might say, ego, that part of us that mediates between our internal realities and the external world. "I act!" is the statement of this center. Physically the third chakra relates to digestion: stomach, spleen, liver, and pancreas. Its energy manifests in the world as personal power, control, and mastery. When this center is blocked, extreme frustration or anger results, often felt as a tightening of the diaphragm and stomach. It is also the center of attachment. Shamans and psychics see and work with the etheric cords that stretch from this center to any object or person in our lives we are attached to.

The lower three centers are concerned primarily with the maintenance of the physical body and life on this planet. As we come up to the fourth, or heart, chakra, we find ourselves in the balancing point between heaven and earth. "I love" are the words of the heart, but if love is thwarted or withheld then anger arises here. The organs ruled here, of course, are the heart, lungs, and circulatory system. A clear green color permeates the heart chakra. Humanity is challenged right now with the task of moving its consciousness primarily from the third to the fourth chakra. The heart chakra has also been the foundation for the message of such luminaries as Buddha, Jesus, and currently the Dalai Lama: compassion, love, and kindness, even at the expense of egoic, third chakra–based power.

The three chakras above the heart move into more subtle and universal spiritual realms of functioning. At the level of the thyroid gland, in the throat rests the fifth chakra. This center has to do with speaking one's highest truth. It is by giving voice to the longings of one's heart that we satisfy our healthy dharmic desires in life, so "I manifest" is the voice of this center. People with highly developed throat chakras can speak to large crowds in such a way that each listener comes away feeling the speaker was talking directly to him or her. Or they might be singers who move large numbers of people. Blockage in the area can cause sore throats, tight necks, laryngitis, vocal cord issues, or thyroid issues leading to hormonal imbalances. The color of this chakra is sky blue. Most clients I see in psychotherapy have significant blockages at this level.

Between the eyebrows rests the sixth chakra, *ajna*, or "third eye," whose color is indigo blue. Some call this the center of Christ consciousness or Buddha consciousness. It is called an eye because of the natural psychic seeing ability we can have via this center. When my daughter was in kindergarten, her teacher was testing for vision dominance and asked her to put a toy telescope up to whichever eye she wanted. Immediately she placed the scope on the third eye center (it had never been discussed with her) and began talking about all the distant things she could "see." When this eye is open or clear, our intuition becomes our sixth sense, available on a daily basis.[5] The pineal gland, sometimes referred to as the master gland because of its important function in regulating the entire body, is governed by this chakra. One could say that the voice of this center says, "I see," when seeing is taken to be clear perception with deep wisdom and understanding.

The final, or seventh, chakra is the crown chakra, the "thousand-petalled lotus" on top of the head. This chakra opens fully only for those who have reached the highest states of consciousness, called enlightenment. It corresponds to the brain and central nervous system, and its color is a beautiful violet. The words associated with this center are the eternal and nondual proclamation "I Am,"[6] or as the Vedantists would say, *Ayam Atma Brahma*: This very Self is Brahman.

Although the chakras are a very important part of the pranamayakosha they are one part of a much larger system. The prana body governs the functioning of every part of the physical body. If there is disturbance in the flow of prana over a long period of time, eventually disease will develop in the corresponding part of the physical body. We can view this energy body as a blueprint much like one you would see around a computer-animated object. It is the structure, the matrix of the physical body. Naturally if the structure is defective, the body is bound to follow suit. One of the primary disturbing forces to the prana energy and structure comes from dysfunctional emotional/ thought patterns. These patterns can be genetic, ancestral, or cultural, or from past lifetimes, from other people (for instance the "aggressive energy" acknowledged in traditional Chinese medicine), or from our own dysfunctional reactions to and beliefs about life.

## The Thinking Mind (Manomayakosha)

The next two koshas are levels of mind, similar yet different. In the Adhara system these are not equivalent to the brain, which would be the physical sheath, but operate through other levels of the human being including the brain. The brain, in this system, is more like a receiver or a filter for mind. So brain is physical and local; mind, in this model, is multidimensional. It can span lifetimes, or, as the ancients say, it transmigrates from lifetime to lifetime.

The two mind sheaths are the kosha of mind and the kosha of intellect, respectively called the manomayakosha and the vijnanamayakosha. They could be called lower mind and higher mind, but for our purposes we will call them thinking mind and wisdom mind. Interestingly, we here in the West once had a similar distinction between what was called *ratio* and *intellect* set out by Augustine of Hippo (known to Catholics as St. Augustine, AD 354–430), who defined ratio as reason and intellect as a higher, or angelic as he put it, mode of knowing. The difference, as he laid out in his writings, isn't in *what* these minds know but *how* they know it. His description is very similar to that of the two koshas of mind in Vedanta.

The manomayakosha, or thinking mind, can be roughly equated to cognitive processes and more concrete thinking processes. This mind is attached to well-being much as Freud described in his concept of the pleasure principle—meaning simply that people seek pleasure and avoid pain. If this mind thinks, then it also doubts. It needs proofs through the senses, through which it primarily operates and gathers information. This mind is informed by physical needs and drives to maintain the equilibrium of the body-mind. Its method is logical although it is influenced heavily by emotion and beliefs. This mind is the one that can be subject to anxiety, depression, trauma, etc. Its ultimate goal is to function well and happily in the world, and in that sense it is akin to ego function. It correlates to the activity of the left hemisphere of the brain (in right-handed people). Contemporary psychotherapy mostly concerns itself with this mind, as do modern educational and scientific methods.

## The Wisdom Mind (Vijnanamayakosha)

The ancient rishis would definitely agree with Socrates that the unexamined life is not worth living. *Vijnana* (pronounced vee-ghee-anna) in Sanskrit means "higher wisdom," or "knowledge." It is a very important concept in the study of Vedanta ("the end of the Vedas," or "the culmination of the scriptures"), a system based on the Upanishads (plus some later texts, including the Bhagavad Gita), and the last of the four stages of the Vedas, a body of ancient scriptures that predate and are the basis for Hinduism. Vijnana yoga, the yoga of wisdom and knowledge, is one of the four branches of yoga and refers to the study of scriptures for higher spiritual knowledge leading to the highest form of self-knowledge, Self-realization.

This higher mind, vijnanamayakosha, literally "the wisdom sheath in the world," is a subtler entity than the thinking mind. This wisdom mind is attached to knowledge and to action. It is not merely content to know things but must actualize this knowledge for the benefit of all. This is the mind that knows without any doubt. You could call it the intuitive mind informed by higher consciousness and awareness. If the lower mind knows by deduction and cognitive processes, this mind knows by leaps of imagination, divine inspiration, and lofty thoughts that some call genius. As you can see in the chart it is getting closer to the core of Being and is therefore able to better reflect the inner core states of joy, bliss, and spirituality, or divinity.

We all have this level as part of our being, but not many of us have consistent access to it. The wisdom mind speaks in a whisper. It can be easily shouted down by egoic opinions, beliefs, judgments, and preconceptions. Access to the wisdom mind is gained by meditation, deep contemplation, imagery, and reverie—the "still small voice." It is hard to come by this access with a distracted, scattered brain (the condition of many of us at any given time!). An academic, intellectualized mind is also a difficult impediment to overcome in seeking wisdom mind, especially because this layer is not easily observable for "proof" of its existence. *You cannot think your way to the wisdom mind.*

Some people seem to be born with easier access than others. People comfortable with abstract or "big-picture" thinking processes are more likely to find their way to wisdom mind. Longtime meditators who have developed their "stillness muscle" become adept at accessing the vijnanamayakosha. Children without highly developed egos or overintellectualized brains naturally access this level, sometimes astonishing their parents and teachers with their innate wisdom. Unfortunately, adults often dismiss their knowledge as the fanciful idealism of childhood.[7] Empathy is often highly developed in those that have reached some conscious awareness at this level.

## The Bliss Body (Anandamayakosha)

Being the innermost of our essences next to the core, eternal Atman, this kosha is very subtle indeed. Without it, life would be a dry, barren existence. It is the very essence of our joy, the juice for our life. I know a yoga teacher who refers to this sheath as the Love Body. This is a level beyond any kind of thought or mental perception, yet we know when we are in it.

Time disappears when we are in the bliss body and so does suffering. As Eckhart Tolle points out in his popular book *The Power of Now*, "In the Now, in the absence of time, all your problems dissolve. Suffering needs Time; it cannot survive in the Now."[8] What does this mean? Some of you reading may never have been to this place consciously. We all go there in deep sleep, awakening refreshed and rejuvenated. But how do we get to this state that we all desire when we are awake?

The Indian scripture Vivekacudamani (Crest jewel of discrimination) is the first document we have describing the koshas. In it the revered teacher Sri Sankaracarya describes the anandamaykosha as "a reflection of the Atman which is Bliss Absolute; whose attributes are pleasure and the rest; and which appears in view when some object agreeable to oneself presents itself. It makes itself spontaneously felt by the fortunate during the fruition of their virtuous deeds; from which every corporeal being derives great joy without the least effort."[9]

I understand virtuous deeds here to be not only, say, working at your local soup kitchen (you don't have to be a saint!), but also the everyday good deeds of our lives: cooking dinner for our family, taking a bike ride or run, helping our kids with their homework, walking the dog—ordinary activities done in a good way with intense focus and forgetfulness of self.

The most important thing to know about the bliss body is that we experience it when our mind's activity is suspended. It is a state beyond mind, the most blissful, joyful state we all go to regularly if we could only recognize it. The fisherman goes there when he is intent on landing his catch, as does the rock climber ascending a particularly treacherous slope, the mother nursing her baby. It is very ordinary and extraordinary, a state we are all striving unconsciously to attain. In healing from trauma there is no better place to be.

---

I realize that on first reading this system is a lot to take in. To review in brief the Adhara system of the koshas, here is what you need to know in order to understand how the different healing techniques are organized in the following chapters:

- physical body sheath (annamayakosha) = our physical body

- energy body (pranamayakosha) = the body that is full of prana or qi and contains the chakras

- thinking mind (manomayakosha) = our ego mind that thinks, believes, doubts, cogitates

- wisdom mind (vijnanamayakosha) = our intuitive mind that knows, is divinely inspired, and is informed by higher wisdom

- bliss body (anandamayakosha) = our innermost sense of self full of love and bliss

All of our interventions for traumatic stress take place within these spheres, each of which has its own chapter.

*You don't have a soul.*
*You are a Soul.*
*You have a body.*

—C. S. Lewis

# Tool 5

# The Annamayakosha: Mending the Physical Body

Trauma hurts! I'm not talking about injuries, and I'm not talking about emotional pain. I'm talking literally about the physical body's reaction to traumatic stress. When the mind becomes overwhelmed, the body follows suit. Universally, people with overwhelming stress and trauma experience these physical symptoms: crushing headaches, gastrointestinal distress (in extreme cases vomiting and/or diarrhea), nonspecific abdominal pain, joint pain, muscular tension, and insomnia. These symptoms can then give rise to other issues, such as nerve pain, autoimmune diseases, obesity, heart disease, chronic fatigue, and overall weakness.

If you have trauma or chronic extreme stress, chances are you have been dealing with several of these issues for quite some time. Unfortunately, many doctors and mental health providers do not understand the severity and reality of the physical fallout from trauma. In fact, due to the compartmentalized nature of health-service delivery, many physicians do not ask about nor really want to hear about the connection of your mental health issues or abuse history to your physical body. Sadly, some trauma patients end up getting labeled by the medical community as difficult, dramatic, or delusional.

I cannot count the number of times patients have complained to me about the reaction of their medical doctors to their traumatic stress. Over the years, my trauma patients have been incorrectly assessed as drug seeking, lacking in will power, hypochondriacal, and that dreaded moniker "noncompliant" (which is often medical-personnel code for "I don't want to see this patient anymore").

One especially pernicious label is that of somatization disorder, a mental illness in which the patient expresses physical complaints in multiple body systems that are not explained by any "general medical condition," as the diagnosis reads. You could call this the "it's-all-in-your-head disorder." After more than thirty years in the mental health business, and with what we know about the trauma-induced disruption of the hypothalamic-pituitary-adrenal axis, I suggest that we need to question whether this classification is a valid one. Too often this label is used to dismiss legitimate patient complaints and stops physicians and mental health providers from looking more deeply into the patient's problems and history. I have yet to see a client meeting the criteria for this disorder who didn't turn out to have a history of a major trauma or serious chronic stress.

Here's my hypothesis about why this problem exists. Doctors self-select as a low-PTSD population. The process of becoming a physician is so difficult and triggering that very few people with florid PTSD end up becoming doctors. If doctors-in-training do have stress and trauma, they learn quickly how to shut it down, and they are encouraged to do so, often losing compassion for both themselves and their patients in the process. Residency, the period of training right after medical school, has for years followed a sink-or-swim model. It is such a difficult part of becoming a physician that divorce rates can be as high as 80 percent in some programs. If aspiring doctors cannot suppress their stress reactions and move forward, they have a very high chance of failing residency.

Patients, however, are a high-stress, high-PTSD population. As you will see later in this book, PTSD itself can give rise over time to numerous health issues, including cardiovascular problems, bowel problems, headaches, neurological issues, and autoimmune disorders. There's the rub: a low-PTSD population treating a high-PTSD population. Unless you have faced trauma head on, it is very difficult to understand. Some doctors believe their PTSD patients are overreacting, especially if memories of the trauma are hazy or from very early in life. In the absence of empathic understanding, negative feelings and judgments arise easily. Symptoms are minimized, and patients can end up feeling bewildered, misunderstood, or belittled.

What to do? This chapter gives you many alternative ways to begin addressing the physical fallout from going through overwhelming events. Do not overwhelm yourself by feeling you have to do any or all of them. Think of this material more as a menu to choose from. Play. Experiment. Try something new. Maybe your friends will think it's weird. Maybe your doctors won't like it; maybe they will. So what! You have nothing to lose except your traumatic stress! Now, let's start with the basics.

## Nutrition

"You are what you eat" is not so far from the yogic saying "The body [annamayakosha] is made of food, sustained by food, and becomes food." Dealing with traumatic stress puts a tremendous load on the resources of the physical body. Our bodies need to be healthy and fit to deal with this tremendous challenge. But for many of us the first thing we let go of when hit by trauma is our nutrition. With the stress hormone cortisol flooding our brains, our bodies cry out for fats and sugars to get us through the calamity.

Did you know that certain foods make your body feel tense and others relax your system? Did you know that digestion is one of the first systems to shut down in the face of an emergency? Did you know that going through trauma can actually turn on genes that inhibit your ability to eat certain foods?

When you go through something overwhelming, food may sink to the bottom of your agenda. Digestion slows; hunger fades, or increases dramatically. Yet, your need for calories and nutrition is no less than before the event and may even be more in the midst of it. You might want to think of this syndrome as the emotional flu. During this initial phase of trauma shock, treat yourself as if you have become ill: rest, hydrate, and eat small, digestible portions of nutritious foods and supplements. In the acute or immediate phase of the crisis a bland diet that includes plenty of nutritious liquids such as soups or stews works well.

Healing from trauma requires your body to be in the best health possible even though it is a time when you can often feel the least like caring for yourself. Resolve to find yourself the best and most nutritious foods available, maybe enlisting the help of family or friends. If shopping at a whole-foods market is too expensive, you can always grow some fresh food of your own or find a local farmer's market. Did you know that many farmers' markets accept food stamps? If you eat meat and fish, find cuts that are naturally raised without hormones, additives, or preservatives. Although raw foods are usually good for you, you may find them hard to digest with a traumatized system. If so, steam, stir-fry, or braise your veggies. With every nutritious bite, visualize your food healing your body and mind, and be sure to bless or give thanks for whatever food you do eat. The quality of your food is much more important than the quantity when healing from trauma.

Some days you won't want to eat well. You'll want to reach for whatever is easy and familiar—comfort food. If you have childhood trauma, your "littles" inside will insist on treats. It's not wrong to eat this food, so don't beat yourself up if you do; it just won't help you physically recover as quickly. And above all, do not create a battle with yourself around food that adds to your stress! It does help to acknowledge you are weak, sick, or wounded in order to mobilize your instinct for caring for yourself. We don't usually fight with ourselves when we have the actual flu, so don't do it now, in the midst of your trauma!

Foods that may stress your body include sugar, alcohol (full of sugars and disrupts your sleep patterns!), fatty or fried foods, processed foods, anything with high-fructose corn syrup (check your labels), citrus, dairy, wheat, or gluten products. Wait a minute, you may be thinking. I get the first ones, but what about those last few? Citrus, dairy, and wheat are foods that many people are commonly allergic to overtly or covertly, meaning you may have had some level of intolerance for years but may not know about it. Under stress these intolerances tend to manifest more strongly.

For example, you may love your morning orange juice but notice it gives you a little bit of a sour stomach. For taste and maybe out of habit, you drink it anyway. But when you are under stress this orange juice could start to become a bigger problem. Just notice. Even raw foods can sometimes tax a delicate and recovering nervous system.

Pay attention to what your body tells you about the food you eat. Here's a miniquestionnaire to help you be aware:

1. Are you more or less energized after eating?

2. Do you have good or sluggish digestion?

3. Are you more alert or sleepy after a meal?

4. Is your mood better or worse after certain foods?

5. How does your body feel after eating—any aches, pains, or stiffness?

I once had a patient who came in and announced calmly, "I had a brownie yesterday, and then I felt really suicidal." For a moment, my conventional reaction was to think she was losing touch with reality. While this patient had an extraordinary amount of abuse in her childhood, she was one of my least dramatic, most levelheaded clients. Usually she understated rather than overstated everything. I took a breath and inquired further. She revealed how she had been managing her anxiety symptoms all these years without medication but with her diet (she had an extreme phobia of drugs). She strongly suspected she was intolerant to gluten. She had noticed that when she ate gluten her blood sugar levels would fluctuate, she would get immediate and extreme fatigue, and *her mood would change.* Hearing her observation was a lightbulb moment for me. Nothing in my training had prepared me for the possibility that foods could affect mood (other than the obvious chocolate and caffeine lift).

## Celiac Disease

In my research I found not only that foods could negatively affect our moods, but that a disorder called celiac disease could be responsible for my client's unusual reaction. Celiac disease is not contagious. It is a genetic disorder that causes gluten to erode the lining of the intestines, literally flattening the nutrient-absorbing villi (those little bumpy things that look like roller-coaster tracks) and blocking the body from receiving the nutrition needed to function normally. Researchers have found that almost one percent of the general population is affected, one out of 133 people of all races and nationalities, making it the most common genetic disease in the world! *Only 5 percent of people with this disorder have been diagnosed correctly*; that means 95 percent of those with this disease are untreated and continue to aggravate their condition (and possibly their mental health) simply by eating foods containing gluten. In people with Swedish or Irish ancestry, the rates of celiac genes reach as high as 30 to 40 percent!

Here are some of the latest facts on celiac disease important to trauma survivors:

1. Research indicates that eating gluten when you have celiac disease negatively affects your mental health, particularly in the areas of depression and anxiety.

2. Celiac disease does not manifest just as a wasting disease. You can be obese and still have it, in which case you absorb calories but not nutrition (and consequently may feel hungry *all the time*).

3. Only 50 percent of undiagnosed people who turned out to have celiac disease had gastrointestinal symptoms!

4. *There is strong anecdotal evidence linking traumas to the incidence of celiac disease.* So far no conclusive research has been done, but the leading researchers acknowledge there are many such stories from patients.

The story with my patient had a happy outcome. She became much more stable and empowered by not eating gluten. As counterintuitive as it may sound, her suicidal feelings clearly receded when she ate gluten free. Currently, many holistic practitioners recommend that people suspend gluten from their diet when they have suffered traumatic stress to see if their symptoms improve. If you fall into a high-risk group for celiac disease, you may want to get the definitive intestinal-biopsy test, but many just go for a substantial gluten-free trial to see how their bodies respond.

## SUPPLEMENTS

As wonderful as whole organic foods are, it is a fact that our foods are less nutritious than they used to be due to the soil depletion of modern farming techniques. Doctors and nutritionists agree on the necessity of taking regular vitamin and mineral supplements in order for our bodies and minds to function healthily. Traumatic stress taxes and depletes the body, so these supplements become *absolutely crucial* to our ongoing functioning and healing. They can even be lifesaving. Top supplements for stress busting are reviewed below.

- *Omega-3 Fatty Acids*: I interviewed several naturopathic doctors for this book. Every single one mentioned adding omega-3 oils to the diet for traumatic stress. These oils assist the functioning of the brain and central nervous system. Evidence from research in Japan and the United States shows that omega-3 supplements can reduce adverse consequences of stress including aggression, PTSD, and depression.[1] They have been shown to reduce depression by increasing the "happy" chemical in the brain, serotonin. Fish oil, flaxseed oil, walnuts, and even algae oil contain omega-3 fatty acids necessary for good brain functioning. These can be purchased as soft-gel capsules or liquid oils, good in salads or mixed into smoothies.

- *B vitamins*: These have earned the name "the stress vitamins." Both medical and holistic doctors universally recommend B vitamin supplements to help strengthen and regulate the nervous system. Deficiency is linked to depression and anxiety. If you have celiac disease or are a vegetarian, there is a good chance you are deficient in B-12. Talk to your doctor about testing and supplementation in easy-to-take dissolvable pills or caplets.

- *Vitamin C*: This common supplement is essential to bolstering the immune system in times of trauma shock and stress. Stress releases free radicals that can damage the body and immune system. The vitamin C works directly to clean up this damage, and many people report a boost in energy when taking it. If you don't like taking pills, there are delicious dissolvable and chewable forms of this vitamin.

- *Vitamin D*: The newest trend in blood testing measures vitamin D levels because many recent studies have found Americans to be deficient in it. Humans make this vitamin, which is found in few foods, from sunlight. According to doctors, if you live north of Georgia you need to supplement the vitamin D you get from sunlight because the strength of the sun in northern latitudes is not sufficient to give you your daily supply, especially in winter. If you do not drink milk you are at additional risk, because vitamin D is often added to milk. Physicians recommend 1,000 mg/day in pill form, but if you are deficient you may need to take many times that amount to bring up your blood levels.

Emerging evidence indicates a link between low vitamin D levels and negative emotional states (depression, anxiety).

- *Calcium*: This essential mineral helps your mood as well as your bones. Make sure you are getting adequate amounts. Calcium supplements before bed can help the body to unwind and sleep. Several studies indicate that calcium supplements help stabilize mood and alleviate PMS (premenstrual syndrome) symptoms aggravated by stress. Nutritionists recommend getting your calcium from calcium citrate because it is absorbed well by the body. Take with magnesium and vitamin D for best effect.

- *Magnesium*: Most of us know that magnesium helps the body absorb calcium. But did you know that the body requires large amounts of magnesium to function well even apart from its role in absorbing calcium? Low magnesium levels are a common problem with people but is hard to diagnose. The adrenal glands need magnesium to help us process stressful experiences, the bowels need magnesium to be regular, and our cells need magnesium to give us optimal energy and relaxation. Many doctors recommend a one-to-one ratio with calcium, although one part magnesium to two parts calcium is acceptable.

All of these vitamins and supplements can be readily purchased at a natural-foods store, pharmacy, or over the Internet. Like all products, some are better than others. The FDA (US Food and Drug Administration) does not currently regulate the quality of these supplements, so you may want to do some research on brands and content or ask your nutritionist, doctor, or naturopath for advice in sorting out your options.

## Medicinal Plant and Herbal Healing

Healing with herbs and plants is possibly the oldest medical modality known to humans. Even animals seek out wild plants to heal their stress, sick stomachs, cancers, and other ailments. Over the centuries herbal healing has gone in and out of favor. In different times and places, herbal healers have been revered and prized above all other community members. Yet, over a period of several centuries known as the Burning Times, the Inquisition of the Catholic Church and leaders in Europe sentenced tens of thousands of herbal healers (most of whom were women) as "witches" to agonizing deaths by fire and other means. For those of European descent these atrocities created a cultural legacy of ambivalence about herbal healing that persists to this day. In other cultures around the world where there was no healer holocaust, no such stigma or ambivalence exists around the use of herbs in healing.

Although herbal remedies from other countries can be highly effective, this section will list several healing plants used commonly in North America and Europe. In the next chapter, Chinese herbs will be addressed under the use of Chinese medicine for healing. All the herbs listed below can be grown in a garden or pot, harvested in the wild, found at a local health-food store, or ordered over the Internet.

Some people like to make their own herbal remedies. The upside of making your own herbal remedies is that it is very cheap; in some cases, no outlay of money at all is required. Also, you can be assured of the quality of the product because you made it. On the other hand, making your own medicine can be time consuming, inconvenient, or even dangerous. You need to be sure to harvest safely and accurately; some healing plants look like plants that will make you ill or kill you!

There are many wonderful books on the market with pictures of appropriate herbs and plants. If you are not sure, just buy the plant or take a guide with you for harvesting.

Proper preparation of herbs enables the body to assimilate safely and effectively the benefit of the plant. Generally, herbal preparations for stress reduction fall into five categories: infusions, decoctions, tinctures, baths, and supplements.

- *Infusions (I)*: Much like a tea, the leaves or other soft parts of a plant are put into either boiling or cold water and then left to sit. A cold-water infusion takes much longer to soak than a hot one.

- *Decoctions (D)*: These are like infusions but use harder, thicker, and woodier parts of the plant that need to be chopped up and boiled for a while in water until they are reduced by half or more.

- *Tinctures (T)*: These use a form of drinking alcohol instead of water as the medium for the plant to soak in. As a result, tinctures can last much longer than infusions or decoctions, sometimes for months.

- *Baths (B)*: Herbs can be strewn in the bath water or put into a linen sack in the bathtub for soaking. This preparation is generally a one-time use.

- *Supplement (S)*: The herb or herbal combinations can be found in pill form in a natural-food store or practitioner's office.

Now we will look at some commonly found herbs and plants used to reduce stress and balance the body in traumatically stressful situations. Although there are many other herbs and plants that can be used to treat the symptoms of PTSD and chronic stress, I have chosen these seven because of their prevalence and agreed-upon uses. Many of them show promise in research studies, and most can be easily grown in your own garden. Next to the plant's name you will find the initial of the method(s) used in preparing the plant as listed above.

- *Chamomile (I, T, B, S)*: Some of us first heard of chamomile as a tea given to the naughty Peter Rabbit, who had been stealing out of Mr. McGregor's garden. No doubt Peter's stomachache was not only from overeating but also from the stress of stealing and being caught. In any case, chamomile gently works to relieve stress and problems with digestion through anti-inflammatory agents. Chamomile has been shown to help adults as well as children with insomnia and chronic tension. In a 2009 study reported in *Journal of Clinical Psychopharmacology*, chamomile was found to alleviate symptoms of general anxiety when given in capsule form.[2] It can be grown in your garden quite easily but also grows wild as a "weed" and can be harvested. The dried flowers make up the teas and tinctures. The whole plant can be tied up in cheesecloth and used for a soothing bath that is good for your skin. As with all plant medicines, if there is any kind of allergic reaction, discontinue use and see a physician immediately.

- *Lavender (B)*: The scent of lavender calms, soothes, and heals. This wonderful healing plant can be crushed and strewn in the bath or placed in one's pillow at night for deep restful sleep. Many people report reduced fatigue and joint pain when lavender is used in a bath. Although it has been used for centuries as a remedy, studies recommend you consult with a knowledgeable practitioner before taking lavender internally, due to possible side effects of headache, nausea, and dizziness.

- *Valerian (I, T, S)*: As early as the ninth century, this herb (known modernly as the "gym-sock herb" due to its stinky root smell) was recommended as a treatment for emotional disorders and hysteria, and its use is verified back to the time of Hippocrates. Today valerian is recognized as one of the leading antianxiety and sedative herbs. Its potency is such that it should not be mixed with other sedative medications, so always let your physician know if you have been taking valerian. Valerian is for short-term use only and can be very helpful for insomnia due to stress. Valeric acid, a component of valerian, has long been used in the treatment of bipolar disorder as valproic acid. Preferred use is capsule form because of the particularly bad taste of the root.

- *Kava (I, T, S)*: This potent herb comes to us from the South Seas, where natives ground the root and mixed it with water for relaxation and sedation. Kava has the unique property of relaxing without being a depressant. The groups of chemicals known as kavalactones (sounds like a rock group, doesn't it?) are credited with inducing feelings of well-being in the user. For nervous anxiety and insomnia, it is considered one of the best herbal remedies available. A few years ago there was a scare around a possible side effect of liver toxicity with kava (the FDA issued a warning in 2002), and it has been banned in Germany, Switzerland, and Canada. However, in Florida and Hawaii and on South Sea islands one can find kava bars that exist to serve kava drinks. Kava is nonaddictive. Several international studies have shown kava (also known as kava kava) to be effective in reducing anxiety levels.

- *Passionflower (I, T, S)*: The National Institutes of Health is in the process of studying the promise of passionflower for reducing anxiety. The results have been deemed promising but inconclusive at this time. Historically, passionflower has been considered a solid remedy for anxiety and other syndromes such as asthma, ADHD (attention deficit/hyperactivity disorder), gastrointestinal discomfort, drug addiction, nerve pain, spastic muscles, and nervous tension. The leaves and flowers are used for teas or other forms of remedies. It is considered a safe herb with few side effects. Interestingly, the plant has been found to contain monoamine-oxidase inhibitors, the same ingredients found in early generations of antidepressants.

- *Skullcap (D, S)*: Varieties of skullcap can be found around the world. Both the Chinese and American varieties are commonly known for their reduction of anxiety. In the United States, skullcap grows most prevalently in southern states and is considered a remedy for nervous tension, insomnia, stress headaches, and digestive disorders. Native Americans used this plant to treat rabies, induce and regulate menstruation, and sometimes to induce visions. Like all herbal medicines, supervision from an herbalist is recommended, because side effects include diarrhea, twitchiness, drowsiness, or even seizures (at high dosages). It is common to find skullcap mixed in with other remedies such as Saint-John's-wort or valerian.

- *Lemon Balm (I, B)*: This herb has not only a long healing history but also a long culinary history. Also known as bee balm, it has antianxiety properties and has been found useful in treating spasms in the digestive tract, colds, flus, high blood pressure, insomnia, and depression. It is very easy to find in tea form in stores, or you can harvest the leaves yourself, since it is easily grown in a container. Many people find the citrusy smell of lemon balm irresistible. It makes a great addition to a bath along with chamomile or lavender.

## ESSENTIAL OILS

Plants and herbs can be used for relieving stress in yet another way, by distilling and using their oils. The use of essential oils for healing is an ancient art. References to healing with oils appear in sources as diverse as Egyptian tombs, the Bible, histories of the Crusades and the Napoleonic wars, and writings of the healing saint Hildegard of Bingen. They have been the subject of research recently at Weber State University in Utah. Holistic practitioners around the globe use these oils in healing every day as they have been used for centuries.

Essential oils can be the extracted oils from a single plant or a blend of complementary healing herbs. A high quality of oil is essential for healing purposes. In Europe the oils are rated for purity based on strict scientific measures. AFNOR (Association Française de Normalisation), the standards organization for France, and ISO (International Organization for Standards) provide these standards. In the United States, to date, there is no regulating body for the use of essential oils, but use of the label "therapeutic grade" generally means the oils meet some quality standards. Unlabeled oils may be entirely synthetic and useless for the purposes of healing.

Current medical research is showing how essential oils can do everything from changing hormone levels to combating cancer. They heal in three main modalities: inhalation (aromatherapy), ingestion, and application on the skin. Of these three, aromatherapy may be the safest method of use. All three modalities have been shown to produce spectacular results in healing from the effects of traumatic stress. Many healing practitioners combine essential oils with other modalities, such as the Emotional Freedom Technique, for powerful results.

The nose connects to the olfactory bulb in the part of the brain called the limbic system, the emotional center. Smell directly affects emotions, evoking a wide range of states, including pleasure, relaxation, arousal, anxiety, and disgust. Of course, these reactions could be produced by learned associations to certain smells, but what is interesting about aromas is that they have their own direct effects on the brain. I interviewed Monique Gallagher, a California-certified essential-oils educator with several years' experience in helping people heal from stressful life events, who identified seven oils that are profound helpers in healing from traumatic stress. Many of them I was already familiar with and use regularly.

- *Lavender*: Called the "universal" or "mother" oil, lavender oil has been used for stress relief for centuries. More powerful than the plant alone, it can be used in the bath or in a diffuser to soothe and relax the nervous system. Some people find that lavender oil relieves tension headaches.

- *Rose*: Rose oil has been shown to help alleviate depressed moods. At the moment this oil is very expensive (it takes a lot of rose petals to make even once ounce of oil!). Practitioners like to use it to help patients open their hearts to life and to love.

- *Balsam Fir*: Aromatherapy with this remarkable oil has been shown in research studies to drop levels of the stress hormone cortisol by 20 to 40 percent, making it a must-have for your trauma toolbox. It can also be taken as a supplement and has a fresh, gender-neutral scent. In other words, all you guys who don't want to smell like ladies' perfume, this one's for you!

- *Geranium*: I am seeing this scent more often in candles and bath products. Geranium oil helps with depression and repressed anger. Monique reports that it helps release negative memories and nervous stress.

- *Cedarwood*: This oil smells similar to balsam fir oil and, like it, helps to calm stress levels. It is also known for providing energetic protection around the body and can be used as a smudge by applying to the hands and wiping around the electromagnetic field of the body. Due to the high level of sesquiterpenes, it has many healing qualities and will help reduce insomnia.

- *Frankincense*: This oil has been around since biblical times and has been traditionally used in Jewish, Egyptian, Chinese, and Tibetan homes. It is *not edible*. Frankincense has protective, antidepressant, and spiritually uplifting properties.

- *Sandalwood*: This oil is increasingly difficult to obtain and is expensive, but it is a powerful healer. Like cedarwood it supports the nervous system. Like cedar, it is high in the healing sesquiterpenes. Some research suggests it can balance the pineal gland (responsible for the sleep cycle and hormones). Traditionally it was used in India to enhance yoga and meditation practices. It can help with acceptance of one's situation and with insomnia.

To apply the oils for aromatherapy, you can place them at pulse points or even right under the nostrils. If a rash develops, get help immediately. Rashes are unusual, but they can occur as an allergic reaction. The safest method is to put the oil in an aromatherapy cold diffuser where none of the its qualities are lost. Other people prefer to make their own spray formulas or use the oils in the bath.

## Naturopathic Medicine

About two hundred years ago, a German named Vincenz Priessnitz noticed a deer that had been shot in the hind end by an arrow. The deer slowly made its way down into a cool stream, where it proceeded to stretch out so that it could immerse the wound deeply in the water. After a period of time, the deer carefully rose and retired to the forest. Day after day for weeks the deer would come to the same spot to bathe its wound. One day Priessnitz noticed that the deer's flank was fully healed. Astonished and intrigued, he decided to apply the same natural principles of cold-water healing to people for various ailments, with much success. Word of the natural water cure spread, and people began to go far and wide to seek treatments. Health spas and sanatoriums sprang up all over Europe. Thus began the modern history of the nature cure in Europe—medicine based upon observations of healing in nature. This knowledge grew and expanded in scope and was eventually imported to America as naturopathic medicine in the early 1900s.

If you live in Seattle; Portland, Oregon; Canada; or Europe, chances are you know someone who has been to a naturopathic doctor. For others, naturopathic medicine may sound strange or even like quackery. Naturopaths are doctors who go for four years to naturopathic medical schools to study the natural healing of the body. They are highly trained practitioners of holistic medicine. About a dozen states in the United States now support or require the reimbursement of licensed naturopathic doctors by insurance companies. In other countries, notably Germany, naturopathy has long been integrated into the medical systems.

Our modern medical physicians can do wondrous things: open plugged hearts, mend broken bones and bodies, do microscopic surgeries, look inside the body, and even eliminate cancer on occasion. If the problem is mechanical or related to invading bacteria, doctors can usually fix it through surgery or medicine. This approach is miraculous when it works, but some disorders baffle physicians and frustrate patients: chronic pain, obesity, autoimmune disorders, allergies, and stress-related disorders, to name a few. Naturopathic doctors excel in treating these and other hard-to-treat conditions.

Whereas medical doctors concern themselves with diseases and calamities, naturopathic doctors concern themselves with the wellness mechanisms in the body. They are interested not so much in the disease itself, but in why and how the disease sets up in this particular body to begin with. Naturopathic doctors look deeply into the ongoing condition of the body, or the *terrain* as they call it. They specialize in mobilizing the body to repair itself and investigate how those mechanisms of healing break down. *Naturopathic doctors consider disease a result of faulty terrain, not so much a result of invading organisms.* They reason that bacteria and viruses are always waiting to invade the body, but not everybody gets sick. Naturopaths ask, why now and why this pathogen (disease)? Whereas traditional physicians ask, which pathogen?

Naturopathic medicine excels in treating stress-related illness. Indeed, in my interviews with naturopathic doctors across the country, all stated that they believe the primary illness of our time is chronic and/or acute stress and trauma. To address all illnesses, including stress and trauma, naturopathic doctors use the following modalities:

- *Hydrotherapy*: the use of warm and cool water to stimulate healing

- *Homeopathy*: a low-risk energy medicine

- *Neuromuscular technique*: a form of spinal manipulation

- *Nutritional supplementation*: minerals, vitamins, amino acids, and others

- *Herbal remedies*

- *Lifestyle counseling and coaching*

- *Acupuncture*: Many naturopathic schools have an acupuncture track.

- *Pharmaceutical medication*: In some states naturopathic doctors are licensed to prescribe medication.

The motto of the American Association of Naturopathic Physicians is "Physicians Who Listen." Unlike modern medical physicians, naturopathic doctors take an extensively detailed history of life events and lifestyle to get to the root of illness. They do not separate emotional healing from physical healing. They investigate all potential factors of disease and disturbance of the terrain of the body: mental, emotional, genetic, environmental, spiritual, social, and sexual. For this reason, traumatized patients often find them helpful and user-friendly, rarely feeling rushed or unheard as they may in a more traditional setting. Many clients who feel traumatized in some way by conventional medicine enjoy trusting and helpful relationships with their naturopathic doctors.

In the United States, public opinion and information about naturopathic doctors is mixed. Some states have made their practice illegal (South Carolina, Tennessee). Most states, however, permit the practice of naturopathic medicine. The state of Washington recognizes the right of a naturopathic doctor to be a primary care provider, and several states are poised to follow suit. These regional differences result from a long history of competition between medical and naturopathic doctors in the United States.

Due to the politics of medical funding, research on naturopathic medicine has been difficult. Recently a shift has been happening in parts of this country towards holistic medicine. Other countries, such as Germany, where Priessnitz began his water cures, already have a long tradition of naturopathic medicine that is fully integrated with other medical services. I encourage you to do your own research about the medical provider that will be best for you (see the resources section for more information).

Dickson Thom is a professor and the chair of naturopathic medicine at the National College of Natural Medicine located in Portland, Oregon. He lectures extensively on naturopathic medicine and is the author of *Coping With Food Intolerances*. He is a highly sought-after teacher and has had some dramatic cures over his many years of practice. I had the privilege of interviewing him about naturopathic treatment of traumatic stress over dinner one night. He stated that when people come to him with extreme stress or trauma, he encourages them to eliminate all sugars and grains, even rice, from their diets immediately. (Although this measure may sound draconian, many of my PTSD patients have found relief by doing it on their own before they even get to therapy.) As a staple diet Thom recommends lots of fresh organic vegetables, especially potatoes, sweet potatoes, and yams for grounding, with fish, chicken, or turkey. The only oils he recommends are fresh butter and olive oil, especially on starchy vegetables to reduce the glycemic index in these foods. Reducing stress and calming down the nervous system require the addition to the diet of two to four tablespoons of ground seeds daily, a B-complex vitamin, and, most important of all, up to thirty grams of fish oil a day. When I said that thirty grams seemed like a lot, he agreed and said that the best way to take the oil was by the tablespoon. I confessed I was a bit surprised and asked him how he got his patients to take that much. He leaned forward warmly, with a smile on his face, rested his hand on my arm and said, "This is going to *really* help you."

Other important strategies he mentioned were sleeping in a totally dark, quiet room, eating and sleeping on a consistent schedule, and getting at least thirty minutes of sunshine every day, preferably in the early morning or late evening to reduce risk of skin damage.

Naturopathic medicine can be an important ally in strengthening the physical body while in states of traumatic shock or extreme stress. To find a naturopathic doctor, you can look online, consult a naturopathic college clinic, or research your local yellow pages.

## Massage Therapy

Massage therapy can be used in a wide range of ways to treat traumatic stress, from relaxing the body to soothing sore tension-laden muscles to safely releasing traumatic memories held in the body. No matter how often you work out or sit in the hot tub, chronic tension related to stress sometimes just refuses to release. In this case, it is useful to engage the services of a massage professional for single sessions or ongoing treatment.

Forty-three states require some form of licensure to practice massage therapy. To qualify, a massage therapist must graduate from an accredited school of massage therapy where anatomy, physiology, and good practice technique are mastered. Hundreds of valid techniques exist to provide relief from stress-related conditions. For stress reduction you may want to consider choosing a medical massage practitioner rather than going to a spa where the massage therapists are more generic and not necessarily oriented to the needs of a patient with a stress condition.

Because of the extremely sensitive, keyed-up condition of a traumatized nervous system, some techniques work better than others. If you have a history of violent or sexual assault, you may find some forms of massage therapy triggering and unpleasant. On the other hand, getting to the place of being able to receive a massage can be a form of healing in and of itself. Here are a few forms of massage that are tolerated well by people with PTSD and other stress-related conditions:

- *Craniosacral massage* falls into the gentle, light-touch category. It works gently with the cranium, spine, and sacrum to facilitate optimal functioning of the nervous system. You can stay clothed. It is very relaxing and highly recommended for PTSD.

- *Reflexology* works with a system of pressure points in the feet (and occasionally the hands) that correspond to certain organ systems in the body. It is gently stimulating and soothing, with a lovely footbath included. Usually clothing remains on.

- *Shiatsu* is another clothes-on procedure similar to reflexology except it works on pressure points all over the body. You lie on a mat or on a table. Stretching and pulling can also be part of this healing-massage experience.

- *Swedish massage* is done on a massage table with cloth draping over a nude or seminude body. This massage can use oils or lotions with or without fragrances, according to your preferences. Characterized by long sweeping strokes, Swedish massage is one of the most common massage forms used in spas and therapeutically. Pressure can be gentle or deep, according to your preference.

- *Rolfing* can be very intense to receive. A deep form of massage, it aims to restructure the body and release restrictive fascia encapsulating the muscles, usually over the course of ten sessions. Warning: Though some people absolutely love this modality, rolfing can be triggering. Good communication with your practitioner is essential for a safe and effective treatment.

- *Pedicures* can help. Don't laugh. When I was recovering from my PTSD, my shamanic counselor, of all people, strongly recommended that I get a pedicure. I found a group of Vietnamese women skilled in pedicures and oriental foot massage. The pedicure was blissful and, for a while, the only massage I could tolerate—kind of like reflexology, but you come out with pretty toenails. Many people find it very therapeutic, and many salons take walk-ins!

To get the most out of your massage follow these steps:

1. Stay grounded and in your body.

2. Speak up immediately if any uncomfortable feelings arise. Massage therapists are not mind readers, and they can be helpful only to the degree you communicate with them.

3. Notice if you are getting triggered during the massage. If so, ask for a break or direct the therapist to work in a different way or area of the body.

4. Know that you drive your own healing process. If it's not working for you or it feels wrong, stop and leave. Feel free to try out different practitioners.

## Chiropractic Care

The stress of PTSD and of the healing process on the nervous and muscular systems in the body cannot be underestimated. Tension creates muscular stress. Traumatic anxiety, with or without some form of intervention, can make muscles tighten without our knowing it. These muscles attach to bones. The pulling forces created by stress can end in a slight displacement of the bones of the spine, skull, or ribs, creating enormous pain and muscle spasms, headaches, or neurological issues for the survivor.

People with PTSD often have back and neck issues they do not always connect to their traumas. I have observed several times in my practice that people's backs can go out when they are in the midst of extreme stress or are processing intense rage or fear. It is almost as if the spinal cord acts like a giant circuit breaker. When people become overwhelmingly angry or anxious, their backs will go out, and they will become immobilized temporarily by bad headaches or neck, shoulder, or back spasms. Even intense tightness in the muscles resulting from stress can pull on the spine, setting one up for a back incident, which can spread, if left unaddressed, to organs, joints, and other areas of the body.

Pain is not the only signal that one should seek chiropractic services. A patient who was processing a lot of painful memories became flooded and started to experience some intense symptoms of vertigo and spaciness, well beyond her emotional reactions. At her chiropractic visit she was surprised to find that the doctor needed to adjust the dural tube, the sheath surrounding the brain and spinal cord. Apparently, it had become so torqued under stress that it was affecting the normal flow of cerebrospinal fluid. After one visit, her equilibrium was restored, and those symptoms did not return.

Many trauma survivors have been through some sort of physical-force injury or trauma along with the emotional wounding of extreme stress. Soldiers who have endured heavy blast shocks to their bodies, rape and assault victims, and car-accident survivors are just a few examples of people who have these types of physical insults. The physical shocks of such events compromise the functioning of the nervous system by misaligning the spine or displacing other parts of the body. The services of a good chiropractor then become not a luxury for survivors, but a necessity.

A slight displacement of the vertebrae or spinal subluxation can create interference in the body's natural neural functions. All of the communication between brain and body passes through the spinal cord and branching nerves. If these nerves are compromised in some way, we do not have optimal health, and we can develop pain, stress, or even lower resistance to diseases over time. Chiropractic adjustments restore the proper alignment of the spine and/or other elements of the skeletal structure. The body then has a chance to heal, reduce or eliminate pain, and maximize functioning.

Chiropractic care is a uniquely American offering, although its roots can be traced to China and Greece between four and five thousand years ago. In 1895 Daniel David Palmer founded the first school of chiropractic care in Davenport, Iowa. Since then, chiropractic schools have sprung up all over this country to train doctors in spinal manipulation. According to the American Chiropractic Association, these doctors must complete four years and approximately 4,200 hours of classroom, laboratory, and clinical education. In order to practice, they must become board certified at the federal and state levels. Once dismissed as quackery, doctors of chiropractic are now considered primary care providers in many states and are considered physicians under Medicare. Many accept insurance.

Chiropractors can specialize in different areas of health. Several chiropractic colleges have postdoctoral training in areas such as neurology, orthopedics, nutrition, sports injuries, family practice, and pediatrics. Chiropractic physicians, like other holistic health practitioners, are trained to look at the whole patient, including lifestyle, to help maximize health. If you see a chiropractor, expect to fill out detailed health forms and possibly receive an X-ray or two to assess skeletal damage and rule out more serious conditions such as a herniated disc.

Through a variety of methods, chiropractors simply help the body assume its best form to promote healing by restoring the position of the spine and sometimes joints, muscles, and tendons. Techniques range from the original bone-crunching method of hands-on manipulation to subtler techniques such as the Activator Method, or controlled force. You may need to do some research about which technique works best for you. Some people love the subtler techniques while loathing having their neck cracked, while others don't feel anything is happening unless they hear and feel a big pop.

Because traumatic stress by definition involves the central nervous system, it is important for your healing that your spinal cord is in good working order! A chiropractor can make this assessment. In addition, chiropractors are experts in holistic health, and they may have other helpful modalities available for your healing process, such as cold laser healing, electrical stimulation, or supplements. I consider at least one chiropractic visit mandatory when healing from PTSD or any other stress disorder.

## Eye Movement Desensitization Response

Eye movement desensitization response (EMDR) has shown positive results in clinical research trials as a treatment for PTSD and related trauma disorders. In 1987, Francine Shapiro, PhD, discovered, during a walk, that she was making eye movements that helped dissipate the stress reaction in her body to upsetting memories. Being a student of therapy and of mindfulness, she was intrigued by this phenomenon. She began asking patients in therapy with her to move their eyes back and forth while recalling distressing material. She saw an amazing reduction in symptoms in her clients and soon after began research trials. Today EMDR is acknowledged as a premier treatment for PTSD. Luminaries in the field of PTSD such as Bessel van der Kolk, MD, strongly endorse her work.

Practitioners of EMDR are almost always licensed psychotherapists or psychiatrists, since it is best used in conjunction with psychotherapy. The exact mechanism of EMDR remains unknown, although practitioners widely agree that EMDR "unsticks" the brain, facilitating processing of unpleasant or traumatic memories.

EMDR seems to work best for people who have had only one or a small number of exposures to traumatic events, for example, a car accident or a single violent attack. The results have been less conclusive for soldiers or patients with complex trauma, people who have had multiple traumatic events throughout their childhood. If you choose to explore EMDR, make sure you find someone who is certified with official EMDR training and is a licensed professional. The first few sessions should be psychotherapy in preparation for the actual EMDR technique. As with any therapy, if you find your symptoms are becoming worse, talk to your therapist and evaluate whether this is the right therapy for you.

## PSYCHIATRIC MEDICATION

Herbal remedies can be wonderful, but for some people suffering intense or complex post-traumatic stress disorder, they just don't provide the necessary relief. Not nearly enough studies have been done yet on psychiatric medication and PTSD, but we do know a few things. One thing we know is that no medication by itself takes care of PTSD. All the medications listed below are best used in conjunction with psychotherapy.

Most of the traumatically stressed patients I have worked with do not want to use psychiatric medications. Some of them have been misdiagnosed in the past and put on medications that made them feel terrible, such as antipsychotic medications or medications for bipolar illness. Others object on principle, stating they are normal and don't want to be treated as someone ill, but as someone wounded. Complex trauma that occurred early in life and profoundly affected the brain's functioning can look like other disorders. Psychiatry, like any field, is still evolving its knowledge in this area, so many patients initially end up misdiagnosed, especially if they don't remember or know about early trauma.

The National Center for PTSD states on its website (www.ptsd. va.gov) that research on medication is inconclusive for children and adolescents with traumatic stress. Bear in mind that the medications discussed below are *for adults only*. There are three basic types of psychiatric medication that individuals with PTSD have found helpful.

- *SSRIs*: Selective serotonin reuptake inhibitors are antidepressant and antianxiety medications. They help to mediate the level of serotonin in the brain. One psychiatrist I know refers to them as "brain grease." For patients with PTSD they seem to help anxiety more than they help depression. They have been shown to help protect and even restore the part of the brain called the hippocampus. The hippocampus plays an important role in emotions and short-term memory, and it tends to shrink in people with PTSD. SSRIs can prevent shrinkage or help restore the normal size of the hippocampus in people with traumatic stress. Some common names of SSRIs include Celexa, Prozac, Lexapro, and Zoloft. If one doesn't work for you, another might; they all have slightly different compositions and side effects. Unpleasant side effects can include drowsiness, nausea, or loss of sexual appetite. A few of these medications have what is known as a short uptake, meaning it takes about four days to go on or come off them, as opposed to six weeks for the usual SSRI. Most of my patients prefer the short-uptake SSRIs (e.g., Lexapro, Celexa) because they quickly feel relief and can come off them rapidly if they don't work or the side effects aren't liked. Although your primary care physician can prescribe them, I highly recommend seeing a specialist such as a psychiatric nurse or psychiatrist to get the most effective treatment. Internal-medicine physicians are not generally up to date on the latest treatments for PTSD.

- *Anxiolytics*: Also known as antianxiety or antipanic medications, these drugs provide powerful quick relief from overwhelming symptoms of an overstimulated nervous system. They can be taken PRN (*pro re nata*, "as needed") or on a regular basis and are often given out in emergency rooms for acute states of panic. Some anxiolytics such as benzodiazepines (e.g., Valium, Xanax, Ativan) or barbiturates (Phenobarbital, Sodium Pentothal) can be highly addictive and are not recommended for long-term usage. Please consider their usage in the short term with a physician's prescription and supervision. They are highly effective and can get people back to functioning in their lives very quickly.

- *Beta-blockers*: These medications are not psychotropic; in other words they do not act directly on the brain. Beta-adrenergic blockers (beta-blockers) were originally developed to help with symptoms of heart disease such as chest pain and high blood pressure, but they have been found to be very effective with PTSD and chronic stress. These drugs lower the ceiling on the physical reaction to stress, rage, and fear by blocking the effects of adrenaline on the brain and body. They have been used effectively with Vietnam veterans in helping modulate rage responses. Many clients who don't like the idea of using psychotropic drugs are open to beta-blockers, drugs that have helpful and minimal side effects. The main reason not to use them would be if you have very low blood pressure or low heart rate. You can get a prescription from a doctor or nurse-practitioner.

- *Antiseizure medications*: Although these types of drugs (such as Tegretol, Topamax, and Depakene) can be very effective at mood stabilization and reduction of irritability and aggression, they can have some very unpleasant side effects, which may include sedation and weight gain. Talk to your physician, psychiatrist, or psychiatric nurse-practitioner about the pros and cons of this class of drugs.

- *Over the counter*: A lot of inpatient psychiatric units use Benadryl as a quick, safe PRN (temporary) treatment for agitation and extreme stress. Benadryl is an antihistamine available in most grocery and drug stores for allergies. The main side effect of Benadryl is extreme tiredness and fatigue. It can help people who are in acute states of anxiety and panic calm down and sleep, but *only in the recommended dosages and only temporarily.* Talk to your physician about an appropriate long-term solution. Dramamine can also be used in a pinch and has a similar profile to Benadryl (antihistamine, sedative effect). Please note that in some people, and especially children, antihistamines can cause what is called a paradoxical reaction, in that the patient becomes more rather than less excitable. If you have this reaction, discontinue use immediately.

• *Street drugs*: Many people have already turned to two prevalent street drugs to work with their traumatic stress, marijuana and ecstasy (MDMA or 3-4-methylenedioxymethamphetamine). The evidence on these two substances is inconclusive thus far, but promising research is being done internationally. In some states you can obtain a medical card for PTSD that allows you to grow and smoke marijuana to alleviate symptoms, but MDMA is still completely illegal in the United States, although it has recently been used in some studies with traumatized veterans. It is unfortunate that patients seeking these substances are labeled in a highly negative way, because it is natural for all mammals to seek substance relief when in pain.

Painkillers (e.g., oxycodone), methamphetamines, and opiates are often illegally used when patients have greater amounts of trauma in their backgrounds. Although these drugs may be tempting, they are dead ends that can ruin or take your life. Some patients I have worked with have described them as dirty or self-abusing drugs. If you are using them now, please get help to get off them as soon as possible.

## BIOFEEDBACK

Biofeedback employs modern technology to teach the body and the brain states of relaxation conducive for healing. Different types of biofeedback use different equipment to provide feedback about how your body is responding to self-training efforts. One of the simplest biofeedback mechanisms is a handheld thermometer, used to teach people how to raise the body temperature. Raising body temperature creates a relaxation response and is often the first step in PTSD protocols for stress reduction.

Heart-rate variability (HRV) responds to stress levels. Biofeedback not only can help you slow your heart rate and lower your blood pressure but can also help to induce deep relaxation. You can do this with a biofeedback practitioner or on your own. The Institute of Heart Math (www.heartmath.org) provides equipment, research, and training to those interested in HRV training. You can purchase a unit to practice with on your own for about two hundred dollars. This technology is rapidly evolving to provide convenience for the consumer. There is now a computer application for HRV training— for about seventy-five dollars you can purchase equipment and an iPhone app from www.ithlete.com.

Neurofeedback is a type of biofeedback that works with the brain. Your brain gives off measurable waves depending on your state (waking, sleeping, etc). It is not unusual for people with traumatic stress to feel unable to relax and to have problems with insomnia. Creative problem solving is constricted, and tension is unremitting. The Peniston protocol[3] is famous for demonstrating how alpha-theta-wave training reduces PTSD symptoms. People with chronic traumatic stress sometimes have trouble generating any alpha-theta-wave activity spontaneously, meaning they are never in a true state of relaxation. If you are one of those people who have trouble relaxing or falling asleep, or if you go right from waking to sleep only to wake up in the middle of the night, this protocol may be for you. Remarkably, not only does this protocol reduce psychiatric symptoms associated with PTSD, but it also improved scores on personality functioning as measured on the MMPI (Minnesota Multiphasic Personality Inventory). Biofeedback research is so promising that it is being used in state-of-the-art trauma facilities, and the military uses it for soldiers returning from war with combat-stress injury.

If you go for biofeedback treatment, here's what you should know:

1. Find a practitioner certified by the Biofeedback Certification International Alliance (BCIA) in biofeedback, neurofeedback, or both.

2. Make sure your practitioner is also at least a master's-level licensed counselor or psychotherapist. It is not usual for memories to come up during treatment or for psychiatric symptoms to emerge (in rare cases, even suicidality).

3. For treatment to work you will need to be highly motivated and self-starting.

4. Shorter treatments for PTSD can be twenty to forty sessions. Longer can be up to sixty or so. How long treatment takes depends on how often you go for sessions.

5. Your insurance may or may not cover biofeedback and/or neurofeedback.

6. An accomplished practitioner will assess for other existing conditions such as traumatic brain injury or tumors.

7. Adults and teens can do well with biofeedback. Effectiveness has not been established for younger children, who have a shorter attention span.

Many people enjoy biofeedback because they can see results very quickly, and they don't have to talk a lot about their feelings.

Also, there are no worrisome side effects to the brain or body from biofeedback, only the normal risks associated with working through traumatic stress.

## Heat Therapies

### Saunas and Hot Tubs

For chronic unremitting tension, a variety of people have found success with heat therapies such as saunas and hot tubs. All of these modalities help in two major ways. First, they force the body into a state of profound physical relaxation, and, second, they help the body to expel toxins through sweat.

Saunas and hot tubs have the advantage of being relatively easy to obtain for personal use. Your local gym probably has one or both of these types of equipment. They are not terribly expensive in the long run to install for personal use and fairly easy to maintain. Regular use seems to bring the greatest benefit.

### Sweat Lodges

Sweat lodges are Native American ceremonies, run by medicine people. The lodge itself is built out of small trees and natural materials made by the hosting tribe, then heated inside with carefully selected wood, stones, and water. A spiritual leader with many years of training conducts the sacred ceremony, which leads to profound healing. Sweat lodges can be safe places to talk because they are dark and contained, but sometimes ceremonies are conducted in silence. Profound releases of stress can happen for participants when sweats are conducted safely and with integrity. The tribes describe sweat lodges as a kind of mental and physical purification. Research done with veterans in sweat lodges has shown a positive effect on mood and muscle tension.[4] Sweat lodges are *not* saunas and should not be imitated by nontribal, unqualified people. In early 2009 a charismatic but incompetent leader held a sweat lodge in which two participants died and eighteen were hospitalized, a highly unusual and terrible outcome. Always follow your bodily cues and leave any event if you start to feel sick or overcome by heat.

All the heat modalities carry some risk. Heat stroke and heat exhaustion should be guarded against with adequate hydration and permission to come and go as needed. A little goes a long way with these powerful healing modalities. Traumatized people can sometimes (understandably) tend to go overboard with things that bring relief of suffering. Consult your physician if you are unsure about how much is too much.

## MUSIC

The often-misquoted William Congreve wrote in his play *The Mourning Bride*, "Music hath charms to soothe the savage breast, / To soften rocks, or bend a knotted oak." Indeed. Listening to music has become so much a part of our culture that our lives have a veritable soundtrack. We use music to get pumped up and music to relax. We connect with friends or isolate ourselves through music. Music is ubiquitous: it's in our phones, our computers, on our televisions, and even in our elevators. With my youngest clients, asking what music they listen to is an important part of the assessment. This discussion connects me in a more relevant and immediate way to their lives and helps me understand their issues and perspectives.

Some people with traumatic stress cannot bear any harsh music. Their finely tuned nervous systems can only handle the soothing strains of New Age or classical music. Others want head-banging, loud, and gritty music, the more shocking and foul, the better. What makes for this disparity? Does it make a difference in healing from trauma?

Like anything else, we can use music consciously or reactively. In contemplating the power of music, I have found two important but very different purposes for healing with music: mirroring and soothing. Mirroring music reflects back to us our traumatic states. Rage, fear, and anxiety all find their place in contemporary music, especially in genres such as heavy metal, punk, and rap. We all need to be mirrored, to feel that someone else understands our condition. It is a basic human need, and it can be very healing. On the other hand, when this type of music is played for plants, at least in anecdotal accounts, they wilt and die within short periods of time. If all a person listens to for a prolonged period of time is music filled with hatred, rage, and fear, the body may be reinforced in these states in a harmful way.

Soothing music cranks down the nervous system and allows us to exhale. It can entrain the brain to softer, more coherent states of functioning and enable us to perform better in our lives. For instance, I never learned to like Bach or housekeeping until I started to listen to Bach when cleaning the house. The orderly square melodies and mathematical roundness somehow helped me to focus and organize in a delightful way.

In other words, music has a physical effect on the brain that leads to changes in our physiology and functioning. I want to be clear here. *There is no right or wrong music to listen to in healing from trauma, but there is music that is more or less helpful, and finding the kind that helps you is a very individual process of discovery.* If you listen to music, start becoming conscious of what you are listening to and why. You can start to enlist the aid of music to lift yourself out of traumatic states.

A few years ago I put together a CD of music for survivors and gave it out in therapy sessions. The feedback was tremendously positive. It began with music by artists that mirrored trauma, despair, anger, and hopelessness (Tool, R.E.M., Sia, punk, heavy metal, or even Gorecki), then moved into fighting back (Seal, Bryan Adams, Peter Gabriel, David Gray, Adele, Carole King, Annie Lennox ) inspiration (Krishna Das or other religious music), uplift (classical, movie, and commercial music), and new vision (Sigur Ros, Enigma, current pop artists, New Age, Adiemus). You can use music as one of your tools to "change the channel" of your moods, to take yourself on a journey, or to be more comfortable in different feeling states. And let's not forget the making of music. Whether alone or together, people have always made music as a form of self-expression, even as a way to give voice to the inexpressible horrors of trauma. Whether you listen, participate, or create, do so in a conscious way and harness the incredible power of music.

## UNWINDING THE BODY

All experiences are ultimately processed through the physical body. When we repress our experiences, we do so with the body. Tension, spasms, and shallow breathing are all signs of stuck trauma within the body itself. You could view this as the body's incomplete response to a traumatic event. Let's say you were hit hard and wanted to hit back but couldn't because you were too little, too scared, too whatever. The body, in its natural biological response, wanted to fight back, but the mind stopped it. After a while you could develop tension in the shoulders and upper back from the incomplete swing your body wanted to take, tension whose origins are forgotten or unknown. These physical responses are often paired with the emotion of the moment. So, if you were too scared to fight for yourself, there may also be repressed rage and fear.

Animals lack the inhibition of a mind over the body, so they tend to react instinctively in a dangerous situation with avoidance, fighting, or freezing, just like humans. Unlike humans, though, animals very quickly discharge tension after a frightening event. If you have a dog, you might notice how it will shake out its tension from head to tail after a fright or a reprimand. Horses neigh loudly and run around discharging energy or, like dogs and other animals, shake vigorously to discharge tension after a negative experience. As culturally socialized humans, we tend to inhibit these natural responses to traumatic stress, instead holding them deep inside our tissues.

Several body-oriented therapies can help release the stored emotions and tensions. Physical therapy, yoga therapy, and massage therapies can address these issues if the practitioner is specially trained. Dr. Peter Levine, who has doctorates in both psychology and medical biophysics, has developed a combination psychotherapy and body therapy called Somatic Experiencing® (SE) in which survivors learn to listen to their bodies and move according to what their bodies need to do in order to discharge trauma energy safely and thoroughly, thus restoring normal functioning to the nervous system. The beauty of Dr. Levine's technique is that it doesn't require a lot of language to do and can be transposed into many different cultures and situations. You can find more information on his SE techniques and practitioners at www.traumahealing.com.

Just placing awareness on the body can begin the healing process for many. Practice noticing where your body is stiff and tight. Are there areas you don't feel comfortable touching or moving? Move through these areas, breathing deeply; notice if any emotions come up, and, if it feels safe, allow yourself to release them in a safe way. A little shaking wouldn't hurt either. In fact, one technique in Chinese healing involves thoroughly shaking the body to get the qi flowing evenly through it. This body energy is intimately connected to the physical body and takes us to our next layer, the energy body, or pranamayakosha.

*Sometimes in your own body the supply of Prana gravitates more or less to one part; the balance is disturbed, and when the balance of Prana is disturbed, what we call disease is produced. To take away the superfluous Prana, or to supply the Prana that is wanting, will be curing the disease.*
—Swami Vivekenanda

# Tool 6

# The Pranamayakosha: Healing Your Energy Body

BEFORE WE LAUNCH into a discussion of the energy body, or pranamayakosha, I invite you to do a little exercise. Rub your hands together very briskly. Rub them until you start to feel some heat build up, maybe ten to twenty seconds. Now quickly separate them wide apart. Now bring them together slowly. Pay close attention to the sensation in the middle of your palms. You may reach a point at which you feel some subtle sensation of resistance, or maybe a tingling feeling or even warmth. Notice at what point that is reached. It is different for everyone. A minority of people will not feel anything. If you are having difficulty feeling the energy between your hands, close your eyes and do it again. You can also try it with a partner. That "ball" of energy you encounter is subtle energy coming out of your activated hands.

What is the energy body, and why do we need to talk about it? As discussed in the fourth chapter, the energy body surrounds and interpenetrates the physical body. The chakras step down and

133

distribute the universal life forces into the body, and these forces are then distributed by subtle nerve currents called meridians in Chinese medicine or nadis in yoga. These subtle nerves of the energy body transport life force to all the organs, flesh, and tissues of the body. They assist in the very functioning of the body systems and are multidimensional.

When there is a blockage or impedance of the flow of energy, disease results. If you have taken a yoga class, you have been working with prana. If you have taken a tai chi or qigong class, you have been working with qi. Both the Chinese and Indian systems assume this energy system as a reality. These systems do have some differences in location, naming, and such, but they both assume there is a functioning subtle energy system animating the body. In fact, most cultures around the world acknowledge and work with subtle energy systems acting in and around the body. Some healers see and/or feel the energy fields of patients as lights, patterns, and even objects. These people are called clairvoyants and are usually born with this ability. Many schools in the United States have been set up to help such gifted healers refine their techniques.

What is often challenging for those of us in the West is the notion that what you see is what you get. If you are one of the majority who can't see energies, it is hard to believe in them. Yet, many of us do have direct experiences of prana. For instance, have you ever felt you were being stared at, then turned around, and there someone was? Or, do you have the ability to walk into a room and feel the "vibe"? What about feelings of creepiness or ickiness emanating from someone? Or someone in whose presence you feel blessed and uplifted? These effects are all the results of subtle energies and their fields.

Trauma deeply affects the flow of energy in the body. Freud famously discovered that some of his patients were so traumatized they had withdrawn all of the energy from certain parts of their bodies, creating abnormal sensations or lack of sensation. He saw people who were "hysterically" (as he called it) blind and paralyzed. When they were able to talk about their feelings, thereby unsticking their energy, the flow returned to those areas, and they were cured. If you look at old movies of soldiers with battle shock, you see men who move with a great deal of spasticity, sometimes to the point of not being able to stand and walk. Nowadays, those symptoms are fairly uncommon. My guess is that because soldiers now have a greater ability to show their feelings and to use language to describe the horrors of war, their bodies are not affected by trauma in the same way.

Although your physician and mental health provider may not feel comfortable talking to you about the flow of your prana or qi, chances are they have heard about it or taken a yoga class! Unless he or she is extremely old-fashioned, your doctor probably has some curiosity about or experience with these modalities. It is not uncommon to see complementary medicine (code for energy, alternative, or vibrational medicine) listed among physicians' interests on their websites. Some medical centers are starting to sponsor residencies or fellowships in integrative medicine. In the fields of both mental health and medicine, professionals can now get continuing-education credits for workshops that discuss energetic modes of healing. Increasing numbers of health professionals in all disciplines, including psychiatry, attend such workshops.

The treatments in this section address the flow of subtle energies in the body. Subtle energies require subtle medicine. People who have worked clairvoyantly will tell you they can see diseases and problems of the body in the energy body long before they finally manifest in the physical body. Think about that. What if we could stop a potential problem before it shows up as heart disease or cancer or another dire issue? What a gift and a blessing!

Trauma and traumatic energies disrupt our subtle-body energies through blockages and impedance. Modalities that unblock the energy body are great complements to other forms of treatment. In many cases they are the only treatment necessary. Harvard Medical School has been a leading proponent of complementary therapies, many of which are energy based; Children's Hospital in Boston was the first to offer pediatric acupuncture. Seattle Children's Hospital sports an entire department of complementary and integrative medicine. The National Institutes of Health (NIH) and the Pentagon have been investigating many of these therapies for PTSD. In fact, the NIH supports the National Center for Complementary and Alternative Medicine, which researches and disseminates information on these modalities (http://nccam.nih.gov/). Many of my patients have found these to be tremendously helpful.

## CHINESE MEDICINE

Although Chinese medicine is thousands of years old, only in the last few years has this practice become more popular in the United States. Acupuncture, in particular, is gaining in popularity for treating various stress-related disorders, disorders that are notoriously difficult to treat by traditional Western methods. A 2007 National Institutes of Health study by Michael Hollifield, MD, showed that acupuncture was as effective as cognitive behavioral therapy in relieving mental and emotional symptoms of PTSD over a twelve-week period.

More than half of the fifty states now license acupuncturists and Chinese-medicine professionals. Most practitioners go to school for three to four years and have to study anatomy, herbalism, TCM (traditional Chinese medicine), acupuncture, and diagnosis. One-year certifications in acupuncture are available for individuals who are already regularly licensed medical physicians. Some states require that insurance companies provide coverage for the use of Chinese medicine for certain conditions, such as chronic pain. Rest assured that if you seek Chinese medicine or acupuncture from a licensed practitioner, you are likely to get excellent care!

Chinese medicine is a vast subject, thousands of years old, and cannot be covered comprehensively in just a few pages. A licensed acupuncturist or TCM practitioner is learned in qi meridians, the function of the organs, anatomy and physiology, the relation of the seasons to disease, herbalism, philosophy, the effect of the mind on the body, and preventive medicine. All practitioners are encouraged to keep their own energy bodies healthy and unblocked through the practice of such exercises as tai chi and qigong,[1] right diet, and right lifestyle in order to be both good role models and effective practitioners.

## Acupuncture

Acupuncture is one tool of Chinese medicine in a treatment plan that might include traditional Chinese herbal decoctions and lifestyle changes. Diagnostic procedures include looking at the tongue for patterns; feeling subtle pulses in the wrists that correspond to the body's major meridians, organs, or lines of qi; and extensive interviewing of the patient about symptoms and lifestyle. Treatment consists of inserting needles into special points along the qi meridians of the body. These insertion points can and do change from session to session based on what your practitioner is noticing from your symptoms and pulses. Now, I know that some of you are scared to death of needles. Let me reassure you that these needles are extremely thin. Many people never even feel them being inserted. Japanese acupuncture needles are so thin they are often no wider than a human hair! But, if you still oppose the use of any kind of inserted needle, there is another technique that can be used for you: acupressure, the use of force applied with the fingers and hands on acupuncture points.

In either case, most people find acupuncture to be highly relaxing and restorative. It is not uncommon for patients to fall asleep on the acupuncture table. After the needles are inserted, the client lies on the massage table waiting for the treatment to take effect. Often people feel symptoms easing as they wait. The effects of one session last anywhere from a couple of days to a couple of weeks, based on your individual constitution and the severity of your symptoms.

Fees for acupuncture range anywhere from twenty dollars a session for a group clinic—usually ear insertion only—to more than one hundred dollars with, for example, a very specialized practitioner in an expensive state. Most people pay from fifty to seventy-five dollars per session, and often that fee can be covered, at least in part, by insurance. Insurance companies vary as to what they will cover. Most acupuncturists are dedicated healers who will do their best to make sure your treatment is affordable.

Because Chinese medicine treats many seemingly different conditions at the same time, it provides for a range of billable options. Most insurance companies that cover acupuncture will cover chronic physical pain conditions that cannot be treated well with Western medicine. Many people with traumatic stress have chronic pain. Even if your insurance company won't allow for your traumatic stress to be treated, you will be covered if you disclose your pain to your practitioner, who can then treat and bill for that. If you don't have insurance and you live near a school of acupuncture, you can often get free or low-cost appointments with students.

I have been privileged to collaborate with an acupuncturist for the last several years. When I see clients with addictions who don't want to take psychiatric medication or who get stuck in traumatic energy, I refer them to my colleague Michael Berletich, L.Acu. Michael has taught Chinese medicine at both the National College of Natural Medicine and the Oregon College of Oriental Medicine in Portland for the last several years. He specializes in traumatic stress, mental emotional disorders, and the treatment of chronic health issues. He has noted that the people with the most trauma are also often deficient in the earth element, that nurtured part of us that helps us stay grounded on this planet. Someone who has not had good parenting when growing up is almost always deficient in this element. This deficiency leads to imbalances in the flow of qi, which leads to pain, anxiety, and, eventually, disease. To treat traumatically stressed clients, Michael drains the energy of trauma while building up the strength of the body. These treatments have invariably speeded up therapy and provided much-needed stability in the body, mind, and spirit while clients have worked through difficult material.

Michael has also helped me understand the symbolic aspects of trauma and dreams from the perspective of Chinese medicine. One patient was a survivor of multifactorial extreme abuse and neglect. In the middle of her psychotherapy treatment she came in with a very disturbing dream of a black, vicious dragon rising out of a black pool of water. In her dream she became almost immobilized with fear, hiding from this beast. In session, as she reported her dream, she became visibly agitated and fearful that it meant something awful about her past and her progress in healing. When I asked Michael about her dream, he said, "Oh, that's a dream about kidney energy."

He went on to clarify that in Chinese medicine the color black is associated symbolically with the kidney, and the kidney organ is ruled by the element water in nature. The emotion associated with the kidney is fear. He pointed out that dragons, in Chinese medicine, are good luck associated with the earth, with water, and with spiritual power and its ability to transform. When I shared this information with my patient, she was visibly relieved and really connected with the interpretation. She had always loved dragons and kept some dragon imagery in her apartment. This new interpretation of her dream gave her strength in dealing with the fears from her past.

In my experience, acupuncture works best with traumatized people when they are in some sort of counseling or therapy program. Otherwise the practitioner can clear and support the body, but the mind may rehash the trauma, re-creating symptoms. Likewise, therapists who work with extremely traumatized people would do well to work collaboratively with TCM practitioners; otherwise the energy of trauma can linger in the system, disrupting the mind and leaving therapy going in circles. The combination of psychotherapy with Chinese medicine is one of the most potent healing forms I have come across in twenty years of doing this work.

## Chinese Herbs

Chinese herbalism is as extensive as it is ancient. Herbs, roots, plants, trees, minerals, and even the body parts of animals make up the panoply of remedies in a Chinese pharmacy, making it seem a little like an "eye of newt and toe of frog" kind of place. But, this is not witchcraft. Although traditional healers in China went through a period of ridicule and discouragement under Communist leader Mao Zedong, he later reversed his position and honored the ancient healing ways as uniquely Chinese. *Unlike Europe, China never went through a multigenerational period of killing off its herbalists and healers. Some families have preserved knowledge of traditional Chinese medicine in an unbroken lineage of training for many generations.* Whereas much indigenous healing knowledge was lost in the West through what has been called the Burning Times, it has been meticulously preserved in the East, to the benefit of all.

Western herbalism and medication focuses on treating symptoms and pathogens with doses of single substances. Chinese herbs are almost always prescribed in combinations. In Chinese medicine, the goal of the practitioner is to treat illness multidimensionally. Chinese herbal prescriptions always work on three levels: the physical body, the energy body, and the spirit body. Each herb has a flavor (sweet, salty, bitter, pungent, and/or sour) and a nature (yin, yang, hot, cold, or neutral). These flavors and natures each have a function that acts directly on the qi as well as chemically upon the physical body. Herbs are always prescribed to restore balance to the body so that not only do the symptoms resolve, but *the whole body is healthier in its functions.*

How does this affect PTSD and other stress-related disorders? Michael described how a TCM practitioner could see PTSD: When someone encounters a traumatic experience or series of events, the body literally cannot digest the experience. The person's digestion becomes affected, not only energetically but physically. This sets off a string of events that changes the body's physiology and creates pathology, so that in the end the body becomes full of phlegm. This phlegm impairs the ability to process events through the senses clearly, resulting in a cognitive feeling of fogginess and lack of clarity and calmness. Severe anxiety eventually results. In addition, the heart sets up barriers for protection, but like all walls these barriers keep out not only negativity but also positivity. They also prevent feelings from being communicated. The person can no longer feel the joy in the world and can't express it either. To make up for this, the stomach, the place of "I want," takes over, demanding more food or more material goods or, at the other extreme, refusing food and comforts. Sound familiar?

Chinese herbs and acupuncture can scour out the phlegm of the malfunctioning digestive system and restore functionality to the various organs involved in absorbing the trauma. These herbs can support and nurture while unsticking various processes that have gone out of balance and become bogged down. And they do their actions with minimal to no side effects, unlike those associated with the powerful modern medicines of the West. The goal of Chinese medicine is to balance, harmonize, and restore the person to functioning in life at every level.

Although some practitioners still use old-fashioned medicinaries with jars full of mysterious substances that people are sent home to boil, many now prescribe palatable medicines that you make into a tea with a little hot water. American TCM practitioners are increasingly turning to gel caps and modern packaging to dispense easy-to-use herbal remedies.

## Tai Chi and Qigong

If you go to any park in China early in the morning, you will see dozens of people of all ages doing exercises together in a deep, slow, and meditative manner. It is a surprising sight for a Westerner. These people are practicing the ancient healing arts of tai chi and qigong. You have already done one of the exercises, the ball of energy exercise at the opening of this chapter.

Tai chi consists of a series of slow movements designed to improve health and concentration while relieving stress and the effects of stress. Although these exercises originally developed in Buddhist and Taoist monasteries, tai chi is also considered a martial art—but think of it as a martial art in super-slow motion. The movements are gentle and smooth, lending themselves to easy learning and low effort. Elderly people benefit greatly from this gentle yet effective exercise, as do people working around a health issue or handicap. Modern research is proving tai chi to be extremely effective in treating and preventing a wide range of modern ailments. It is excellent for those with exercise intolerance, commonly seen in people with traumatic stress and PTSD.

Qigong and tai chi are usually taught together. Qigong literally means the cultivation of the living energy of the universe, qi, within living organisms. It is also spelled chi kung or chi gung, due to various interpretations of Chinese pronunciation, but don't let that trip you up. Like tai chi, qigong is gentle, noninvasive, and easy to learn. It helps balance the energy body and can restore flow into constricted areas through movement, breath, visualization, and meditation (intention). Don't confuse gentle with weak, though. These exercises are powerful tools for bringing in healing and balance to stressed-out bodies and minds. Another benefit is the coordination and strength they bring to the physical body, creating a feeling of lightness and safety as one moves through the world. In some cases your TCM practitioner may prescribe certain movements or breathing exercises to facilitate the healing process.

A new form of rehabilitative tai chi called tai chi easy can be done while seated. Several different forms of tai chi are taught in classes and on a multitude of DVDs available for purchase. Most people like to get started in a class setting for the more in-depth instruction and opportunity to ask questions. After you learn one of the forms, tai chi can be done anywhere, solo or in a group. Your local college, senior center, community center, or city classes are likely to offer tai chi or qigong or both at reasonable prices. If you want more in-depth instruction, there are entire schools devoted to teaching these forms. Some people with traumatic stress feel triggered or socially anxious in groups and do not want to take classes. If you are one of these, there are dozens of videotapes and online programs offering instruction.

## THOUGHT FIELD THERAPY AND EMOTIONAL FREEDOM TECHNIQUE

Thought Field Therapy (TFT), developed by American psychologist Dr. Roger Callahan, and the Emotional Freedom Technique (EFT), developed by Gary Craig, an engineer who studied with Dr. Callahan, both rely on tapping on acupuncture meridians to dissipate symptoms of trauma and other disorders. Many therapists have trained with one or both of them and may prescribe tapping on certain points in the body as homework to eliminate distress. I have seen symptoms dissipate rapidly with this technique, and there is much anecdotal evidence to support TFT and EFT. However, the research has not been conclusive, and what little research has been done has not been done with scientific rigor. That said, different people will respond differently. Patients with extremely sensitive nervous systems may find benefit in these techniques. No harmful side effects can come from tapping the body's meridians, other than perhaps not getting your money's worth. If you are interested you can find many practitioners of these techniques on the Internet. Gary Craig retired in June 2010, but many of his students still practice around the country.

## Energy Healers

Barbara Brennan, a NASA scientist turned energy healer and teacher, runs four-year schools in the United States, Europe, and Japan that have attracted students from more than forty countries of all ages and walks of life. Her bestselling books *Hands of Light* and *Light Emerging* have become classics in the field of energy healing, with detailed descriptions of the energy field and its dynamics, complete with color pictures and diagrams of energy dynamics. She describes how trauma can rip open and scar chakras, disrupting the body's flow of life force. Over time this chronic disruption creates instability in the health of both mind and body.

There is an additional side effect of chakra damage, especially damage to the second chakra, the one just below your navel, often damaged in sexual abuse, and that side effect is psychic ability or extreme sensitivity to others. This sensitivity can take the form of any of the extrasensory gifts of perception. When people realize they have access to this sensitivity for a reason, they start to feel less crazy and helpless in the world. With training, these gifts can be a tremendous boon to one's life.

Healers who have completed Brennan's program know how to bring balance back to the chakra system and restore functioning and flow in depleted areas. You can find practitioners who have graduated from her program at www.barbarabrennan.com, and her books are available at any bookstore or online.

Similar energy healers who work with prana and chi with varying degrees of talent and training can be found in every state. Although energy healing has been around as long as human beings have been, because it is not recognized as an official healing modality, it is also not regulated or licensed. The best way to find talented energy healers is by word of mouth and experience. Spiritual bookstores and natural food stores often serve as clearinghouses for information about healers in the community. Ask to see their community bulletin boards or binders for referrals. Once you go to a healer, trust your gut. If you like the person and feel helped afterward, great. If not, try someone else or some other modality. Working with the energy body is very personal work and should feel safe, comfortable, and respectful both of your experiences and of you as a person.

## Reiki

Reiki is a specialized form of energy healing brought to the United States from Japan, where it was discovered and developed in the early part of the twentieth century by a Buddhist monk. Reiki practitioners undergo regular study and "attunements" in which they adjust their energy fields to healing work under the tutelage of a more advanced practitioner called a Reiki master. There are an estimated five thousand Reiki masters and half a million Reiki practitioners worldwide.

While medical research on Reiki is inconclusive, most people who receive it report tremendous experiences of relaxation and sometimes spontaneous healing of various conditions. What's nice about Reiki for trauma survivors is that minimal touch is involved. Reiki practitioners channel healing energy through their palms into the client's energy field without skin-to-skin contact being necessary. Reiki treatments can be received sitting or lying down with clothes on and eyes open. People who cannot tolerate massage often do well with this form of treatment. As with many other forms of healing, the results of Reiki will not fully take effect without healthy lifestyle changes by the patient.

## CRYSTALS AND STONES

From ancient times through today, crystals and stones have been effective tools used by healers. Although sometimes made fun of in American media, healing with gems, crystals, and stones has an unbroken tradition in several cultures. Indians have used gems and crystals as a modality in their healing methods for ten thousand years. Tibetans shape crystals to make their famous "singing bowls" that produce healing wavelengths of beautiful sound. Native peoples the world over have utilized crystals and stones in healing sessions and ceremonies. The knowledge of their use was often handed down to medicine men or to special keeper families from generation to generation within the tribes. This information has remained relatively secret until recently. Due to the advent of the Internet and the recent willingness of healers to disclose their knowledge, we now have unprecedented access to this special form of healing.

There is remarkable agreement across these different cultures on the properties of stones and crystals and what they are used for. Among cultures that employ rocks and minerals for healing, all include healing from mental trauma as a prominent function of crystals. In my practice, I direct clients who are open minded and in an acute phase of trauma shock to certain stones and crystals in my office for clearing and grounding, often with profound and immediate results similar to smudging. It is not unusual to find clients intuitively drawn to holding certain stones even if they are not aware of the stones' healing potential or don't believe in crystal healing.

If you are drawn to crystal healing, I encourage you to explore and play with the stones and crystals you are drawn to. If you are not used to working with crystals, begin by working with just one at a time, and observe proper protocol. Most crystal healers commonly agree upon these procedures:

1. Wash and clear your crystal before using. Crystals absorb negative energies around them and can then reradiate these same energies or, at the very least, lose their effectiveness in healing. Regularly clear your crystals by immersing them in sea salt or placing in sunlight for a period of hours to days. Smudging them with sage is also effective. Some crystals, like selenite and quartz, will literally clear up before your eyes when you do so.

2. Bless the crystals or find someone to bless them and express gratitude before using them. Be sure to set some kind of positive or holy intention with your stone or crystal. Crystals used with wrong or unconscious intent can make you more ungrounded, spaced out, or even troubled, the opposite of what we want when healing from trauma.

3. As a general rule, do not sleep with them, and do not wear them all of the time unless you feel strongly guided to or are working with a crystal practitioner.

4. Work with only one crystal at a time until you get a feeling for this kind of treatment. Some people will feel nothing at all; some will feel instant relief, and a few sensitive souls may become dizzy and overwhelmed. As with all energy therapies, more is not necessarily better. Results can be subtle, especially in the beginning. Watch and wait!

Noncrystalline stones such as those you find in rivers or at the beach are fairly hardy and need cleansing only rarely. When they do, you can immerse them in natural water (ocean or stream) or place them in sunlight. Crystals tend to readily absorb and transform our negative energies. Your crystal may darken as you work with it or change color in as little as one session. Under extreme circumstances I have seen them fracture or crumble spontaneously. Remember to cleanse and rejuvenate your crystals on a regular basis, not just when you get them. If you use sea salt as a cleansing agent, throw it away when you are done; do not reuse!

The crystals and stones listed below rank among some of the most helpful for working with traumatic energies. Their qualities and purposes are based on research, interviews with crystal healers and shamans, and my own experience. These are rough guidelines. If you are intuitive, go with your own intuition on how to use them. Each person's energy field is completely different, and the combination that works for you may look very different from someone else's. You don't have to be psychic to find what is helpful—gut feelings and hunches work great too!

## Rose Quartz

Rose quartz is beautiful to look at and to feel. Universally loved for its soft pink color and its gentle healing aura, it works wonders with children and adults alike. Rose quartz gently heals the heart chakra in the areas of love, gentleness, and compassion. Practitioners like its cleansing properties as well as the way it helps the body gently shed outmoded energies and beliefs. Because it is hard to get overwhelmed by rose quartz, it is the ideal stone to wear daily as jewelry or to have in your bedroom or anywhere throughout the house. Young children tend to be drawn to rose quartz, and it can be placed near even the youngest babies who have experienced stressful births, illnesses, and other stressful events. (As with all small objects, please do not place small stones within the reach of small children who could choke on them.)

## Hematite

In the first-aid chapter I talked about the importance of grounding as the very first step to dealing with trauma by getting your attention fully into your body. Hematite is the ultimate grounding stone, an iron-oxide mineral with a shiny steel-gray color. It is very inexpensive to buy, and you only need a small stone to ground yourself effectively. While you can find it in jewelry, I recommend a small palm-size piece you can pick up and hold or put in your pocket. When you are starting to feel dissociative, fearful, or worried about your reality testing, hematite can help you to get calm and focused.

## Calcite

I am very partial to calcites for the powerful yet gentle ways they help people heal from overwhelming stress. Calcite comes in several forms and colors: clear (Iceland spar), blue, green, orange, honey, opaque pink, transparent pink, red, stellar beam (yellow), and white (merkabite). Found on almost every continent, calcite makes up the bulk of marbles and limestones.

Green and pink calcites share many qualities with rose quartz in gently working with healing the heart chakra. They are very gentle crystals with applications to every age group. If you are experiencing medical illness or self-directed anger around your trauma, these stones may help you with forgiveness and acceptance. The energy of green calcite is refreshing and cooling, helpful if dealing with anger issues.

Orange and honey calcites are particularly suited to working with sexual abuse. They are both orange hued, the color of the second-chakra sexual center. You can put a largish-sized orange calcite in a mineral-salt bath to help drain off the extremely toxic energies of sexual abuse. Honey calcite is reputed to help with glandular imbalances caused by extreme stress.

## Selenite

Shaped like a long, thin wand, selenite is a powerful clearing and attunement stone found in Mexico. It helps to raise the individual's consciousness while dissolving emotional and spiritual blockages. Sweeping the wand from head to toe around the body's energy field works to dissipate traumatic energy quickly while helping patients connect with the best parts of themselves. Cleanse regularly!

## Lithium Quartz

This special quartz crystal is found in only one location in the world, in Brazil. It is a pinkish-colored, quartz-shaped crystal, usually small enough to hold in the palm of your hand. This stone gently but powerfully stabilizes emotions and facilitates calm and peaceful states. It is gentle enough to use with children. Practitioners use it to decrease extreme anxiety and panic attacks, and it can be used effectively in conjunction with antianxiety medication.

## Smoky Quartz

If you have trauma or are working with those who do, I highly recommend having this remarkable crystal in your arsenal. Like hematite, smoky quartz is a master grounding stone, but it is also tops for clearing negative energies. When my patients are reliving terrible memories or have gone through something dark, I ask them to hold the smoky-quartz crystal that I keep in my office. The results are immediate and palpable in bringing them back to earth and lifting their mood. This crystal just siphons off negativity. If I could choose just one stone to have in my office, it would be this one. Cleanse after each use.

## Magnetite

The only magnetized rock, magnetite is prized for its ability to move out strong negative energies, including physical and emotional pain. It is a very strong grounding and cleansing stone prized by energy healers the world over for its powerful ability to extract pain and negative emotions.

## Apophyllite

Apophyllite is a beautiful seafoam-green rock. Best used for those with spiritual awareness or intention, this crystal beautifully raises the spiritual vibration of whatever it is around and puts people in touch with their spiritual nature, thinning the veils between human and divine nature. It clears blockages in the crown chakra and helps people realize the divine oneness of all—the ultimate cure for stress and trauma. If you are drawn to it, use it.

## River Stones

Stones found in rivers or in the ocean are wonderful aids in grounding. Unlike crystals, they are not as intense in the energy field and can be lived with twenty-four hours a day without any adverse effects. Put them under your pillow, under your bed, or under your feet as you sit at your desk; they work for stability in your body on the earth. If you are intensely dissociative you can lie flat on your back with a good-sized rock under each hand and foot and under the pillow, breathing gently and deeply until you feel yourself return to your body. Stones that come out of pristine areas in natural water will have a much cleaner vibration than others.

## SMUDGING

One of the most effective tools in clearing traumatic energy is also one of the strangest for modern scientific minds to accept. Native Americans have been using sage, sweetgrass, and cedar in smudging ceremonies for thousands of years and have passed their knowledge along to modern healers. In Portland, Oregon, where I practice, it is very common to find practitioners of all kinds who smudge themselves, their offices, and their clients on a regular basis. Those of us who are sensitive to energies always feel a palpable difference in the room and in the people we work with after smudging. If I could use only one alternative-healing modality in my practice, this would be it. It is simple and benign, and people can get instant relief from their distressing symptoms.

One of the most common herbs for smudging (and many say the most powerful) is white sage, also known as California white sage, bee sage, and *Salvia apiana*. The word *salvia* in Latin means "to save," and for good reason; this potent herb brings profound and instant relief from intense suffering. Traditionally, the healer burns a few leaves in an abalone shell, invoking the four elements of water (the shell), earth (the ash), fire (the fire burning in the sage), and air (the smoke). An important ingredient in the ceremony is thanksgiving for this sacred healing gift. Commonly, a feather, prayer fan, or partial bird's wing is used to disperse negative energies while sweeping the sage smoke through a person's energy field. An attitude of reverence and gratitude when using sage is essential as intention lingers in the environment long after usage.

Today white sage is sold loose leaf or in sticks, bundles of sage held together by twine. You can find smudging sticks in a spiritual bookstore or online, or you can make your own. You only need to burn a very small amount to get the desired effect. I often burn just one leaf if I am clearing a patient or myself.

To smudge, place a lit leaf on a rock or in a small bowl (if you hold it in your hand, burning bits can drop off and mar your flooring or burn the person being smudged). Gently move the leaf completely around the outline of the person, making sure the smoke reaches all parts of the energy field front and back, from the toes to the crown of the head. It is equally effective to smudge yourself or to be smudged. Take your time to be thorough and mindful in this intimate process. Usually, being smudged is experienced as a very pleasant and nurturing experience. Belief is not required for the treatment to work.

A good indication that you need to smudge is the feeling that you are in the "trauma vortex," that swirling, nauseating, disoriented feeling that comes on in the midst of a trauma or in a powerful flashback. Most people I have worked with report a 40 to 60 percent reduction in the intensity of their symptoms when smudged at this time, giving them the help they need to stabilize emotionally and feel empowered. I strongly encourage you to have sage on hand at home, in your car, and in your office to provide instant relief as needed, especially if you have suffered a traumatic event. If you are not in a place where you can burn something, it is also surprisingly effective to crush a sage leaf and inhale its aroma deeply.

Sometimes your whole space can feel congested with stagnant or depressed energy; sensitive people can feel this as darkness, fatigue, or a sticky goo. To clear and lighten your work or home environment, light the whole end of the smudge stick or several leaves in a bowl, so that a good amount of smoke is put out. Always keep a window or door open when doing this so that the negativity has somewhere to go. When you are smudging your space is also a good time to clear crystals or other healing objects you use by holding them briefly in the smoke. A note of caution here: sage can smell like marijuana to the uninitiated. If you are in a shared space, communicate with your neighbors, ventilate, and use the smallest amounts possible.

Another commonly used smudging herb is the abundant sagebrush plant (*Artemisia tridentata*) that grows all over the United States, especially in the southwestern states. You can buy smudge sticks made from sagebrush or harvest your own. Harvesting is best done with an attitude of appreciation and awareness. Always harvest with regard for the health of the plants and respect for the local inhabitants! Native Americans commonly include sweetgrass (for positivity) or cedar (for cleansing) in their sagebrush bundles. Last year I bought some sticks from the Pueblo Indians in New Mexico that included lavender —very sweet smelling and effective.

## HOMEOPATHY

I interviewed three different naturopathic doctors from New York City for this section. They all use homeopathy regularly in their practices, and they all worked in the aftermath of 9/11 using homeopathy. To my surprise, they all recommended the same four remedies as effective in dealing with PTSD and overwhelming stress. Dr. Lauri Grossman, DC, CCH, RSHom(NA), currently chairs the Department of Humanism at the American Medical College of Homeopathy in Phoenix, Arizona, and also has a longstanding private practice in Manhattan. She revealed that evaluating stress-related exhaustion is a key component of her work in New York and that many of her patients have symptoms of PTSD *even if it seems as though they have not been exposed directly to a trauma.* She related that chronic overwhelming stress in daily life can have the same effect on people's bodies as does PTSD and that homeopathy is an excellent way to address these issues. All the practitioners I spoke with revealed that they often work in conjunction with psychotherapists in New York City.

Homeopathic remedies consist of extremely dilute solutions of ingredients, so dilute that there may be only a couple of molecules of the substance in any given preparation. It is a true energy or vibrational medicine, and as such there is no possible danger of overdosing. Although homeopathy was developed in the 1700s in Germany and has been in continuous use since that time in Europe and elsewhere, there is still a fair amount of controversy about its effectiveness. Research studies have failed to show any effect greater than placebo. However, positive anecdotal accounts of these remedies are legion, and naturopathic doctors have seriously questioned the methodology of the current research studies. In December 2010 Nobel Prize–winning scientist Professor Luc Montagnier surprised the scientific community with his interview in *Science* magazine in which he stated that homeopathy "is not pseudoscience. It's not quackery. These are real phenomena that require further study."[2] Homeopathy is taught in every naturopathic school in the United States, and specialized programs are available for homeopathic studies only.

Four commonly prescribed remedies for traumatic stress are listed below. They are available over the counter at health-food stores and holistic pharmacies. Boiron makes some of the most commonly found remedies. Do not be fooled by their labels, which list other conditions they treat. Dr. Grossman and her colleagues assure me that they use these homeopathic medicines most frequently for issues related to traumatic stress. These remedies come in little sugar pills.

For best results use the lid to dispense, not your hands, and place under the tongue until dissolved.

- *Aconitum* deals with the energy of shock and is a good remedy for panic disorder. Shock can result from a physical, emotional, or spiritual jolt, and, as you recall from the first chapter, is the very first stage of psychological trauma. For one to move forward in healing, shock needs to be released, and aconitum can help move that process along. Among the practitioners I interviewed, it was one of the most universally prescribed remedies for people affected by the New York attack on 9/11. Aconitum is highly recommended and safe to use according to the directions on the label.

- *Arnica* is an all-around first-aid remedy. It can be found in creams and gels as well as in homeopathic tablet form. Arnica addresses the physical aspects of trauma and acts to reduce bruising, swelling, and any internal inflammation incurred in the injuries that commonly accompany psychological trauma.

- *Staphysagria* is prescribed for people who have suppressed the anger of a trauma or series of traumas and now find themselves stuck. It is particularly helpful for meek people who cannot find their way out of a bad situation or relationship. But be forewarned, this medication does work, and often that repressed anger will come leaping to the surface shortly after the patient begins this remedy. For this reason, all the naturopaths interviewed stressed that it is best if a naturopathic doctor supervises its use. In my own practice, I witnessed a patient stuck for months in therapy around leaving her destructive marriage move into action suddenly after she started this remedy under the supervision of a local clinic. If you are a person who says, "I never get angry," or goes out of your way to avoid confrontation, staphysagria may be the remedy for you.

- *Stramonium* is used when terror and dark energies are involved in the trauma. For instance, a terrorist attack, a psychopathic encounter, war, or even a scary movie could necessitate the use of this remedy. For many homeopaths it is the "go to" remedy for PTSD. Stramonium is a night-blooming flower, and this remedy is designed to work in the darkness. I have seen it clear up people's energy fields when nothing else would touch them. If you are struggling with the fallout from heinous abuse or a terrifying incident, this remedy is worth trying. As with staphysagria, stramonium is best used under the supervision of a licensed naturopath.

## Flower Essences

Unlike essential oils, which work through the olfactory system to the brain, flower essences work directly upon the energy body. In the 1930s the English physician and homeopath Edward Bach developed dilute solutions of flowers in water and brandy to be taken in small amounts internally. He found them to be especially effective for disorders of stress. Today the Bach Flower Remedies are sold all over the world to balance and soothe distressing emotional states. The best-selling formula Rescue Remedy was designed to reduce symptoms of trauma and extreme stress in close proximity to a traumatic event. Many people carry this formula in their purses or cars.

Like all energy remedies, the effects of flower essences are subtle and not immediately discernable to the average client *without making an effort to track and rate symptoms.* A practitioner friend calls this "time-space medicine," noting that the cause and symptoms of the disease as well as the effects of healing have to be tracked carefully over space and time because of their subtlety. It is not uncommon for people to think nothing is happening, only to find over the next couple of days to weeks that symptoms have gone into remission. With flower essences, the more sensitive the person, the more easily and immediately the results are felt.

Research studies have been inconclusive, yet flower essences are widely used. Some people cannot ingest the brandy used to suspend the remedy, and other companies, such as Perelandra, have addressed this intolerance by using vinegar as a base for the essences. Today there is a proliferation all over the world of companies that produce flower essences and practitioners who specialize in them. To find flower essences, look on the Internet or in your local health-food store, or talk to a practitioner (herbalist, naturopathic doctor, etc.). If you are intuitive, you may be able to feel out for yourself which essences will be the most helpful for you. As with homeopathic remedies, it is impossible to hurt yourself with these remedies. They can be mixed and matched in bottles as needed.

## ANIMAL THERAPIES

It is no secret that animals are sensitive to energy. What is not so well known is how animals affect our energy fields. Many traumatized people find human interaction so uncomfortable that they turn to the relative safety of animals. This is healthy! Dogs and cats, and even more unusual pets, can provide great sources of comfort both emotionally and physically.

Rick Yount runs the healing program Paws for Purple Hearts in California, which trains veterans with psychological scars to train service dogs for other veterans with physical disabilities. In the process of training these dogs, the veterans report improvements in their sleep, mood, impulse control, emotional regulation, and sense of purpose, and *a reduction in PTSD symptoms.* Yount's successful program has been featured on several television shows. One veteran recalled how he had not had a single full night's sleep since his return until he took his dog home to train. That first night he slept deeply, secure with the dog next to him on the bed.

Horses, too, seem to have a mysterious healing effect on people. Many books have now been written on the subject, and certification programs are springing up nationally and internationally for working with horses and stress-related disorders. Being around horses grounds the body's energy, often resulting in a feeling of deep, peaceful relaxation that I call "barn bliss." People who work for years with horses recognize their almost telepathic abilities and emotional connectedness to one another and to the people they love. In one workshop I attended, a woman with DID (dissociative identity disorder, formerly known as multiple personality disorder) related how her therapy horse would look down lower at her when she was in her child personalities and at her full height when she was functioning as an adult—talk about feeling seen!

Animal therapy and service programs are springing up all over the United States and internationally. Here in Portland, our local animal hospital offers service dog training. The Equine Assisted Growth and Learning Association (EAGALA) offers international workshops and certification in equine-assisted psychotherapy for licensed therapists. You can find qualified practitioners at their website, www.eagala.com. Likewise, Epona Equestrian Services (www.taoofequus.com) offers therapeutic equine programs for PTSD and related issues, with one program focused specifically on returning veterans, based on

Linda Kohanav's work as laid out in her remarkable book *The Tao of Equus*. Whether you are a therapist seeking to expand your repertoire or a person in need of healing, both programs are wonderful places to connect with horses as healers.

## HEALING IN NATURE

For centuries in Europe, people would be sent to sanatoriums for healing from "nervous exhaustion" as well as other depleting conditions such as tuberculosis. Invariably, these sanatoriums were located near healing natural resources, such as in mountain wilderness, at the shore, or near healing springs. Native Americans and indigenous people everywhere have long known of places that seem to be charged with a mysterious healing power. Many people debilitated by stress conditions naturally gravitate towards wild places full of healing energy such as Hawaii, mountainous areas like the Rockies, or even deserts. Like animals, we seem to have an instinct that will direct us to the place that is right for us. In the United States we are fortunate to have such areas in abundance. To find them, look for liminal areas to visit, that is, areas of nature that border each other, such as ocean and shore, meadow and forest, mountain and valley, or places of upwelling, such as cold springs, mineral hot pools, geysers, and volcanoes. The further away from human population centers, the better.

As the body is full of energy meridians, so is the Earth. In England, these energy lines were named ley lines, due to the many villages along these lines whose names ended in "ley."[3] Many major cathedrals in Europe have been built upon the intersection of major ley lines that were discovered and measured by dowsing or particular astronomical alignments. They contain powerful healing energies.

The Kealakekua area of the Big Island of Hawaii; Sedona; Arizona; and the Mt. Shasta area of California are examples of such places. Sometimes you will hear talk of "vortexes" where the healing power is particularly strong. Visiting these places can accelerate one's healing tremendously. But beware, not all vortexes are healing; some have strong negative energies. Investigate them carefully before you visit.

Despite what you may think about tree huggers, close contact with our forest friends can quickly restore calmness to an overtaxed nervous system. The sesquiterpenes found in the sap of pines, cedars, and balsam are so powerful in calming the body that they are distilled into essential oils. Oaks have a nurturing solidity that the sensitive can feel. Birch and aspen groves have been considered sacred around the world. Sit under or against these trees, and let yourself drift into a state of relaxed openness, letting the trees absorb the toxic energies you want to release. In Chinese medicine, trees are said to thrive on this negative qi, much in the way they take in our poisonous carbon dioxide and convert it to oxygen. I once had an extreme-abuse patient whose only safe contact in the world was with trees. Only after several years of intensive therapy could she move out of tree relationships and into the world of human relationships. Sitting under a favorite tree can also be a great place to write in your journal about your trauma, both grounding and releasing for your body.

Unless you have a phobia of water, you have probably noticed its beneficial effects on stress. A yogi friend of mine describes swimming in the waters off Hawaii as "swimming in a great ocean of prana." Pristine waters can charge up and cleanse the energies around and throughout your body. Cold mountain lakes, sparkling forest streams, waterfalls, hidden warm springs, and clean oceans charge up the body and mind when you are healing from trauma. They also seem to help reduce physical symptoms of distress. When seeking such places, be sure to avoid areas that attract carousing and dangerous activities, not only for your safety, but because water tends to hold the vibration of those around it. Masaru Emoto, famous for his best seller *The True Power of Water*, has spent more than two decades researching the vibratory imprinting of water crystals. He shows, in dramatic before-and-after photos, the effect of words and thoughts on water crystals. Positive vibrations produce beautifully formed ice crystals; negative energy causes the water crystals to fall apart in ugly mutations. Emoto has been a modern leader in the healing power of waters, both taken internally like medicine and used to bathe in. He puts it this way: "We must pay respect to water, feel love and gratitude, and receive vibrations with a positive attitude. When water changes, you change and I change. Because both you and I are water."[4]

Time is a powerful component in nature healing. Whether it is different seasons, different years, or different times of day, all bring subtle energies to bear upon the mind and body. In our go, go, go culture, we do not stop to acknowledge the differences between the outward-moving activity of summer and the dormancy and ingathering of energies in the winter, the awakening shakti energies of the spring and the contemplative, melancholy fall. We are expected to ignore our connection to nature and to life and *produce*, expelling our psychic energies at all times to serve our family, our businesses, and the insatiable demands of our economy. In itself, this lifestyle is enough to produce profound stresses on the energy body of an individual. For someone with stress damage, it is not a sustainable or healing way to live. The person who complains or wants to slow down is often ridiculed, reprimanded, or rejected.

*In order to heal from stress, the energy body needs to have a new relationship with time itself.* In the practice of *lomi-lomi*, the healing modality taught in Hawaii by kahunas, medicine people, an important exercise involves going outside at sunset. One is encouraged to watch as the sun kisses the ocean at the end of the day and then to *consciously release all of the day's negative energies into that union.* In India the time of dusk is considered to be one of the most auspicious times for meditation and communion with the divine, as is sunrise. As in physical nature, the liminal in time opens the portal to healing and sacred energies. Equinoxes, solstices, sunrises, and sunsets all offer experiences to shift and heal the energy body. I invite you to pay close attention to your energy patterns during the seasons and during the day. What times are you filled with energy? When are you called to rest and go inward? When can you feel the presence of healing power or spiritual connection? Resolve to join with the power of nature for your own healing. You may find resistance from those around you, but you will also be teaching them and modeling a saner, more conscious, and sacred way to be in the world.

## YOGA

Thousands of Americans now take yoga classes, go on yoga retreats, and wear trendy yoga workout clothes, but how many of us know that yogic practices were designed to balance the flow of prana in our energy bodies? Hatha yoga, the practice of physical postures called asanas, help the body to unblock and inflate the subtle nerve currents called nadis. Traditionally, asanas were just one branch of the eight-limbed yoga outlined by the father of yoga, Patanjali. The end goal of yoga was supposed to be enlightenment. Today most yoga teachers advertise the end goal as health, comfort in the body, and longevity, which are not at all bad, but do sell yoga short. To get to the truly powerful benefits of yoga we need to look at the energy body and prana.

## Pranayama

The practices of pranayama and hatha yoga go hand in hand. In 1995 I obtained certification as a yoga teacher through the Kripalu Center in the Berkshires of Massachusetts. We were taught that specific breathing exercises, called pranayama, form the very foundation of yogic practice. If control of the breath is not practiced throughout yogic practice, then yoga becomes just another set of physical exercises. With conscious use of the breath, the effects of postures are multiplied exponentially. Not only that, but pranayama can be an entire type of yoga in and of itself.

*Pranayama* literally means "control of the life force." We know today, as did ancient yogis and yoginis, that breath lies at the intersection of the conscious and unconscious minds, at the interface of the sympathetic and parasympathetic nervous systems. The body always breathes until death. We can breathe consciously, or the breath can breathe us unconsciously. We can breathe to wake ourselves up and energize our bodies, or we can breathe to bring relaxation to every part of our body. Pranayama is gaining in popularity in Western countries. The iPhone even has an app for it called Pranayama, which is getting great reviews.

In the first-aid chapter I gave three breathing exercises for crisis drawn from very simple pranayama exercises. There are a few more I would like to share with you here. They can be done before or after yoga postures or as a stand-alone practice. Many of the breaths can be found on YouTube as demonstrations. Beware! These practices are very powerful in moving energy in the body and purifying the nadis. They should not be done for extended periods of time without a great deal of prior purification of the body and mind, or else the mind and/ or body can begin to feel unbalanced. If you are new to pranayama, practice only a few minutes each day, *building up to* maybe fifteen to twenty minutes per session. Because trauma tends to linger in the body, it naturally stands to reason that unblocking the body could feel uncomfortable. This process is like having a bowel movement after days to weeks of constipation: challenging, uncomfortable and icky. Be in your body and get grounded, then try these exercises. If you become light-headed, triggered, or uncomfortable, then *stop* and try a different practice or consult with a qualified yoga teacher.

*Ujjai*: **The Ocean Breath**. This breath moves pranic energy throughout the body and is sometimes used in conjunction with or in between different postures for grounding and strengthening. It is considered a heating breath. To do ujjai, partially close off the back of the throat as if you were to whisper, then breathe deeply, slowly and rhythmically. A steady roaring sound should be made in the back of the throat while practicing this breath, like the sound of the ocean far away. It is both relaxing and energizing, making it excellent for people recovering from stress-related disorders.

*Nadi Shodhana*: **Alternate-Nostril Breathing**. Most of us don't know it, but we already do alternate-nostril breathing throughout the day. Science has shown that people tend to breathe through one nostril dominantly for about three hours before switching to the other one. The nostrils are aligned with different major energy channels along the spine called the ida and the pingala, which run beside the central spine channel, and the sushumna, which runs along it (my teacher refers to them mnemonically as the *Nina*, the *Pinta*, and the *Santa Maria*). You don't need to memorize them, but you do need to realize that *unbalanced breathing leads to an unbalanced flow of energy throughout the body.* Alternate-nostril breathing restores balance to breath and body through forced intervals of single-nostril breath. Recent research in India and other countries has shown that nadi shodhana is good for increasing lung capacity, calming down the nervous system by supporting parasympathetic processes, and increasing both calmness and alertness in the brain. It is one of the most highly recommended yogic practices for stress reduction.[5]

To begin, bring your hand up to your face. Pinch off the right nostril and inhale four beats through the left nostril. Switching fingers, pinch off the left nostril leaving the right open and exhale *gently* to a count of eight. Leaving your hand in place, then inhale through the right nostril again with a count of four for the inhalation. Lastly, exhale gently for eight beats through the left nostril. This four-eight-four-eight pattern makes up one set. Variations on this pranayama include holding the breath for four counts (one to two seconds) after each inhalation. When you first begin doing rounds of nadi shodhana, do only a few at a time, maybe only one to three. Your body will need time to adjust to this exercise. If you tire, stop. Forcing should never be a part of pranayama.

***Kapalbhati*: Breath of Fire.** This powerful breath purifies nerve channels, organs, and the chakras themselves (see tool 4). When you are feeling very angry, jealous, or toxic to yourself or others, this breath can give you a way to safely vent the energy of those feelings. To do kapalbhati, sit in a chair with feet firmly on the floor or sit cross-legged with a straight spine as for meditation. You will be blowing air vigorously out your nostrils engaging the stomach muscles and diaphragm. It is like blowing out a candle with a strong puff of air, only you will keep your mouth closed, with air exiting the nostrils. You might want to blow your nose before beginning. Do not do this exercise if you are congested! Some yoginis feel that women on their menses or pregnant women should not do kapalbhati. Focus on a strong exhalation *with no effort at all on the inhalation.* Air will naturally get sucked back into your emptied lungs. For maximum effect, aim for about one breath per second. Some yogis recommend visualizing blowing out negative thoughts and feelings for added benefit. Do only a few of these in the beginning, building up to as long as fifteen minutes per day. If you get dizzy, slow down or stop. If you find that this exercise is too triggering or that too much energy is moving, then go to another, more calming pranayama.

### Asanas: Yoga Postures

Recovering from traumatic stress can sometimes be a delicate operation. The body will often become achy or have unexplained muscle spasms. Cardiovascular exercise can become intolerable and set off panic attacks. The diaphragm can contract painfully underneath the ribs, shutting down breath, or the psoas muscles deep in the hips can spasm, causing back and gut pain. The energy body starts to block off and shut down, closing off prana to important areas of the body such as the ovaries or testes, stomach, or colon. Along with pranayama, yogic asanas, or postures, assist in keeping the flow of energy going and in rejuvenating the physical body. It would be ideal to consult with a local yoga practitioner who can recommend what's best for you. Alternatively you can start with the few simple postures below.

**Child Pose (*Balasana*).** This easy and simple posture will help gently stretch the spine while creating a nurturing space for rest. To bring yourself into child pose, kneel down on something soft—a yoga mat, folded blanket, or rug—and slowly bring your head down onto the floor. Essentially, you bring the body into the fetal position while facing the belly down towards the earth. If you have a round body or an inflexible one, you can place pillows beneath the head or hips until comfortable. Allow your hands to lie either in front of the head or along the sides of the body. Lie in this restorative and grounding posture for as long as comfortable. If you wish, you can do ujjai breath for increased relaxation.

**Modified Shoulder Stand (*Sarvangasana*).** To do a normal shoulder stand you lie on your back and roll up onto the shoulders with the feet in the air. This posture promotes toning and strength; it is sometimes called the mother of all postures for its beneficial effect on the brain and glandular systems. In the modified position described here, we are looking for restoration and relaxation. Lie against a wall with your buttocks a few inches from it and your legs extended in the air and resting on the wall. For maximum relaxation, it helps to put a small pillow or blanket underneath the hips to raise them gently. This posture helps with circulation, relaxation, and restoration. You can even put an eye pillow over your eyes and turn on some delicious music. Ahhh!

**Wind Relieving Posture (*Pavana Muktasana*).** I'm not kidding; it really is called that. This posture helps with peristalsis (an action of the intestines), a universal trouble area for trauma survivors. Rolling onto your back, first pull your right knee *gently* towards your chest. Yoga is no time for machismo; for maximum effect, movements should be smooth and gentle. We don't want any strain in the lower back. Hold over or under your knee and take a few deep breaths. Slowly bring the leg back to the floor. Repeat with the left leg. Finally, bring both legs slowly up in a bent position towards the chest. Wrapping your hands around your knees, tuck your chin slightly to straighten your neck and then pull gently back. Unfold your legs back onto the floor and feel the effects of your posture. Always remember to begin the sequence with the *right* leg for the correct effect on the colon.

**Knee to Floor Stretch**. This pose is heavily modified from traditional yoga to make it safe for all levels of practitioners while giving the body a gentle twisting stretch. Lying flat on your back, bring your left foot up to your right knee with both knees pointing towards the ceiling. Extend both arms out into a "t" at shoulder level. On the exhalation bring your left knee over to the floor rolling onto your right side, *yet leaving your shoulders squarely flat on the floor*. Do not force your position; few people can get their knee to the floor on the first try; it can take years of practice to do so. This position is great for the all-important central psoas muscles and opening up lines of energy in the core of the body as well as in the breath. Slowly bring your left knee back to pointing at the ceiling by rolling the left hip down to the floor. Extend the left leg and breathe for a few seconds. When you are ready, repeat on the other side.

**Tree Pose (*Vrikshasana*)**. The tree pose is a great grounding and focusing posture that will help with balance. It will also call you out on dissociation; if you are ungrounded you will have a terrible time maintaining this balancing posture. Begin from a standing position with your hands pressed palms together in front of the breastbone. Fix your gaze on something that doesn't move; this will help your balance. Slowly turn out your right leg and bend your knee so that your knee is pointing to the right while lifting your foot to your ankle. Pause, if your balance is good continue to raise your foot until the instep of your right foot is resting along the inside of your left knee. Stabilize your posture by making sure both hipbones are pointing forward (sometimes I call them your headlights). With your right hipbone facing forward, rotate your right knee slightly further outward; this should bring further stability. Breathe! If you cannot balance, then rest the toes of your right foot gently on the floor. With practice your balance will improve tremendously. When ready, lower the foot *slowly* to the ground. Gently shake out your legs and arms and repeat on the other side.

Many other postures are excellent for traumatic stress and can be looked up on the Internet or learned in a yoga class. In addition to these simple postures, I highly recommend downward dog, the cat-dog stretch, triangle pose, pigeon pose, and warrior I and II. Proceed slowly. Even if you have done yoga before, your physiology is totally changed by trauma, and you may need to relearn or modify previously done postures. Be sure to breath rhythmically throughout each posture and *never force or overdo* your yoga postures. With patience and time, asanas can unwind traumatic energy patterns, restoring you to perfect health in mind and body. Your ability to meditate will improve, too.

## BLESSING FOOD AND WATER

Every culture and religion has rituals for blessing food. Christians say grace. Jewish people make a blessing before eating. Indigenous peoples universally consider giving thanks to Spirit to be an essential part of mealtime. In India, there are different types of blessings, one of which is for ordinary meals. For special occasions, a puja ceremony blesses food and turns it into divine food, called *prasad*. Eating prasad in small amounts is considered very auspicious. Swamis often keep supersweet candy prasad they will push on you like Italian grandmothers. But have we ever stopped to think deeply upon these practices?

Sri Sarada, an Indian saint who lived at the end of the nineteenth century, touched thousands of Hindu lives with her teachings and initiations. She used to say, "First offer to God whatever you eat. One must not eat unoffered food. As your food is, so will be your blood. From pure food you get pure blood, pure mind, and strength."[6] It has also long been part of Indian thinking and medicine that eating when you are upset taints the food you eat with negativity and negatively affects your health.

It is not necessary to believe in God to bless one's food. There is a Celtic blessing that consists of visualizing a pure white rose superimposed over the food. A shaman I know simply says "Thank you" before eating. We need to start connecting the dots of how our attitude affects our physiology as well as the vibration of the food we ingest. This also applies to preparation of our food. You can infuse the food you make with love and gratitude or anger and resentment. It's your choice, so make that choice with awareness.

To return to Masaru Emoto's work for a moment, remember that all food is mostly water. Our bodies are water. His work shows that our thoughts and intentions can actually affect the crystalline structure of water, either positively or negatively. Logically, then, it stands to reason that our thoughts and intentions will affect the very structure of our food, both energetically *and physically*. If we are serious about clearing and balancing our energy body, then blessing food and water before meals becomes a necessary component of our healing. Even if you are feeling toxic, it is a helpful practice to say grace. Just make a conscious effort at every meal to offer some kind of blessing of thanks, even if it's "Rub-a-dub-dub, thanks for the grub." Some people find it helpful to post a blessing or keep a book of different blessings on the table. This small, time-honored technique will make a big difference over time in your healing. It surely couldn't hurt!

There are myriad ways to restore the flow of energy, prana, or qi to the body in order to heal the body and mind. This chapter has sampled a few of the most common methods for regulating the flow of prana in the body. Modern medicine is well on its way to recognizing these realities: energy-medicine research is being stepped up from the National Institutes of Health to Harvard Medical School to naturopathic colleges around the country. They are the future of medicine. The benefits of these modalities are profound for people who suffer from traumatic stress, as shown in the many stories in books and on the Internet of the healings that have taken place using them. Understanding how the mind affects the flow of prana and the physical body is our next stage in the multidimensional healing of trauma.

*We are what we think.*
*All that we are arises with our thoughts.*
*With our thoughts we make the world.*
—The Buddha

# Tool 7

# The Manomayakosha: Enlisting Your Thinking Mind

---

THE PATHOLOGIZING OF THE MIND has been a real obstacle to trauma survivors seeking and getting treatment. In the field of mental health, we have not yet made any real distinctions between mental illness and mental wounds. At a visceral level, many people resist psychotherapy and counseling for traumatic stress due to their indignation over being treated as ill, when they are, in fact, injured. Being treated as though one is sick, crazy, or "other" when one has been injured (often by a sick and/or crazy person) just adds insult to injury. Can you relate to this scenario? I know I can. Too often I have had clients who have come into my practice labeled as drug seeking, noncompliant, somatisizing, histrionic (dramatic), borderline, difficult, or overreactive when they are just intensely frustrated and helpless in the face of a medical system that does not understand their needs or know how to treat their problems effectively. By the time they get to me, their problems have compounded. Not only do they have the original injury and its profound impact on their bodies and lives, but now they have the additional problems of being neglected, offended, and untreated by a system that is supposed to help them. Sound familiar?

Thanks to the good work of people like Dr. Andrew Weil and Dr. Deepak Chopra among many others, we have all been hearing about the mind-body connection for years now. Western medicine has finally begun to acknowledge the profound connection between the mind and the body but still does not completely understand it. Prana is the missing link. Mind, prana, and body are intimately related. Each affects the other in subtle and not-so-subtle ways. The diagram below shows how the influences of each can flow in either direction. Injuries and problems can begin in the body, the prana body, or the mind, but inevitably spread to all three. The good news is that healing can begin in any of these places, positively affecting the others in turn. In severe traumatic stress, the best results occur when all three are engaged in the healing process.

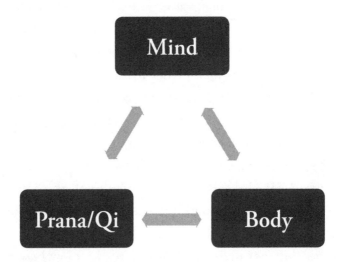

In many traditions of healing, the mind is considered the strongest component of healing because it has the ability to override the mechanisms of prana and body. As a psychotherapist, I have seen people's chronically sore throats, stuffy sinuses, back pain, chest pain, and headaches disappear during the course of their therapy. Chronic lack of expression of one's truth almost always leads to problems in the body. The latest research in PTSD is showing profound links to heart disease, diabetes, fibromyalgia, and chronic fatigue. Now, don't get me wrong; I am not blaming the patient for "bad thoughts." But I would be remiss if I did not point out the untapped potential for healing in the mind. In this chapter, I will give you several ways to work with your cognitive-mind layer, your manomayakosha, to move quickly through traumatic patterns of stress, thus freeing up the entire body for healing.

## COUNSELING

Although many good techniques for working with trauma are now emerging, the fact remains that many counselors and therapists do not have good training in trauma. I graduated from one of the best clinical schools for social work in the country. I had teachers and supervisors known to be at the top in their fields, and yet my training in PTSD and trauma was severely lacking. Why? The field of traumatology is actually quite new!

The term *post-traumatic stress disorder* was coined in the 1970s. In the mid-1980s the very first information started to emerge about the prevalence of child abuse resulting in trauma, and that was only in certain progressive centers of the United States. Oprah Winfrey and Phil Donahue started featuring more child abuse survivors on their shows, and we can thank them for bringing this important public health issue to national attention. Most survivors do not realize how recent the information is on child abuse and trauma in general. Did you know that most pediatricians in the 1970s thought that the rate of incest was one case in a million? Due to the difficulty of researching this issue, it is still hard to get accurate figures, but some recent research is showing rates of incest at 10–20 percent of the general population![1]

The greatest gains in our knowledge of psychological trauma have been made in the last couple of decades. At the same time, insurance companies have been cutting down reimbursement for therapeutic programs and sessions. This trend has been unfortunate. Right at the moment we discovered the technologies to help survivors manage, the resources for providing those technologies were cut. For professionals and for clients, these have been difficult times for meeting important mental health needs. What this means to you, the consumer, is that your need for competent practice in the areas of trauma may not have been met.

If you have had a bad experience with a counselor or therapist, this chapter is for you. If you have been lucky enough to have great trauma counseling, perhaps it will give you ideas for deepening that therapy or coming at your problems from a different angle, always helpful when therapy stagnates (which it inevitably does). All the exercises below can be done either on your own or with a competent, engaged therapist. If your therapist is not willing to work with you actively on these issues, is neutral or remote, or interprets nondirective psychotherapy as being passive, you may want to consider changing to someone who is open to learning new techniques and/or becoming trained in the field of trauma.

## FINDING SAFETY

All trauma patients have safety issues by definition. You must find your safe places as a prerequisite to healing. Must! This safety must be accessible in your mind, body, and environment. All safety begins in the mind, with consciously contemplating your circumstances, thinking about what is safe and right for you.

Writing or drawing can help incorporate this exercise into your consciousness. If you are working with a therapist, safety should be a part of your discussions together from day one. If your therapist never mentions safety, perhaps he or she does not know how to work with trauma appropriately. I have just spent two chapters giving you all kinds of recommendations for working with traumatic stress in your mind and body. Without a safe place to land in your mind, body, and environment, none of those techniques will be helpful for you for very long. *Safety work is foundational and not optional in healing from trauma.* Otherwise it's like trying to stitch up a cut while your hand's still in the buzz saw; it doesn't work, and it's painful and messy for all involved.

Find a quiet and safe place to sit. What is safe? Safe means you will not be hurt, triggered, or distracted in any way from your work of healing. Home is not always someone's safe place. In fact, many people were hurt in their homes and are deeply triggered into anxiety by being home. Find a neutral place like a park, library, or even the inside of your car. Mentally traverse the environments you move through during your day: your workplace, the trip there and back, the stores where you shop, and especially your home environment, which I want you to go through *one room at a time*. Notice where you are triggered and, more importantly, notice where you are rarely or never triggered. If you need help clarifying your thoughts, rate these places on a one-to-ten scale if one is not safe at all and ten is the safest place you could ever imagine. Or you can draw them and color-code them. If you discover areas that do not feel safe to you, such as a part of town you cross on your way to work or a certain area of your house, ask yourself what you need to do to create safety there. If you are not sure, work with a friend, family member, or counselor. As we will see in the skiing story later in the chapter, avoidance can also be a healthy solution—as long as it is done with awareness.

The second level of safety to assess is safety in your body. Trauma happens to the body. If it came about because of something you saw, maybe your eyes are traumatized. If something was done to you, the trauma is in the affected part of your body. Maybe the way your brain works traumatizes you (e.g., making you jump all over the place, ruminate, or brood). Find the areas of your body that are safe. Just as Earth has her safe places and dangerous places, so does your body. Sometimes people tell me initially that they do not feel safe anywhere in their body. We're not going for a large area here; it could be the size of a postage stamp. It could be the mitochondria inside your cells or the space between your molecules. Just find the beginning place of safety. I once had a patient who could only find a spot on the bottom of her foot the size of an eraser. It's a start! And you have to start somewhere. Once you discover your body has some safe places, you can expand from there, annexing, as it were, other areas of safety for your body and clearing trauma from unsafe areas. You need that grounding of a safe place in the body to help heal.

Last, we look at the mind (or maybe first; the order, of course, is up to you). We all have safe and unsafe places we go to in our own heads. It's your mission to find those places. What thoughts make you sick with trauma? What thoughts feel good and safe to you? Can you keep your brain focused on the helpful thoughts and memories? Or are you constantly pulled into negative thoughts and flashbacks?

Of all the muscles we have in our body, our mind is often the weakest one. Okay, I know you don't have any actual muscles in your brain, but you do have thinking habits. Mapping your safe places in your mind will help you have a place to anchor when the storms hit. Did you know you can create safe spaces in your own mind? Try this exercise:

*Sit or lie down in a comfortable and safe location where your body can be totally supported. If you like, put on soft, nontriggering and relaxing music. Good.*

*Now let yourself travel in your mind's eye to a favorite place, a healing place. It could be somewhere you have been to long ago or recently. Maybe it's somewhere you have always wanted to go. It might exist in the real world or in a world of your imagination. What matters is that it makes you feel peaceful, happy, and safe. Now, in your mind's eye, look around you. What does this place look like? Know that you can adjust this place to suit you however and whenever you want. Are there people, or are you alone? Are there creatures, trees, plants, or flowers? Maybe you are near water or high on a hill with a beautiful view. Take it in. What is the air temperature? Are you sitting, standing, or lying down? Feel the safe ground underneath you, supporting you. Choose your favorite weather. Listen for sounds all around you. Maybe birds are singing, maybe you hear the splash of dolphins frolicking, maybe you are in a vast and silent temple; just notice the sounds. And as you are there, drink in the safety of this place, this place of your creation. Nobody can come there without your permission. There are no demands in this place, only nurturance and peace, peace, peace. Feel this safety deep within your being. Know that wherever you go in the outside world, this peaceful place always lies within you, and you can return again and again. Now when you are ready, gently allow your consciousness to return to this body, the external world, maybe wiggling fingers and toes when you are ready. Good. Feel the effects in your body as you return from your safe place.*

If you wish you can record this visualization with music of your choosing and play it to yourself. If you have difficulty with imagery, that's okay. You will get better after the first few times. Not only does this safe-place visualization help create more safe spaces in the mind, but it also helps it to calm down and focus. This focus becomes essential for pulling the mind back from traumatic journeys it wants to take during flashbacks. I highly recommend this sort of exercise. As with the other exercises, visualization is something you can work on with your therapist or even a coach or chaplain.

## MAPPING TRIGGERS

If you have traumatic stress or PTSD, you have triggers. You may not know what they are, and you may not even have heard of triggers before, but you definitely have them. Have you ever heard of Pavlov's dog? The famous scientist Ivan Pavlov paired the sound of a bell ringing with the presentation of dinner to dogs he was studying. After a few rounds of ringing the bell at the same time the dogs' dinner was presented, Pavlov rang the bell without presenting dinner and observed the response of the dogs. They salivated copiously when the bell was rung *even though there was no dinner they could smell or taste.* Since the sound of the bell was paired with dinner, the sound was enough to *trigger* the physiology of digestion to begin, even in the absence of actual food.

Likewise, when we suffer a trauma, the circumstances around the trauma get paired to our physiological reaction to the trauma itself, only instead of salivating, we get panicked, frozen, dizzy and lightheaded, headachy, filled with rage, or any of a number of other traumatic stress symptoms. These triggers are often not obvious to us or to the people we live with. Some are obvious, though. If you are old enough, perhaps you remember Colonel Oliver North at trial ducking at lightning speed under the defense table when he heard the sound of a car backfiring. It's easy to imagine a soldier misinterpreting that sound as gunfire.

But a trigger can be *any stimulus that was previously paired with the trauma, whether we remember it or not.* The body does not lie. Only the mind is capable of denial. The truth of what we experienced is stored in the body, which is why mapping triggers is so helpful. It helps keep us safe from re-experiencing traumas. At the same time, triggers inform us about what traumas we have lived through, *even if we do not remember the original traumatic event.* The relationship of triggers to traumas in descending order of healthiness and healing are:

1. We can remember all our traumatic events and know all our triggers (best-case scenario).

2. We can remember our trauma(s) and not know all of our triggers.

3. We can know our triggers but not remember our trauma(s).

4. We can be ignorant of our traumatic experiences and not realize that we have triggers to them (making us and others feel crazy).

Since triggers often lead to the body's re-experiencing the trauma state, it is no wonder we avoid them both consciously and unconsciously!

We know that the stimulus for Pavlov's dogs' salivating was a bell. But what can traumatic triggers be? Simply put, they can be anything at all. For some people they feel like everything. When the whole world feels triggering to someone, that person is often an agoraphobic recluse, or, conversely, he or she can be out in the world but dealing with daily, persistent, and severe anxiety. If your abuse was sexual, you will have sexual triggers; that is obvious to most people. But what may be less obvious is the trigger of the scent of the cologne worn by the abuser, the feel of stubble on your face, a certain tone of voice, a word choice, or the look of a ceiling, room, or environment. For a prisoner of war from Vietnam, triggers could be rice, bamboo, humid warmth, or the need to take a shower, among many others. Perhaps that POW's wife serves him rice one night for dinner, and he goes ballistic, tearing apart her cooking. That would be a case of number 2 on the list above. He may not even realize that rice is a trigger for his experience. Triggers do not excuse our abusive behaviors, but understanding triggers will certainly help us get a handle on working on them and help us feel more in control.

The more aware we are of our triggers, the more we can work through them or help others to understand our needs in the environment. If our friend the POW knows rice is a trigger, he begins to have choices and more control over his symptoms (and so does his spouse). He can choose to work through that aversion, or he can shape his environment to avoid having to be presented with rice.

Some triggers are worth working through and some aren't. A few years ago, I broke my leg very badly downhill skiing, a sport I never really enjoyed anyway. I could have worked through my triggers around skiing to get back out there, but why? I don't really feel a need to ski again in this lifetime and don't have to. I chose not to and recently gave away all my ski equipment to a young woman who was thrilled to get it. Problem solved. For more severe traumas, however, there are usually multiple and unavoidable triggers. Some will fade with awareness; others we have to work on, and there are lots of ways to do that. The first step is mapping them.

I recommend writing down or drawing your triggers, getting them down on paper in some form or fashion. Some triggers you will know right away; some you will have to ferret out. Triggers fall into six categories: the five senses of taste, touch, smell, sight, and hearing, plus feeling states. Let's start with the senses, because they are the easiest. You can divide your paper into different sections reflecting each of these senses. It will help jog your memory to go through each sense modality individually. Let's say you are working in the smell category. Ask yourself what smells really bother you. All of us have smells we do and don't like. Generally we all like floral scents and dislike the smell of feces, but I am not talking about ordinary aversions here; I am talking about radical reactions. Nobody likes the smell of poop, but if that smell sends you into a panic or frozen numbness and dissociation, it's a trigger. Or maybe the scent of lavender makes you want to rip someone's head off. That's a little unusual; write it down. Take your time working through each category. Do not attempt to do all of this work in one day! If you are in therapy, it can feel safe and reassuring to do it with your therapist. Or it may not, depending again on your triggers, but find some way to do it anyway.

Feeling states are a little trickier to map. A common trigger for abuse victims is the feeling state of sexual arousal. Just getting aroused can become a trigger in and of itself if you were repeatedly violated against your will, especially if you were a child. Another triggering feeling state can be fear itself. Let's say you are watching a scary movie, and all of a sudden you go into a blind panic with your heart racing and a feeling of doom. The fear generated by the movie can activate intense feelings of fear related to suppressed memories of traumatic events. Even the feeling state of vigorous exercise can mimic a panic state and send a person into a full-blown panic attack.

The more triggers you have, the crazier you are likely to feel—especially if you cannot relate your triggers to solid memories. People with many triggers are often pathologized by their friends, families,

traumas onto less severe experiences or get triggered as described above. But the core traumas are never overestimated. That's just not how the mind works.

The trauma timeline is a useful tool to help people come into alignment with how their lives have actually played out. To make a trauma timeline, get a large piece of paper and divide your life into years along the paper. If you are older than thirty, it might be easier to do five-year increments. But do it however feels best to you. Be colorful. Be expressive, but don't feel that this has to be the Mona Lisa or anything. Nobody needs to see this except you and, maybe, your therapist. Sometimes it can be helpful to share it with your spouse or partner too.

Put a deep line through the year(s) in which your trauma(s) occurred and label it (them). If you have multiple traumas, color-code them. For instance, put all sexual abuse in one color, all physical violence in another, etc. If you are not sure whether something qualifies as a trauma, it does for this exercise; that's the rule. You may find you need to come back to this paper a few times as more incidents come to you. I find it helpful to mark your age at the time and a couple of pertinent circumstances. For example: age 10, grandmother beat me, left bruises on my behind; age 22, convoy ran over mines, buddies killed; age 38, terrible car accident, thought I'd never walk again.

The timeline will help break through any denial you are holding. It is also helpful for noticing patterns to the traumas and can help you gauge your progress in healing. It is a fantastic tool to use in therapy, and *I highly recommend sharing it or even making it together with your competent therapist.* All good therapies work with the timeline concept in some fashion or other. This version is just one you put down on paper.

Like all the suggestions in this book, timing is everything. If you are averse to this exercise, you might want to explore why, but you don't have to do it right away or at all. Also, do not meditate upon the negativity in the timeline. It is meant to validate your feelings and put things in perspective, not to ruin your feelings about your life. Equally healing can be creating a balancing timeline of all the fortunate events and healthy and fun things you have done for yourself.

## The "I Want" Exercise

People sometimes ask me what question I ask most frequently as a therapist. I think they are expecting to hear, "How do you feel about that?" They are surprised when I tell them that by far the most common question I ask, and often the most difficult for people to answer, is, "What do you want?"

This question is foundational for the human being. Here's why. During infancy the sense of self is merged with mother and the environment; as we come into toddlerhood, the very first glimmers of sense of self and ego begin to appear. Let me clarify something here. For a therapist, *ego* is not a dirty word. Egos, like physical bodies, are absolutely necessary to function on planet Earth. The function of ego is what helps connect the internal world of the individual with the external world of objects. Otherwise we'd all be walking around in a continuous infantile state of self-absorption, and we wouldn't last very long here in the body. So the ego I am talking about here is not negative but absolutely necessary.

Anyway, you have this little toddler developing a new ego. This emerging ego is based mostly on "I want" and "I don't want." The toddler also has locomotion now, so is cruising around discovering objects it wants and doesn't want. Ideally, parents make an effort to understand what their child wants (likes) or doesn't want (dislikes). Even if they can't or don't want to gratify the child's desires, a good enough parent has empathy for the little one, as in, "No, you can't play with the shiny Christmas ornaments, but don't they look lovely; I can see why you'd want them." An impaired or abusive parent disrupts the child's discovery of its own self: "Bad boy/girl! I paid a fortune for those ornaments; I don't even want you looking at them!" Now the child is not only sad about not getting the ornament, but is made to feel bad for even wanting it in the first place. Children in such situations become confused about whose self they are. If they are themselves, they get into more trouble. If they adopt the parents' point of view they are safer. So, in an extreme case (and most survivors of childhood abuse qualify as having had extreme experiences), children naturally adopt the parents' view of the world instead of their own. Children who grow into adults that are disconnected from their own sense of self can develop many different mental health issues: eating disorders, addictions, depression, and personality disorders, to name a few.

If you grew up in a family in which your needs and wants were trivialized or you were abused, chances are you have trouble with your core sense of self. A simple exercise to overcome this deficit is to start asking yourself, "What do I really want?" Be specific. Be persistent. Write it down. I have never worked with a childhood-trauma survivor who did not have tremendous challenges in sense of self. Trauma always distorts sense of self in children and often leads to a lifetime of problems in relationships. *Your inner self is your spiritual self.* If you find out what that inner self really wants and how to feed it, you are well on your way to permanent relief of suffering.

## EXPRESSIVE THERAPIES

Some of the most helpful aids in healing from trauma are those that reconnect us with our emotions. For decades the hallmark of successful therapy was considered to be the release of emotion, called *abreaction*, seen as necessary for the therapeutic process. This area in trauma treatment is tricky because emotions like fear or rage are so intense that we can start to feel unbalanced and hopeless as we go into them. Big reveals and emotions may make great television or movies, but they often don't make great therapy. When trauma survivors dive too deeply and too quickly into their emotions, the effect on healing can be chilling rather than helpful, sometimes even scaring people out of their healing process.

Yet, when we do connect with those emotions, our being cries out for expression. There are many ways we can do this safely and in manageable doses. Any kind of art, be it painting, music, dance, poetry, clay, or other medium, will relieve this need for harmonization of the inner experience with the outer expression. Journaling helps lend a voice to the inchoate emotions struggling to burst out. This art can be purely personal, or it can be brought to therapy sessions or even exhibited. Some masters spin their traumatic straw into literal gold—consider author Stephen King, Oprah Winfrey, the band Tool, or the book and film *The Lovely Bones*, born out of the author's survival of a brutal attack.

There are many organizations that promote healing through artistic expression, as well as professional therapists who offer their services in these modalities. All survivors I have met struggle with the ineffability of their experience and their frustration in communicating it in a way that does not harm others. Art provides a safe, productive release from the torment of inexpressible emotion. You can find these organizations locally and online. There are also many websites that post survivors' art online for sharing.

## THE WORK OF BYRON KATIE

For ten years Byron Katie battled suicidal depression, rage, and paranoia. One day, as she lay on the floor of a halfway house for people with eating disorders as a cockroach crawled on her foot, she woke up into a profoundly shifted identity. Her previous sense of self fell away, leaving only delight in her existence. She realized that all the pain she had suffered, all the depression, had one source. From that day on, she lived in a profound state of peacefulness and joy. Her family was astonished at the change. People started to notice something different about her. They called her "the lit lady of Barstow." Soon people were coming from far and wide for her teachings.

Today Byron Katie has an internationally known school that attracts hundreds each year for workshops, seminars, and encounters, and her work has reached millions. She has written five books and produced many CDs and DVDs of her talks and workshops. She has appeared in a lengthy interview with Oprah and travels internationally giving talks and workshops. What does she teach? She teaches what she calls The Work.

Byron Katie realized that all her suffering resulted from her stressful thoughts that ultimately were not true. In other words, get to the root of an untrue thought, and misery disappears. Her technique is exceedingly simple: four questions and a turnaround statement (one or more). She encourages her students to shine the light of truth and awareness on their stressfully untrue thoughts. The darkness of the mind's contorted beliefs ultimately cannot contend with the clear light of true awareness. With this work, untrue thoughts melt away like snow in the sunshine, leaving only the freshness of a purified and peaceful mind.

To do The Work, one gathers up judgmental thoughts about anything or anyone—a husband, a coworker, PTSD, even your abuser (although I wouldn't start with that one first; that's the advanced course!)—and puts these thoughts into statements. You then ask yourself the following four questions about your statement, followed by a turnaround statement:

1. Is it true?

2. Can you absolutely know that it's true?

3. How do you react when you think that thought?

4. Who would you be without that thought?

5. Turn the thought around by rewriting your statement from an opposite perspective.

Let's take a common thought from PTSD that causes much suffering, such as "I'm so broken that I'll never be fixed," and subject it to The Work. This hypothetical example is based on dozens of conversations I have had with survivors. If you wish, try it first yourself, and then read my example. It's up to you!

1. Thought: I'm so broken that I can never be fixed. *Is it true?* Yep, that's how it feels.

2. *Can you absolutely know that it's true?* Hmmm, absolutely is a strong word. Maybe I can't *absolutely know* that I'll *never* be fixed.

192

3. *How do you react when you think the thought "I'm so broken that I'll never be fixed"?* I feel terrible, hopeless, like life is not worth living. Sometimes I don't feel worthy to be alive. If I'm so broken, who could love me? I feel unlovable and like a burden when I think that thought.

4. *Who would you be without that thought?* Wow, that's a hard one. I usually live with that thought all the time. Okay, let me close my eyes . . . without that thought . . . I think I would feel hopeful about the future, motivated to get better, and like life might be worth living again.

5. *Now turn your statement around. How many turnarounds can you get from your statement "I'm so broken that I'll never be fixed"?* Well here's one: I'm broken, but I can be fixed. *Good, can you think of another, more radical turnaround?* I'm fixed, and I'll never be broken. *Yes, excellent. Now just quietly let yourself be with that exercise. Without judgment, just notice how you are feeling now.*

The best way to imbibe Byron Katie's work is in person, but if you can't make it to one of her workshops, she has posted several free videos on her website (www.thework.com). In addition, all the forms you need to do this work are on her website as downloadable pdf files, with audio instructions, also free. Her online store sells several inexpensive CDs, DVDs, and books. Like any technique, The Work is not for everybody. If you have a bad feeling about it, honor your feelings first, or maybe seek certified facilitators who are graduates of her training program. You can even have a session by Skype! For many people, however, insight and change have come with lightning swiftness through this radical technique applied alone with pen and paper. She has even posted several letters from prisoners who have been profoundly helped by The Work. Is it true? Yes!

## Loving-Kindness Meditation (Metta)

I love teaching metta, also known as loving-kindness meditation, because it is easy to do and has been shown in research studies to change how the brain functions in a positive way. Metta comes to us from the Theravada line of Buddhist teachings. Its benefits can be summed up in this famous saying by the Dalai Lama: "If you want others to be happy, practice compassion. If you want to be happy, practice compassion."

According to tradition, the Buddha first taught this meditation as an antidote to extreme fear in the moment when fear arises. As such, it is perfectly suited to people who have panic attacks and/or PTSD. Metta is not religious, being closer to modern affirmation techniques than to a prayer, especially in the early stages of practice.

Metta consists of four simple statements repeated over and over in a relaxed and meditative state. No special equipment or technique is needed. This practice can be done as easily in a hospital bed as on a meditation cushion or a chair. To do metta, just settle yourself into a comfortable position in which you will not fall asleep. Repeat these four phrases in your mind, or you can say them out loud.

1. May I be free from danger.

2. May I have mental happiness.

3. May I have physical happiness.

4. May I have ease of well-being.

That's it. Easy peasy—oh, except for one hitch. After you become comfortable extending loving-kindness to yourself, the second stage of practice is to extend metta to others, beginning first with the people closest to you and then out into the world. So the second stage of metta might be extending loving-kindness to your partner:

1. May my partner be free from danger.

2. May my partner have mental happiness.

3. May my partner have physical happiness.

4. May my partner have ease of well-being.

After your partner, then focus on maybe your children, your friends, your parents, your business associates, your grocer, etc. The most advanced and powerful stage of the practice of metta involves extending loving-kindness to your enemies and abusers. It may be years to decades before one is truly ready for this stage of advanced metta, but what healing you will achieve in the process!

If you are new to metta, just begin with yourself. You might stay with this stage of the practice for weeks, months, or years. Do not skip over extending loving-kindness to yourself! Most of us with stress disorders have ambivalent relationships with ourselves at best. Metta will help you clear out all the areas in which you may have self-loathing, replacing them with a sweet self-love. If those words just made you cringe, you have lots more work yet to do. Go slowly, go gently and without cynicism for maximum benefit.

According to the Buddha, benefits of the loving-kindness meditation include deep, restful sleep and sweet dreams, the love of people and animals, protection from harm, a radiant face, a peaceful mind, a beneficial death, and rebirth into happier realms. Recent research has confirmed the Buddha's predictions by showing that metta practice does in fact confer more positive affect (emotion) in the practitioner as well as activity in the brain centers correlated with happiness and well-being.[2]

## ECKHART TOLLE NOW

Like Byron Katie, Eckhart Tolle suffered years of anxiety and depression prior to a sudden and complete awakening into a new existence free from suffering by coming into what he calls "the Now." His books *The Power of Now: A Guide to Spiritual Enlightenment* and *A New Earth: Awakening to Your Life's Purpose* have been international best sellers. You may have seen him on Oprah Winfrey's show when she highlighted her webcast series with him.

Tolle's teachings are simple and very relevant to those of us with trauma. First, he talks about the mind's tendency to live in the past, filled with brooding and depression, or the future, filled with fear and anxiety. When you bring the mind fully into the present moment, anxiety and depression drop away, leaving only your true peaceful nature. I have written earlier about how trauma disorders can be viewed as time disorders. A huge problem with survivors is the inability to stay tethered to the present moment. We often find ourselves catapulting back into traumatic memories or forward into highly charged anxious anticipation, sometimes to the point where our life becomes paralyzed. Mr. Tolle's firsthand experience of living in the Now is a powerful antidote to the helpless back-and-forth of the mind.

When caught up in flashbacks or anxiety, I have often found it helpful to ask the question, "What is happening right now?" to bring attention back to the Now. Often the answer is "I am sitting in my kitchen drinking tea," or "I am driving my car," or even "I am sitting in meditation." If we develop the habit of bringing our minds back to the

Now, we find that the vast majority of the time our lives are perfectly normal and we are safe; we just miss seeing this because of our mind's preoccupation with past and future. As I write this, my children are stressing over their homework and a busy schedule to the point of tears, *and school hasn't even started yet!* We all do this to some degree.

Another key concept in Eckhart Tolle's teachings is that of the pain body, similar to the concept of the shadow in Jungian psychology. The pain body is the dark side of the ego that has accumulated and identified with painful experiences from your life and from the culture around you. This pain body has a life of its own, driving us to behave in ways we ordinarily would not. It feeds off our unconsciousness, our lack of awareness. Sometimes it is dormant, and sometimes it roars into life with a ferocious and destructive power. All people and even collective egoic entities such as corporations, churches, and governments have pain bodies.

The pain body of someone with trauma is particularly heavy and burdensome. According to Eckhart Tolle, this condition is not necessarily a bad thing. A heavy pain body is sometimes the very thing that awakens people out of their suffering, as he and Byron Katie did. It's as if the ego finally just gives up and disintegrates, leaving only the shiny core of pure Self or Atman. The antidote to the darkness of the pain body is the light of awareness. The mind does not need to take a long time to shift. As a sage once put it, "If a cave has been dark for ten thousand years, how long does it take to get light once you bring in the torches?"

Eckhart Tolle travels around the world teaching constantly. He maintains a website at www.eckharttolle.com, where you can find books, a workbook, DVDs, and audio books, as well as audio and video downloads. His teachings are very simple, gentle, and to the point. I highly recommend them for trauma survivors.

# Tool 8

# The Jnanamayakosha: Mining the Wisdom Mind

THE BRAIN THINKS thoughts, and it is those thoughts that we examined in the last chapter. But what is the mind, really? Is it just the brain or something much vaster and deeper? In yoga and other Eastern spiritual traditions, mind persists from lifetime to lifetime. We can think of the accumulation of lifetimes of habitual thoughts and experiences congealed into an iceberg. Imagine, for a moment, this iceberg. The part above water is you, your individual self in this lifetime. If the iceberg represents your mind, then, the very top of the iceberg is the conscious mind, the thoughts you know you are having, the memories you can recall at the drop of a hat. These thoughts make up what we think of ourselves, our self-concept. As you move down to the intersection of ice and water, you come to an area that is still available to you as thinkable thoughts, but maybe these memories need a little prod. They are what Freud called preconscious thoughts, thoughts that are ready to come into awareness at any moment. If you meditate, you might notice lots of these preconscious thoughts manifesting in an annoying and distracting way when you become silent. Notice that there are far more preconscious thoughts congealed here than conscious ones higher up; the iceberg widens the lower it goes.

The waterline marks the beginning of the parts of our selves that are under water, so to speak. Have you ever seen a picture of an iceberg? The part under water is *huge*, almost unimaginably so. This is where the unconscious mind lies, with thoughts, memories, and experiences that are not easily available to us. When people first start doing spiritual practice or go into a depth therapy, they are often amazed at what eventually comes up from these depths: unacceptable feelings that have been shoved down, unbearable memories, unusual awarenesses outside of our ordinary cultural conditioning, and more. *The unconscious mind is what we don't know that we know.* It is almost impossible, by definition, to access these levels of the mind without assistance, yet it is important that we do so in order to free ourselves from persistent traumatic stress. Freud's genius was in pioneering ways to access this important part of the mind, ways that he called the Royal Roads to the Unconscious, and they were through dreams, slips of the tongue, and free association, the very basis of psychoanalysis.

Truth will out. Significant unconscious thoughts, feelings, or memories are like whales. They can stay submerged only for certain periods of time. Eventually they have to come up for air, however briefly—and this is why it is helpful to have a vigilant therapist who will call, "Thar she blows!" In that moment when they surface, we have a chance to learn something important about our histories and ourselves. In accepting these hidden parts of our minds we also extend to ourselves acceptance and a healthy self-love, a love that has perhaps been denied to us because of trauma.

Jung, Freud's famous pupil and successor, went even deeper. He found in the depths of the unconscious mind a shocking surprise. He found that at our deepest levels our minds are no longer our own but are communal. The iceberg swims in a vast sea of interconnection. All water merges with every other part of the water. Where the ice meets the sea, it too returns to water and absorbs the water. Jung found that the mind is not a closed system, something that our quantum physicists are also now proclaiming. At the deepest level of our minds we mysteriously hook into the mind of humanity, animals, and even the cosmos, something our shamanic indigenous ancestors have said from time out of mind. When we come to the edges of the iceberg, water does not disappear; it only morphs into something more liquid and movable, something that is the matrix of consciousness itself. We can tap into this matrix for healing, for wisdom, and for the expansion of our own consciousness. Such is the power of the vast realms of the jnanamayakosha, the wisdom mind.

## CORE BELIEFS AND QUANTUM PHYSICS

Have you ever noticed how our beliefs tend to shape reality? Years ago, *Saturday Night Live* did a hilarious parody of the self-help movement with depressed self-help guru Stuart Smalley (Al Franken) "helping" the famous basketball player Michael Jordan.[1] Stuart says, "The night before a game, you must lie awake thinking, 'I'm not good enough . . . everybody's better than me . . . I'm not going to score any points . . . I have no business playing this game . . . ,'" to which Jordan, visibly amused, replies, "Well, not really." We all know that if there is one thing a famous basketball player is not doing the night before a game, it is visualizing missing baskets and being worse than everyone else.

Traumatic events change our perceptions and beliefs about reality. They are so powerful, so seared into our memory, that their effects on our thinking linger on, long after all traces of the event have passed. There is a good reason for this, biologically speaking. Nature has designed us to respond more powerfully to fear than to almost any other stimulus. Let's say you are a hunter-gatherer, walking through a beautiful meadow filled with luscious berries, roots, and fruits. You are enjoying the blue sky, the scent of grasses and trees. All of a sudden, a predator, all teeth and claws, lunges at you. You get away, but only just. The next time you walk through that meadow, what will you remember, the beauty or the beast? Of course, it is the beast, and that's a good thing for the human species; otherwise, you might just walk into hungry jaws the next time you go looking for berries.

It is inevitable that over the course of our lives traumatic events will imbue us with thoughts and beliefs that are neither true nor helpful. Based on these unfortunate experiences, we develop core beliefs around the scariness and danger of life, until all we can think about is avoiding danger. If we are constantly thinking about that predator, we can never enjoy the beauty of gathering the fruits of our lives: joy, wonder, love. These false core beliefs need to be found, acknowledged, released, and replaced, so that we are free to live a joyful life.

Core beliefs are often formed very early in life and create a kind of template in the mind through which all experience is filtered. These beliefs are so much a part of us that *they are often unknown and therefore unquestioned*. Because they are unquestioned, they form the very basis of our identity. Sometimes these beliefs are helpful and benign. Sometimes they prevent us from getting the help we need in recovering from traumatic stress or even get us into dangerous situations.

After several years of working with a man with a very traumatic history, one day he blurted out a core belief in my office, "People are f***ers, and they'll f*** you over if you give them half a chance!" He reported feeling that way for as long as he could remember. Of course, since he is one of the "people" and so am I, his exclamation provided lots of grist for the therapy mill. But more importantly, he could start to see how he had been living in a reality that doomed him to ill treatment and possibly to treating others the same way. Needless to say, he had few close relationships, and the ones he did have were in crisis. Other popular core beliefs of victims of traumatic events include "I cannot get the help that I need"; "No one can understand what I've been through"; "Life's a bitch, then you die"; and so on.

Quantum physics shows us that in reality nothing is what it seems. The chair I am sitting on seems solid, but in reality it is full of space, tiny particles held together by electromagnetic glue, barely substantial. In quantum experiments the attitude of the observer has been shown to affect the outcome of the experiment. In other words, intention literally creates results. What if our core beliefs actually shape the reality we live in?

Years ago, there was a television show called *It's a Miracle*. Hosted by Richard Thomas, it chronicled fantastic rescues and recoveries of people in peril. After watching several episodes, I noticed a pattern. In almost every case, the person in an impossible situation prayed or asked for divine assistance before help arrived. Whether or not there is a divine being that came to the aid of the person is beyond the scope of this book. What struck me, as a therapist, was that the people were open to receiving help and had a strong belief that help could come, even in dire circumstances. These were people who had not given up, who believed in the possibility of deliverance. Their core belief, even in the midst of deep pain and fear was, "I am lovable, loved, and protected. I can get the help I need."

Do not mistake my intentions here. I am not out to blame the victim by saying that somehow you have manifested all of your ill fortune and if you just change your mind, things will magically get better. I do not believe that. We are on planet Earth, after all. People do crummy things to one another. Victimization, unfortunately, is a fact of life here.

What is important is looking at your core beliefs now. Do you have any beliefs, overt or hidden, that would prevent or impede your recovery? Pay special attention to those hidden ones. For example, some women who want to leave an abusive relationship might think to themselves, "I deserve a better life. I want to be safe, loved, and happy. I need to leave and start over." Underneath the conscious mind, though, might lurk a core belief from childhood that says, "I am worthless. I deserve all the abuse shown me. It's all the attention I will ever get." Guess which belief will win out? *In my experience, the unconscious negative core beliefs trump the positive affirmations every time.*

Sometimes, we may need psychotherapy to get at our hidden core-belief structures. But you can start now, even without a therapist, by writing out your core beliefs. This will take time and a commitment to introspection. Make a weekly appointment on your calendar with yourself. Sit down with pen and paper and go spelunking into the ancient caves of your own mind. When you release old negative beliefs and integrate your positive hopes and wishes for the future, you will have healed yourself at your deepest levels and freed yourself for the life that you really want.

## RAISING THE OPPOSITE WAVE

There is an old yogic technique for freeing the mind from negativity that looks remarkably like some of the cognitive-behavior techniques used in modern counseling today. This technique is called raising the opposite wave, or in Sanskrit the impossibly long *pratipakshabhavanam*. The rishis were aware that opposite states of consciousness cancelled each other out. As mentioned earlier, the sympathetic and parasympathetic nervous systems are mutually exclusive. We cannot be anxiously relaxed or calmly fearful; they are literally opposite bodily states.

To raise the opposite wave, we first need to cultivate insight and awareness to know which state we are in to begin with. Think about the roadmap from the first chapter; this is an example of looking for that "you are here" place. If we are in a great place, wonderful, enjoy it! If not, the ancients say, do something about it. The longer we persist in negative states, the more they persist in us. For those of you old enough to remember record players, think of a record filled with grooves. The needle moves smoothly through the musical grooves until it catches one that is slightly deeper than the others. The first time this happens, there is a small hiccup, but the music goes on. Each time the needle catches in the groove, the groove gets deeper, until one day you try to play your beautiful music, and you can't; the needle is stuck in the groove, endlessly repeating the annoying sound and unable to complete the song. Our brains are like that record. If we allow negative states to recur persistently without challenge, they can trip up our joy, become annoying habits and eventually persistent states of being that keep us stuck in misery.

The opening stanza of the Prayer of St. Francis is a beautiful example of the practice of raising the opposite wave:

> *Lord, make me an instrument of your peace.*
> *Where there is hatred, let me sow love.*
> *Where there is injury, pardon.*
> *Where there is doubt, faith.*
> *Where there is despair, hope.*
> *Where there is darkness, light.*
> *Where there is sadness, joy.*

Most people hear this prayer as something to be practiced in the external world (a beautiful thing to do), but first we have to practice it within our own minds. If there is hatred within, cultivate love; if there is despair, cultivate hope. And, we could add, if there is anxiety, create calmness; if there is depression, cultivate joy. Where there are internal judgments, we can deepen understanding; where there is bitterness, we can forgive. The list truly is endless. We can engage our own will to lighten our internal load, and when that load is too heavy, prayer or affirmations can be a wonderful way to help lift and lighten our spirits. Fortunately, we live in a remarkable time when all the resources we need to do this practice are available to us. On the Internet, in bookstores, in workshops and therapy offices, the wisdom of all cultures has been released for our benefit and healing. Ask, and you truly shall receive. Are you ready to give it a try?

## GIVING WHAT WE NEED TO RECEIVE

When we live in states of extreme traumatic stress, life becomes an arduous struggle for survival. We can become so consumed with our feelings of pain, separation, rage, and despair that it becomes hard to go on living our lives. Suicidal or homicidal feelings can emerge, or we can just give up, what I call sitting down on the curb and refusing to move. We might not hurt anyone, but we also can't move forward in jobs, relationships, or life. In this state, people ultimately lose hope and respect for themselves. Giving up becomes a negative spiral that, at its worst, can end in addiction, homelessness, loss of one's family, or even death.

What would you say if I told you there was a pill for this state, one that would magically take away these feelings and give your life meaning and purpose? You'd want it, right? Well, there's good news and bad news. So far as I know, there is no such pill. The good news is that there is a powerful antidote to states of self-absorbed hopelessness and negativity that is guaranteed to work, because it has been taught and used throughout human history. You don't need anyone to help you with it, and it's free. It is called selfless compassionate service to others, and it is an express one-way ticket out of hell.

That reminds me of a story of a man who almost died but didn't. While he was in the out-of-body state, an angel offered to give him a free tour of the afterlife, a preview of coming attractions, so to speak. The angel first took him to a room where there was a big boiling pot of food in the middle of a table surrounded by gaunt, hungry figures with spoons. However, their spoons were too long. Every time they desperately tried to get the food into their mouths, they couldn't. The food scalded their faces, stained their clothes, and only dribbled occasionally into their mouths. These people screamed and moaned, by turns irate and despairing. Horrified, the man turned to his angel guide and asked, "What is this place?" "This is hell," the angel replied. At their next stop they encountered a very similar looking room, again with the pot of bubbling food and the extra long spoons, but at this table people looked happy and well fed. They were relaxed and joking, enjoying their delicious meal. When the man looked closer, he saw them feeding each other with the long spoons. "This is heaven," said the angel.

Every major religion teaches active compassion through service for others. Jewish teachings call it *tikkun olam*, repairing the world for the good of all. *Seva*, or selfless service to others, is a cornerstone of yogic practice in Hinduism. Christians call it *acts of charity*. Buddhists focus on developing *bodhichitta*, the heart of compassion for all suffering beings.

When we are in pain, we can collapse into ourselves, to the point where our world gets smaller and smaller and our pain gets bigger and bigger. On the other hand, we could let our suffering inform us about the extent of other beings' sufferings. We may not be able to relieve our own suffering in the moment, but we can reach out to others and help them. By taking action on behalf of others, we soon realize we are feeling better, too. Many people instinctively know how to do this already. Some of us have children who force us out of our shell of suffering and into service whether we want to or not. But many people with traumatic stress isolate themselves, feeling they are of no use to anyone in their painful condition.

Here is my recommendation to alleviate your suffering and despair. Find someone to help every day, in a kind and selfless way. Your gesture does not have to be grand. You don't have to build a homeless shelter or serve on the streets of Calcutta like Mother Teresa, although if you want to and have the means, far be it from me to discourage you. Otherwise, start small. Smile and say thank you to the grocery clerk during checkout. Look around you in your apartment building, neighborhood, or workplace and start to notice who is suffering and why. Offer to carry someone's bag of groceries. Give up your seat on the bus to someone who needs it more than you do. Give a few hours a week to a local volunteer program—especially if you are out of work. Call a family member who is lonely and say you love them. Smile warmly at people you pass on the street. The possibilities are truly endless.

You may not feel better immediately, but keep at it. Several research studies have proven the benefits of selfless service with compassion over time. You will find that selfless service results in the following:

- Greater self-esteem

- A sense of meaning and purpose in life

- Less anxiety and/or depression

- Increased capacity to love and care for others

- More connection and feelings of belonging

- Lessening of chronic pain

In the beginning, keeping a journal of your actions may help to remind yourself of the good you have done. Whether or not you feel good while doing the action does not seem to matter. A lot of people wait to feel better before they do better. In fact, the process of healing is just the reverse. *Doing better creates better feelings.* It's a little like exercise. At first you just feel tired; then you notice yourself getting stronger, and then after you persist in your goals you find yourself fitter than ever. Along the way, you will create a better world for all of us.

## SHAMANIC PRACTICES

In my practice I have found that people with significant trauma histories feel unusually open to shamanic healing. For many, regular psychotherapy just doesn't address the depth of wounding a trauma survivor feels. Concepts like soul retrieval of fragmented parts, journeying, and power animals seem eerily natural to those who have depth wounding. Trauma pierces through all layers of our psyches. The pain is intense and unremitting, making people open to nonordinary interventions. But I think the affinity goes even deeper than relief of pain. Traumatic injury and recovery has been a part of shamanic initiation in every culture around the world.

The word *shaman* comes to us from the Russian steppes and Siberia. According to the *Collins English Dictionary*, the word has its roots in the Sanskrit word *srama*, "spiritual exercise." It has become common to use *shaman* to describe any medicine person from an indigenous ethnic group or any healer who works with what has been termed nonordinary reality to provide healing for individuals and groups. A small sample of names for these healers includes medicine people, curanderas, witches, aboriginal healers, druids, manbos, and gatekeepers. For ease of recognition and convenience (if not linguistic and cultural accuracy) nonordinary indigenous healers will be referred to here as shamanic. But please realize that many indigenous people would not identify themselves by the name shaman.

A surprisingly large number of people in the United States have gone to a shaman for healing, are familiar with shamanic techniques, or have even studied some of those techniques themselves. A generation ago shamanic healing was considered ignorant by the scientific community, irrelevant by the masses, and satanic by many Christians (and still is in some parts of the country). Fortunately, with tolerance, exposure, and a greater understanding of our native brothers and sisters, as well as our own indigenous ancestors, attitudes are changing.

One of the best-kept secrets of psychotherapy (even from clinicians) is that *survivors of extreme trauma almost always have experiences in nonordinary reality.* Of course, the psychiatric community labels them with dry, clinical-sounding names, but I think it's a case of you say tomato and I say tomahto. If someone experiences trauma while out of body, floating on the ceiling, we therapists call it *dissociation*, never astral projection. If a client forms a telepathic link with the therapist, we call it *unconscious communication* or, even worse, *projection* (especially if the therapist is in denial of his or her own baggage), never clairaudience or direct knowing. Psychoanalysts don't journey; they go into *reverie*. Clients don't withdraw their pranic aura from an object; they *decathect*. Gifted empaths have *permeable boundaries*, never clairsentience. And so on. So, if you have had some, shall we say, *unusual* experiences, you are definitely not alone; in fact, you are probably in the silent majority. What these experiences mean for a survivor of trauma is that *by the very nature of your traumatic experience you may have access to nonordinary realms of healing to assist you.* Strange as such an experience may be, it is very good news! You have the power to heal!

Below are some shamanic techniques, proven over centuries, that can augment your healing.

## Power Animals

Most indigenous cultures consider animals to be sacred elements in the hoop of life equal in worth to the life of humans. While indigenous people may eat animals for survival and use their bodies to provide shelter and clothing, there is a reverence and acknowledgment that the beingness of animals transcends their bodies. All animals are seen to have a unique archetypal spirit, qualities that can be called upon in certain tasks, like hunting, healing, or spiritual protection. Many Native Americans, or First People as they are called in Canada, affiliate their clans or tribes with certain animals, so whole families can be from the wolf, bear, eagle, or raven clans, among others. Encountering certain animals at certain times, either in ordinary reality or in the dreamtime, has meaning for shamanic healing. These animals are sometimes called power animals, and they are considered to be tremendous aids in healing and ceremony. Some say all human beings have their individual power animals that watch over them.

I counseled a patient who, for several years, had no sense of personal safety anywhere due to early and ongoing severe abuse. Sometimes the fear got so bad that she had to sleep in her car at night, even though she had a perfectly fine place to live, in the physical sense. She came to one session with an unusually vivid dream that two buffalo had moved in with her and were watching out of the windows, guarding her. This dream was extremely comforting to her, and her sense of safety in her personal space increased. I encouraged her to acknowledge the buffalo as her power animals and not to write off the experience as just a dream, but to embrace the sense of safety they brought. Were they "real"? Does it matter? This powerful dream really made a difference to the client in a felt sense of protection and safety.

Jamie Sams is a Native American healer of Cherokee and Seneca descent who has cowritten, with David Carson, one of the most popular books on power animals ever, *Medicine Cards: The Discovery of Power Through the Ways of Animals*. The book is an interpretation of the cards, each of which shows a power animal. Millions of people around the world have used this tool for emotional healing and guidance through animal guides and totems. The book and card deck remain one of the easiest and most pleasing ways to access connection to animal archetypal wisdom. Aside from providing readings with card layouts, the book is an excellent reference for animals that show up in dream imagery and in strange encounters in everyday life.

If you have an animal you have a strong affinity with, or one that keeps showing up in your life in unusual ways, it could be a power animal (and, yes, you can have more than one), your archetypal animal companion or helper. Allow yourself to connect with the energy of this animal. What is it trying to tell you? What qualities does it embody? Are they qualities you need for yourself, for your own healing? Allow this sacred assistance with gratitude and humility.

## Soul Retrieval

Perhaps there is no more apt metaphor for healing from trauma than the concept of soul fragmentation, soul loss, and soul retrieval. Indigenous cultures consider soul loss or fragmentation to be a terrible condition that gives rise to all sorts of diseases in the mind and body. Soul loss (or even soul captivity) can occur under conditions that are not life threatening but still result in traumatic stress, such as bitter divorces, the loss of loved ones, abusive relationships, or betrayals. Our language describing these relational events reflects this concept even in modern culture:

*They took a piece of me with them.*
*I'm not myself.*
*I'll never be whole again.*
*She won't let me go.*

And, of course, soul loss can happen under classic PTSD conditions such as on a battlefield or in a car accident:

*A part of me died out there.*
*I left that person on the battlefield.*
*I don't recognize who I've become.*
*I can't find my way home to myself.*

Psychology actually has a vocabulary for soul loss and fragmentation. If someone is disconnected from a sense of self, we say that person is dissociative. Fragmentation is a clinical term for the condition in which various self-states are not integrated into a cohesive whole. Alters (distinct personalities within the person that are unaware of each other) occur when the fragmentation is so extreme that important parts of the self holding the keys to memories and the continuity of life experiences can't be found. This extreme condition, previously known as multiple personality disorder, is now called dissociative identity disorder (DID). Repressed memories also involve aspects of self (or soul) that have been split off and forgotten.[2]

Soul retrieval in psychotherapy can look a lot like memory retrieval. The more awareness brought to the process in feeling and understanding the immense energies involved—that you are bringing back not just a cognitive state, but an entire soul state—the more powerful and complete the integration will be. It is important to acknowledge the age of the part being integrated and to recognize that the part holding the memory may not be aware of the current year and age of the victim. This process can be a visual experience for the client or a felt one. One of my patients reported experiencing the part coming back as swollen and inflamed, tender and fragile upon return. It is not unusual for people to experience changes in their energy, mood, and outlook while adjusting to the new reality. Such experiences are always positive in the long run, but they can be challenging in the initial stages when accompanied by such phenomenon as sudden spurts of energy alternating with fatigue, spaciness, or changes to how the world is experienced such as colors being brighter and feelings being more vivid.

Of course, traditional shamanic practices incorporate radically different techniques that look strange to a traditional Western practitioner, but are no less powerful than familiar ones. Sandra Ingerman's famous book on the subject, *Soul Retrieval: Mending the Fragmented Self*, introduced thousands of Americans to this practice. The shaman, usually in a trance induced with rattles, drums, or chants (and in some cultures with plant substances), journeys into an alternate reality where a soul fragment is residing. The shaman brings this soul fragment back and "blows" it back into the body where the patient can then integrate it, overcoming the depression, PTSD, or other state of dis-ease that has resulted from soul loss. It is a journey fraught with difficulties, especially if that piece is being held captive by another being with some powers of its own (dark magic, sorcery, or ritual abuse). If this is the case, traditional therapy may not be enough, and I recommend that the victim seek out an accomplished spiritual shaman or medicine person with integrity to help reclaim the stolen and captive parts.

Just as others can hold onto certain fragments of our selves, we can unwittingly suffer from holding onto others' pieces. I have often found in my practice with adult survivors of child abuse that victims have held on to and unconsciously "owned" energetic fragments of their perpetrators, the most common of these being the shame of the perpetrator, which energetically has a thick, heavy, dark, and gooey signature. When victims are overcome with shame, I ask them how much of this shame feels as if it is theirs, and how much feels as if it belongs to the perpetrator. I have never in several years of practice had a patient answer that 100 percent or even 80 percent is his or her own. Patients are always surprised to find that they own only about 40 to 60 percent of the shame and that the rest is the split-off and projected part of the abuser they have unconsciously owned. At this point I advise them to return to sender the shame that is not their own. I have met other therapists who work in a similar way, but instead of sending the energy back to the perpetrator, they send it over the horizon, burn it up in a fire, or send it to the sun. However you do this shamanic exercise, it is healing and instantly relieving. You can try it yourself and be done in an instant. Be sure to set up some sort of block to the energy bouncing back to you by getting clear on what was not your fault and by visualizing a powerful barrier (yellow crime tape, orange cones, a guardian, etc.).

## The Screen Exercise

According to clairvoyants, we connect to everyone around us via light cords that attach in the region of the solar plexus. If we are sensitive to energy (and many of us with traumatic stress are) we can not only feel the energies of those around us, but unconsciously and at a young age learn we can actually manipulate others' energies. It comes naturally to some of us and sometimes is a matter of survival to calm down an anxious parent or alleviate someone's intensely violent rages. This unconscious energy work is very draining, and when we carry it into adulthood we can add to our own psychic burden the weight of others' sorrows and emotions. Initially, most people don't even realize they are doing this work.

One of the most singular and powerful exercises I've run across to deal with these negative attachments is the screen exercise. Part of the burden we carry with traumatic stress is waltzing around with other people's energies, which engages our compassion but also our egoic striving (however unconscious) to change the energy. Being in this condition drains us. Here is an exercise for releasing it:

> *Imagine that you have become a giant screen as in a screen door or a screen window. Feel yourself letting energies pass through you like air through the screen. You will still be able to read energy and use your knowing, but those energies will no longer stick to you like Velcro. The holes in the screen can be as big or as fine as you want to make them, with structural integrity remaining intact. You can even coat them with Teflon. Any negativity you encounter will blow right on through without any effort on your part. Just be willing to release all the energy you encounter while retaining the information left behind. Send the negative energy off to Spirit, to God, to the sun, or to a tree outside, (Remember, they like negative qi.)*

This screen exercise replaces the need to shield or defend. I have met very few sensitives that can effectively shield. Women, especially, tend not to shield effectively, and shielding is often not deemed desirable in certain spiritual groups. Many Buddhists, for example, encourage opening the heart of compassion and discourage shielding, even from negative energies. With the screen exercise we can be present and aware of others' sufferings without taking them on. For maximum effectiveness, practice this exercise consciously and regularly. Don't forget to remember! Otherwise, as one clairvoyant told me, people will continue to chuck their trash into your energy field for processing, and you will feel inexplicably burdened.

As for those pesky cords to undesirable people in our lives, if you have them, you may be tempted to rip them right out. Don't! Even if—and especially if—you are corded to an abuser. Ripping out connections before they are ripe for release can leave an ugly energetic wound in the prana body and affect the stability of the mind. Instead, visualize yourself pinching off those cords and have an intention for them to fall off (somewhat like an umbilical cord). Some people like to look to religious figures such as the archangel St. Michael or the goddess Durga with their swords to help cut the cords. It is always safe to ask for divine help. The combination of gradual cord release and the screen exercise will bring back a sense of sanity and safety if you are drowning in negative energies.

## Journeying

As a therapist, I journey a lot in my work with clients. It takes only a moment for me to close my eyes (or not) and zoom into a realm with answers that often come in the form of a singular image I may or may not understand. Amazingly, the client understands what the image means even if I don't and usually has a big "aha" moment. It is a great shortcut for healing and bypasses all the negative aspects of being in the manomayakosha (cognitive-mind layer), such as doubt, disbelief, and confusion, as well as egoic motivation (because I really cannot take any credit whatsoever for what I am shown and neither can the patient).

Journeys are very similar to the concept of fantasy, or reverie, in psychoanalytic thought. You might know them as daydreams. However, in shamanic types of practices thoughts are things and have effects (measurable in some experiments) in ordinary as well as nonordinary reality. You can think of a journey as a directed and focused daydream—at least in the beginning. As you progress, you may need some assistance moving about in realms you are unaccustomed to. The more control you have over your own mind and attention, the more effective your journeying will become. You also need to develop the capacity to dissolve your own resistance or, as we say in theater arts, suspend your disbelief.

If you decide to journey, create an intention for yourself. For instance, "I want to heal my relationship with my partner." The safety meditation laid out earlier is also a kind of a journey. Ask to be taken and shown exactly what you need to heal for your *highest purpose only.* You can request the company of a spirit guide in angelic or animal form for guidance and protection. Find a safe and peaceful place where you will not be disturbed. If you wish, you can also have a friend, counselor, or someone else you trust with you to "hold space" as you journey. Some people like to light a candle as they journey to symbolize their process and as a focal point for return. Censor nothing. Let the images come; if it gets scary you can always stop, but if you ask for protection it is highly unlikely you will have a negative experience. Afterward, be sure to record what you experienced through writing, sketching, or talking to your companion or even into a recorder. If you want in-depth instruction or feel safer with a human guide, there are many workshops and facilitators of the journeying process that you can work with in a group or one on one.

When you get information, work with it. Integrate it as soon as possible. *Many people get information on healing that they fail to implement. We need to embody the healing process, or our visions will amount to nothing but an interesting story.*

## Past-Life-Regression Therapy

Another way people can journey is through time. When people journey into their deep past, they can find themselves in what may seem like another lifetime. In 1980, Dr. Brian Weiss was head of the psychiatry department at Mt. Sinai Medical Center (Miami Beach) and a psychoanalyst skilled in hypnosis when he stumbled into a patient's past-life memories. What convinced him that something extraordinary was happening was not so much the historically accurate details of her memories but the information she brought back from the state between lifetimes. Incredibly, she told him about his own family members who had passed and shocked him with the knowledge of a baby he had lost in this lifetime, an intensely personal event that was not public knowledge at the time. His deep exploration of his journey with this patient led him to write the international best seller *Many Lifetimes, Many Masters: The True Story of a Prominent Psychiatrist, His Young Patient, and the Past-Life Therapy That Changed Both Their Lives.*

Today, by conservative estimate, about one-quarter of people of all religious faiths in the United States, including Christianity, believe in reincarnation. Dr. Weiss's books have continued to grow in popularity, and he was even featured on *The Oprah Winfrey Show* in the 2008 season. Currently he speaks internationally and along with his social worker wife trains facilitators in past-life-regression therapy (PLRT). I had the privilege of completing their course for therapists in the fall of 2009 and have conducted a number of past-life regressions since then.

What is amazing about PLRT is that it seems to work whether one believes in past lives or not. You can think of this work as being about genetic heritage, race memory, Jungian mind fields, or just plain fantasy; the results are the same. But if you do believe in reincarnation, the impact on trauma is this: we all carry trauma predominantly in our minds, because it is a universal human experience. That mind transmigrates from body to body over lifetime to lifetime. Traumas give rise to complexes and core beliefs (*samskaras* and *sankalpas* in Indian philosophy) that we carry forward and manifest, or at least lay the groundwork for, in our subsequent lifetimes. Until these traumas are released and beliefs adjusted to a healthier state, we will continue to repeat unconsciously the situation of trauma in our lives even into future lifetimes. That's the bad news. The good news is that death is an illusion (albeit a painful one) and that we have an infinite number of chances to heal and "get it right." The great news is that with a few sessions working in the deep mind, much trauma can be cleared from this and other lifetimes. *PLRT is a powerful healing shortcut, a wormhole through the psyche that collapses time and provides nearly instantaneous relief of suffering.*

I counseled a patient who was struggling to get past a lifetime of insecurity and trauma about having been abandoned in mid-childhood by her parents—one physically and the other emotionally. When she came to me for therapy, she was in an abusive marriage, one she clearly knew she had to leave, but she carried intense fear about finding happiness alone. This fear of abandonment and being alone kept her from moving fully into the divorce process. She was deeply stuck and in a state of chronic traumatic stress. In PLRT she relived two lifetimes in which she had been extremely happy and content as a young single woman. In a lifetime in New York City she experienced herself as happy and free to live her life as she chose. There was no sense of lack of fulfillment by not being with a man, only a sense of freedom and exhilaration in the possibilities for her life. The other lifetime was as a native woman in the Far North in an indeterminate time and place. She had a beautiful vision of herself under the cold northern sky, independent, strong, fearless, and confident about herself and her abilities. Prior to this regression, she had never experienced herself in this way (in this lifetime). The felt experience of those lifetimes became a polestar for her in her emerging sense of self and of possibility for a new life free from her dead marriage. Today she radiantly embodies those qualities as a single woman who has stepped fully into herself, a radical shift from the fearful, constricted life she had been leading when she first came to therapy. Although traditional therapy was also part of her treatment, I suspect that our PLRT session shortened her therapy by several months to years.

Dozens of clinical hypnotists and psychotherapists have been trained to do this kind of depth work by Dr. Weiss (www.brianweiss.com) and also by Roger Woolger, PhD, another pioneer of regression therapy. Dr. Woolger, a Jungian practitioner originally from England who now lives in the Hudson Valley in New York, lists practitioners he has trained on his website (www.rogerwoolger.com). If past-life regression sounds as if it is for you, you can book a session with a clinician trained by one of these pioneers or even go to their workshops. Dr. Weiss and Dr. Woolger give group trainings around the world, but do not see individual clients as far as I know. Both have published books and DVDs that facilitate regressions in the comfort and safety of your own home.

# WISDOM TEACHINGS

Every culture has its wisdom teachings. When they are written down, they are sometimes called scripture. They can be the very highest offerings of the mind, and some call them the Word of God or divinely inspired. For many, these teachings are wonderful aids to turn to when we are in the depths of despair or caught up in anxiety because they lift up the vibration of the suffering mind. They can focus our mind on what is good, beautiful, and true and remind us that suffering is a universal condition for which there are many answers and solutions.

An old joke has Job, who in the Bible suffered so many horrible trials, finally asking God why. Why was he, a good man, subjected to so much suffering? As the joke goes, God leans in and whispers, "Because you just piss me off." This joke reflects our worst fears about why we suffer from traumatic stress—that somehow, somewhere, we deserve what has happened to us, and now we are being punished for our sins or transgressions.

Reading wisdom teachings helps us go beyond the cogitations of our thinking minds, our worries, doubts, and fears; they remind us that the experience of suffering is universal. Normally, we tend to restrict our reading to material dictated by our culture and upbringing. But many have found succor and awakening in reading a variety of the world's great wisdom texts. Because of the openness of the Internet and our global lifestyle, we have more access to these teachings than at any time in recorded history. And not only ancient wisdom scriptures are available, but also books by modern sages. One can find talks on the Internet by everyone from the Dalai Lama to Ram Dass to Native American elders.

If you are open to the idea, I recommend reading many or all of the major religious texts, from the Bible to the Koran, the Bhagavad Gita

to the Tao Te Ching. Find poems and writing by mystics like Meister
Eckhart or Rumi, or read the lives of the saints. Many people are unaware
that the greatest spiritual breakthroughs have happened to those who
have suffered the greatest: St. Francis, who rebelled against his wealthy,
stifling family; Rama, who, as a young man, was sick unto death of the
world (what we might now trivialize as teenage angst); Paramahansa
Yogananda, a modern saint and mystic who was propelled by the early
death of his mother into a search for God; or Saint Teresa of Avila, who,
under backbreaking difficulties, famously said, "If this is how you treat
your friends, Lord, no wonder you have so few of them." A modern
teacher of peace and liberation, the Vietnamese monk Thich Nhat
Hanh, saw his village burnt to the ground three times by Americans.
Three times he helped to rebuild it. Later he came to America to work
with veterans and teach peace. His book *Anger: Wisdom for Cooling the
Flames* is one of the best I have ever read on the subject and is highly
recommended for survivors of trauma.

Reading about (or listening to) wisdom reinforces our own deep
knowing. It turns our mind away from brooding on our suffering
and lifts our mood. Wisdom teachings do not have to be based in
any single religion. They work just as well for atheists as for believers.
Atheists, of course, can choose uplifting teachings that align with their
nonreligious beliefs and values, such as the Tao Te Ching. Getting
your daily consumption of wisdom (my favorite time is just before
sleep) is highly recommended in healing from traumatic stress, as are
the following practices of prayer and mantra.

## Prayer and Mantra

Cognitive therapy sometimes uses a technique called thought
substitution, in which one replaces, or pushes out, a negative thought

with a positive one. I find it rather mediocre as a healing technique—in part because it only engages the level of the cognitive mind and frustrates as often as it helps. Prayer and mantra, on the other hand, are like thought substitution on steroids. These powerful practices call in all the subtler energies and, in the case of mantra, powers said to be at the very foundation of the universal mind, to lift the human mind up and out of the darkness of trauma.

Prayer is found in every spiritual culture and religion. Prayers, in their highest forms, can be affirmations, requests, blessings, or communion with the divine. They can even manifest in the form of healings. What is not as helpful is prayer done in a rote way, without concentration or sincerity, or on a sporadic timetable. The traumatically stressed mind naturally tends to want to fall into grief, anger, brooding, and resentment. Prayer, when done with intensity and consistency, gives the mind something else to focus on, a helpful practice especially for those who find meditation impossible or undesirable. Spontaneous prayer opens up a relational connection between us and the divine, whether it be directed to Jesus, Mohammed, Buddha, Mary, Kali, Quan Yin, or Great Spirit. Take one step towards God, as the saying goes, and God takes two steps towards us. This sense of personal connection can be a saving grace in times of despair. Use your connection: pray, talk, and commune on a regular basis.

Mantra, a set of words repeated for spiritual growth, is a little more mysterious and foreign to the Western mind than prayer. India has a famous story about mantra practice. A man sought a sorcerer to obtain a genie that would grant him all his wishes. The sorcerer was reluctant to tell the man about how to obtain the services of the genie, for it was quite dangerous. The man was not to be deterred and left with the genie and a mysterious warning about keeping the genie busy. If the genie were not kept busy, it would destroy him. No problem, the man thought, I have many requests to keep this genie busy for a lifetime. His first request was to be made rich. The genie whisked away and was back within minutes handing him a bank statement that showed an account full to the brim with cash. Okay, the man thought, and he sent the genie out to obtain some land and build a magnificent mansion for him to live in. The man was dismayed to see the genie back within the hour, rubbing his hands with glee because it knew it would get to destroy the man if not kept busy. As quickly as the man set up tasks for the genie, they were completed, until the man was utterly exhausted and desperate to think of new tasks. He saw an old sadhu (holy man) with a dog watching him out of the corner of his eye and decided to swallow his pride and ask for help. The sadhu smiled kindly, bent over and plucked a curly hair off of the dog. "Here, give this to your genie and tell him to straighten it," said the sadhu. When the genie returned the man asked him to straighten the hair, but every time the genie straightened it, the hair sprang back into its curly shape. "There," said the sadhu, "that will keep him busy until you need him again; now go and get some rest!" The man in the story is us; the genie is our mind, which can manifest everything we wish, but which destroys us if not properly directed, and the curly hair represents the power of mantra to keep the mind focused and out of trouble.

In India, mantra is traditionally given by an illumined teacher in a ceremony called *mantra diksha* and is considered a sacred transmission of spiritual power or energy to the student. Often the divine syllable "Om" or "Aum" is included along with a powerful word, or *bijam* ("seed" in Sanskrit), and the name of a deity. There are many kinds of mantras for health, wealth, spiritual realization, compassion, or steadiness in meditation, among others; there are even some for good marriages! Buddhists also confer and utilize mantras for purification of the mind.[3]

Mantra, like prayer, is a repetitive practice. It can be done anywhere and anytime. Sometimes practitioners like to use mala necklaces consisting of 108 beads, each representing one repetition of the mantra, just as Catholics might say the rosary, only instead of reciting mantras Catholics say prayers on their rosary beads. Mantra is said to clear the mind, prepare the way for deeper meditation, and ameliorate the effects of one's karma. The classic example of this lessening of karma says that if you were supposed to suffer a sword blow to your leg, you would get only a pinprick instead. People who practice mantra or prayer for extended periods report it to be a powerful tool to heal and focus the mind. People can experience profound visions and divine experiences during these practices. A single authentic spiritual experience is a powerful antidote for even a lifetime full of trauma.

## MEDITATION

Swami Vivekenanda, the famous spiritual teacher who first brought yoga to America, compared the human mind to a drunk monkey being stung by a scorpion while drowning. And that's a "normal" mind! With PTSD we can add to the monkey mind the distractions of flashbacks, intolerable anxiety, irritability, and depression. We are not trained in this country to focus our minds on anything except homework and, eventually, "grown-up" work. When our minds are not focused on work (or the Internet or television), we generally let the monkey have its way with us, which is sometimes fun but usually miserable.

I have often said that Western psychotherapy ends where Eastern spirituality begins: with a calm and focused mind. But how do we get to practice a calm and focused mind when our minds and bodies are so besieged with traumatic stress? The same way you get to Carnegie Hall: practice, practice, practice. I don't mean to sound glib, but *the only way to learn how to meditate is to practice meditation.* If that sounds hard, consider how much time you spend every day in "have-to-do" tasks. Brushing teeth: 10 minutes; bathing and styling: 30 to 40 minutes; eating meals: 10 to 60 minutes each; commuting to work: 20 minutes on average; walking the dog: 10 to 20 minutes; meditation: priceless. Is it really true we do not have the time to build in 10 to 60 minutes a day of meditation? Can we afford not to? As Gandhi is said to have quipped, "I have so much to accomplish today that I must meditate two hours instead of one."

If there is any magic in the world to heal us from PTSD and traumatic stress, it is meditation. The more time you spend doing it, paradoxically, the more time you have. Meditation focuses and concentrates the mind so that it runs much more efficiently when you do get up off the mat. Longtime meditators often see their need for sleep decrease by one to two hours, and they see their productivity increase. Other benefits include:

• You lower the overall "anxiety basement" of the body, that is, your lowest chronic level of anxiety. If the needle on your stress gauge is constantly in the yellow to red zone, it will lower to the green to yellow zone. In that way, when you do get hit with a trigger you are not automatically in the red-hot emergency zone.

• Clarity is gained as the mind presents you with its contents. At first this can feel unpleasant (much as in psychotherapy), but there is no way to clear the mind without knowing what is in it. The only way out is through!

- Over time, the tension in the body and mind will unwind, leaving room for profound upwellings of peaceful, loving, and blissful feelings. Thich Nhat Hanh has said that the main purpose of meditation for Americans is to learn to tolerate peaceful feelings, and from my professional experience that is a true statement.

- The peace gained in meditation practice will stay with you physiologically and mentally throughout the day, not just while you are on your cushion. After several years of practice, this peace becomes nearly unshakable.

- Meditation has been shown to promote growth in areas of the brain responsible for happy and contented feelings and to decrease activity in areas of the brain associated with stress and unhappiness.

- Meditation strengthens the "mind muscle." Most of us have flabby mind muscles because we have so rarely challenged our minds for control. When flashbacks come along, they yank us back in time along with them. The more power you have over your mind's activity, the better you will cope with PTSD activation when it comes along.

People initially resist meditative practices for several reasons. One has to do with religious concerns. There is a rumor in some Christian communities that meditation opens the mind to negative or demonic influences. As someone who is spiritually trained, I would never dismiss such concerns outright. In answer, I have to say that I think people are more at risk of their minds hanging wide open to negative influences in front of a television than they are in meditation. But, if this is a concern of yours, during meditation surround yourself with reminders of divine protection: pictures of angels, the deities of your choice, or other icons. You can also hold a picture of your protector in your heart chakra and meditate on that. If you are a Christian, for example, hold a beautiful image of Jesus or Mary in your heart during your meditation and ask for complete and divine protection in your meditation space.

Another thing I hear a lot of people say is, "I could never do that; I can't make my mind go blank." *Meditation is not making your mind go blank!* There are actually many different meditation techniques that go well beyond the scope of this book. There are single-pointed meditations, mantra meditations, and meditations on the breath or on different chakras, and, yes, there are formless meditations. There are Christian meditations, Buddhist meditations, Taoist meditations, and Hindu meditations, and they all have different purposes for and effects on the mind. They do require some instruction. Meditating in a group can be quite powerful: the collective mind helps calm and deepen the mind of the beginning meditator.

Here is a simple meditation you can begin to work with:

*Find a comfortable place to sit with a comfortably straight spine. It can either be a cushion or a chair; just find a place where you will not fall asleep easily. We do not want to condition the mind to fall out during meditation but to wake up! Rest your hands on your legs, and balance your head upon your neck for minimum stress. This meditation can be done with eyes open or shut. If you have a tendency to space out or dissociate, it might be best to keep your eyes half open, focused on a spot on the floor about three feet in front of you. Otherwise close your eyes. If you wish, you can lightly touch the tip of your tongue to the roof of your mouth; this will strengthen your energy and focus during meditation. Rest your right hand lightly on top of your left hand, palms up in your lap. Notice the flow of air moving in and out of your nostrils; try to feel each separate sensation connected with the breath, but do not try to change or force the breath in any way. Good. If your attention begins to wander, just bring it lightly back to the breath. As you sit, you will notice different feelings and urges come up in the body. Notice them without necessarily giving in to them. If your nose begins to itch, just notice it; watch it as it intensifies and decreases. Notice how long it takes for the sensation to fade. Notice if you have any emotions coming up around those sensations.*

*You should be fairly comfortable. If you really need to move, because you have a knee injury, for example, gently shift to a more comfortable position, and then bring your attention back to the breath. See if you can observe without acting. Become aware of your thoughts and the nature of things happening in and around you. When thoughts come, let them drift through your consciousness like a leaf floating downriver. Try not to grab them or censor them. This is very hard to do in the beginning. Our thoughts will run with us, and we may be several paragraphs into a fantasy or thought before we realize we are even having one. This is perfectly normal. When you do notice your thought has run away with you, just bring your attention back to the breath and be happy that you noticed it. This noticing is the beginning of true awareness and meditation. When you are ready to come out of meditation, take some deeper breaths, wiggle fingers and toes, and fully open your eyes. Notice how you are feeling at the end of meditation compared to how you felt at the beginning, without judgment; just be aware . . .*

In the beginning your meditation sessions may be just three to five minutes long. I recommend picking a regular time and place for meditation. Many people set aside a place in their bedroom or house for a shrine or altar, but any dedicated space will do. First thing in the morning and last thing at night are often good times. Traditional meditation times are daybreak and dusk. Some people like to begin their meditation time with mantra. As time goes on, slowly increase your daily meditation time to a minimum of fifteen minutes a day. More is not necessarily better in meditation; the mind takes time to acclimate to such a new and powerful practice. You don't want to climb too high too fast. As questions arise you may want to find an experienced and gentle preceptor to help you adjust to this new world of practice. If you are results oriented, consider keeping a meditation journal at your altar or place of meditation and jot a few notes after your meditation about the quality of your experience, the length of time, and how your body felt. Everyone I see in my practice with PTSD who has learned to meditate has benefitted enormously from the practice. Now you can too!

*Nothing is more important than reconnecting with your bliss.*
*Nothing is as rich. Nothing is more real.*

—Deepak Chopra

# Tool 9

# The Anandamayakosha: Ecstasy and the Bliss Body

---

TAKE A MOMENT and reach back, far back into your childhood. Find an age before you hit puberty, perhaps somewhere in early childhood or just before all of the great changes of adolescence. Maybe you already had a lot of trauma by that time, but for the purposes of exploring bliss, it doesn't matter. All children naturally go into ecstatic states of being whether they have been traumatized or not. Maybe you were staring at a bug or a flower for an infinite second. Maybe you were lying on your back in fragrant grass, gazing at the clouds slowly changing shapes. Maybe you were floating in a lake warmed by the summer sun, warm at the top and cool at the depths. Find a moment when all thought suspended in the flow of beingness, and reach deeply into that moment. Perhaps you even had a feeling of being catapulted into a reality much larger than yourself. Unless your opening was huge and cosmic (it does happen that way for some people), you probably took no notice of it at the time because the very nature of such moments suspends thought. Only after the flow recedes can we recollect a perfect state of blissful harmony. Such moments can be dismissed and forgotten altogether as we age. Adults collude with this forgetting by denying or minimizing children's profound experiences of connection. Do you remember . . . ?

In thinking about the words *bliss* and *ecstasy* today, what come to mind for many are sex and chocolate or even drugs. It is an unfortunate reality that advertising has co-opted these words and their energy in an ever-expanding quest to sell us something. The media's constant hyperbole of experience has dumbed down our experiences of bliss as a culture. I would now like to reclaim these powerful words and our birthright to them. We can have access to those experiences now, without ingesting the potentially toxic effects of food, sex, or drugs. Now, this view is not meant to be puritanical. Seeking ecstasy through substances is a time-honored practice throughout the world, but doing so is fraught with dangers, especially for those with a trauma history that often includes sexual and/or substance addictions. In this chapter we will discuss how to discover and dwell in the bliss that is the very essence of your nature as a human being without resorting to potentially damaging or addictive practices.

Ecstasy as spiritual experience reaches back deep into the very roots of Western history and culture. In ancient Greek, *ekstasis* literally meant to stand outside one's self and generally referred to intense spiritual states of rapture and bliss. Until recently, ecstasy was considered a necessary part of spiritual life and experience. Many coming-of-age rituals in indigenous cultures induce a state of ecstasy, as do many religious practices: Sufis twirling, Hindus in *samadhi*, Christians fasting and praying, and so on. Important as these practices may be, they are not the only way to access bliss. *The experience of bliss is as natural as breathing and not confined to*

234

*the realm of spiritual ecstasy.* Bliss is a very ordinary experience, so ordinary and subtle that it is easy to miss. Spiritual practices merely show us the way to notice and prolong those states until they become a way of being in the world.

In our yogic system of the five bodies, the innermost circle around the eternal core of the true self is the anandamayakosha, literally the body appearing in maya as bliss (*ananda*). Although one might argue philosophical differences between the words *bliss, ecstasy,* and *flow,* they are interchangeable, *bliss* being more of an Eastern spiritual concept, *ecstasy* springing from Western mysticism, and *flow* being a modern term not necessarily related to religious experience at all. These states exist beyond the activities of mind. When you are in flow, you are, by definition in a state of no thought. *The experience of bliss always transcends mind and thought.* It is only *after* we have been in a state of flow that we process it through the mind. This state happens all the time, if only we can notice it. So then, why aren't we in bliss all the time? Our minds, full of pain, complaints, judgments, and commentary, drown out the still small voice of bliss. Bliss is like a hidden cave in a large rock wall. It's easy to miss, but if you go inside it opens up into vast caverns of overwhelming beauty that stun the mind and nourish the heart.

The good news is that our capacity for ecstasy, for noticing blissful opportunities, can be increased. Certain activities are almost guaranteed to bring a feeling of flow, ecstasy, or bliss if we open to them. For a trauma survivor, there is no greater gift than being showered with joy, because the loss of the capacity to feel joyful can be one of the most painful consequences of traumatic experience. Moving into ecstatic states restores our ability to experience the fierce joy of living and breathes us back into life.

If you want to experience ecstasy, follow these steps:

1. *Engage in a healthy ecstatic activity.* Activities that activate dormant bliss involve beauty, truth, spirituality, and/or extreme sensation. You will know from your past experience what "lights you up." It is very personal. For some people horses are blissful; for others they are terrifying, unpredictable creatures of doom. Pick an activity that at minimum you enjoy and at best can alter your state of being in an ecstatic way. When we are traumatically stressed, it is easy to let our mood dictate our activity. We might let a beautiful, warm leaf-falling autumn day go by without even going outside. The first step is setting the intention to maximize ecstasy by putting ourselves in the condition in which bliss becomes possible. If you are really stumped, some activities are inherently blissful for large numbers of people. Some of these will be listed and explored later in this chapter. Just do it, as the saying goes. Engage your will to move the body into the necessary experience for bliss. What do you have to lose?

2. *Pay full attention to your senses.* Be fully present in your body. Attend to every sensation on your skin, what you see with your eyes, what you can hear, and what you feel. Focus through the senses. Feel your way into the experience. If you are listening to a beautiful piece of music, for example, close your eyes, put on the headphones, and focus only on the music. Notice where the music hits you in your body and how those sensations move around. If you are leaf gazing, note the colors, feel the sun on your face, smell the crinkly dried leaves, and hear the crunchy sound they make as you walk through them. When you engage your senses, your feeling brain takes you out of your thoughts and out of your left brain and into a place where bliss becomes possible.

3. *Surrender the illusion of control.* You cannot dictate when and where ecstasy will happen. All you can do is set the necessary conditions for it to happen to you and through you. The more you

try to control the experience, the more it will slip away from you, like a slippery bar of soap you squeeze so hard it pops out of your hand. *Bliss is not something we do; it is something we allow.* Bliss arises spontaneously within us, a glorious bubble of well-being that rises to the surface. So, acknowledge to yourself at the outset that you cannot force it to happen, and then follow steps one and two, waiting patiently for bliss to arise.

Although you cannot control the experience, you can control your mind. If you find your mind wandering into negative thoughts, acknowledge them, thank your mind for being so vigilant, and then return to the sensations of the experience. It is no accident that accomplished meditators have more experiences of bliss than ordinary people. In fact, holy people of India always have bliss as a very part of their ordained names, which invariably end in *ananda*, Sanskrit for "bliss"; Paramahansa Yog*ananda* (the bliss of yoga) and Swami Vivek*ananda* (the bliss of wise discrimination) are two examples.

*4. Engage your inner child.* Self-consciousness is the enemy of ecstasy. Like Adam and Eve, we start life in a garden of delights where it is okay to run around naked in the sunshine. Children live in the moment and do not have the capacity for self-reflection. Initially, they learn inhibition through rules, not because they are self-aware. This lack of self-awareness is why it is so easy for them to be in the moment, going from one blissful state to another, whether it is building fairy houses, kicking a soccer ball, wrestling with the dog, or eating a Popsicle. Only in adolescence do we "eat of the fruit of the tree of knowledge of good and evil." The veils fall. We become self-aware and want to cover our nakedness, our transparency. As teenagers we learn to hide from ourselves and from others, especially if our family lacks joy or is dysfunctional. Sadly, this hiding often continues into adulthood, and the loss of childlike joy becomes a permanent condition that we rationalize with the labels "responsible," "mature," "realistic," or "intellectual." How sad for us! How boring!

If Jesus really did say that the only way to the Kingdom of God was to become as little children, I believe this joyful spontaneity is what he meant. Literally, we cannot experience the condition of heavenly bliss in our being while still holding on to our adult ego's sense of self-importance and self-consciousness. We need to lose our judgments, our negative self-talk, and our all-around adult uptightness in favor of silly, blissful, ecstatic joy. So what if we burst into tears upon hearing that song, or do a little dance while walking in the sun, or kiss our horse's fuzzy lips! Who cares if you are a big burly man who talks to his dog in a squeaky schoolgirl's voice or a proper society lady who casts off the high heels and skirts for a shot at hip-hop in low jeans and sneakers? Lose the identification with who you are supposed to be and let your freak flag fly. After years of being a therapist, I can tell you with certainty that nobody cares except you, anyway—yes, really!

5. *Cultivate the attitude of gratitude.* If you have ever been in a genuinely blissful state, you will notice that gratitude arises naturally as an unstoppable emotion. *Gratitude creates the conditions in the mind for the acceptance and acknowledgment of joy.* Guess what? States of flow, ecstasy, and bliss are happening in the mind every day, several times a day, but we are generally too preoccupied with our thoughts, fears, and distractions to notice. If you have even a nanosecond of relief from destructive thoughts and emotions, notice it, and give thanks. Over time those nanoseconds will become seconds, then minutes and even hours. Some rare beings, with much practice of the gratitude of presence, live in an unbroken state of bliss known as enlightenment.

In a radical way these five steps are how we take back our own mind and being from the experience of trauma. As the saying goes,

"The best revenge is having a good life." When the brain is exhausted from the rigors of trauma, accessing these states can be harder to do. Cultivate patience. Your ability to feel joy and bliss will return as surely as spring follows winter. Know that if you have difficulty feeling much of anything, your body and brain are still in recovery. But, I promise you, the feeling will return. It has to because *joy is the very essence of your being.*

Now, if you have your own ideas of how to be in the flow, go for it. Close the book, get up, and do it! Otherwise, read on for ideas of how to cultivate the ultimate healing states of bliss, flow, and ecstasy. Without them life becomes a burden and a chore, but with them all manner of ills can be overcome and healed.

## FISHING

Rivers of Recovery (www.riversofrecovery.org) is an organization that leads veterans with PTSD on fishing retreats. They published a study in 2009 that showed an immense reduction of PTSD symptoms during their fishing expeditions with veterans.[1] The data showed significant decreases in depression, anxiety, and body-based stress symptoms, such as insomnia, in the soldiers after a two-day, three-night fly-fishing retreat in scenic Utah. The participants reported feeling significantly happier and more peaceful after this brief weekend of fishing.

Men (and some women) often go fishing to wash away their cares and find moments of peaceful solitude. Fishing is the ultimate flow activity in many ways, from the single-pointed focus on the rod and reel to the beauty of the surroundings, the sound of flowing water, and the solitude. Men who fish rarely engage in idle chitchat and may even fish to get away from it. This silence is healthy and necessary to rejuvenate the mind and reconnect with internal peaceful states. Now we have the research to prove it!

## Dolphin Encounters

Dolphins swim in a perpetual sea of ecstasy. They are masters of joy and connection, their ability to heal so powerful they have even broken through the barriers of autism. Many traumatized people have been profoundly healed by dolphin encounters because of their reconnection to meaning, joy, and bliss. For some, such an encounter is the first time they realize they are capable of these feelings. Dolphins seem to have an intuitive sense of how to approach people who are in healing processes, whether physical or mental. When they swim with dolphins, people feel as if their hearts have opened, they have been deeply seen and understood, or they have reconnected to their own ability to be playful. Some say that the dolphins' sonar clicks and chirps work directly on the physical body for healing.

There are two basic types of dolphin encounters: in captivity and in the wild. Dolphin encounters in captivity have the advantage of being reliable and immediate. They can be pricey and are often found in fancy hotel settings in Hawaii or Florida. Because they are highly structured for safety, they can be wonderful first experiences, especially for children, the timid, the disabled, and the elderly. The disadvantages are that the dolphins are constrained in their movements by the smallness of the pool, the interactions are highly regulated by the trainers, and the dolphins are often kept in captivity all their lives.

Wilderness encounters lack the safety-control features of captive encounters, but they offer a deeper and freer experience for all involved—dolphins and humans. On the down side, they are not as reliable as the scheduled experiences with captive dolphins.

Kealakekua Bay on Hawaii's Big Island is famous for its local pod of friendly spinner dolphins, but the pod can be elusive even if they are in residence. In the wild, dolphins pick and choose their own encounters. If you go on your own, ask the locals about the best times to find dolphins, and then approach your encounter with humility, respect, and an open heart. Marine laws prevent swimming up to these animals, but they are free to approach you at any time. Just hearing them communicate under water or seeing them glide twenty feet below you can be a thrilling and joyful experience. Be sure to bring your snorkel, mask, and fins!

If you have some money to spend, a structured wilderness encounter can be the best of all possible worlds. Knowledgeable guides take guests out for one to several days and boat into areas of dolphin activity. Dolphins are sometimes more likely to approach these groups because of their familiarity with the leaders and the schedule of swims. These retreats can be life changing, and intense bonding usually happens among the participants. Because these excursions are supervised, they tend to be much safer than random wilderness experiences, if more expensive. If you need an experience of explosive joy and reconnection to move you back into the center of your life, I urge you to consider an encounter or retreat with these playful, loving beings.

## EXTREME SPORTS

When you have a history of traumatic stress, you become accustomed to a certain amount of adrenaline flowing through your system. In its absence life can feel dull, dry, and dusty by comparison. When I worked in extreme mental health settings, my coworkers and I used to joke nervously about being adrenaline junkies, because most of us came from highly traumatically stressed families. Of course, most people who seek an adrenaline high don't do so by working with psychotically violent clients; they do it through extreme sports. Whether the motivation is adrenaline addiction, a need to master one's fear, or a denial of fear, many people with trauma histories naturally gravitate towards risky adrenaline-producing activities like bungee jumping, mountain climbing, skydiving, deep-sea diving, ATV riding, skiing, motocross racing, and even some extreme forms of horseback riding.

The army has recently noticed that returning soldiers suffer from this kind of adrenaline-withdrawal syndrome, so they have started a new program called Warrior Adventure Quest. In this Northwest-based program, returning soldiers are sent through a series of high-adrenaline adventures such as paintball fighting, whitewater rafting, mountain biking, snowboarding, and other intense activities. After each event, the soldiers go through a debriefing designed to help them acclimate to the slower pace of living in a peaceful community. Data on the program's effectiveness is still being collected, but the soldiers seem to love it.

When engaged in dangerous situations, the mind is forced to focus down to a single point, a moment-by-moment experience sometimes termed flow. There is no time for thought or rumination, just the exhilaration of being in the moment. Mastering the difficult event leads to a rush of endorphins, the addictive "I lived!" moment. For people stuck in depression or anxious cycles, these moments point to a possible way out. An ecstatic rush can do wonders for a stuck psyche. The downside is that after each high the cycle can end in a crash in which the mood drops again. For people who are highly dissociative, that is, who space out rather than focus when in danger, extreme sports are contraindicated and could lead to serious injury or death. If you are inclined to go this direction, make sure you are grounded in your body, have good safe support for the activity, and have a competent group leader or therapist to debrief with afterward.

## COLLECTIVE ECSTASY

Around the world people have used song and dance for healing and to unite and uplift entire communities after traumatic events. Anyone who has been in a theater production, a choir, a band, or a dance company can testify to the powerfully uplifting vibrations that are generated when people come together in a common, joyful purpose. Native peoples in the Americas have held and continue to hold powwows, gatherings of ceremonial dance and song. African slaves sang spirituals to survive backbreaking work in hot fields and to keep their spirits up in unlivable circumstances. European ancestors had folk dances and celebrations. Collective ecstasies have arisen spontaneously around the world out of communal celebrations of both joy and suffering.

With the advent of around-the-clock entertainment on television and the Internet and the ability to download music using applications like iTunes, collective art and uplift has taken a backseat to individual gratification. In Western culture, we are generally too busy, too self-conscious, too immersed in what we think we want, to unite with other human beings in the act of ecstatic creation. Yet, being united with other human beings in an upwelling of joyful music, movement, and celebration can be the most blissful fulfillment available on planet Earth, tremendously healing for those who feel separated from humanity by their personal traumas.

In the 1980s raves were tremendously popular with young people in the United States. Fueled by drugs, techno music, and lasers, participants would allow themselves to be swept into ecstatic and out-of-control states. Modern-day rock concerts offer people a chance to go beyond their individual boundaries into a state of collective frenzy. Why have flash mobs[2] become so popular lately? People are hungry for this experience of ecstatic connection.

In the West, art forms such as theater, music, and dance still offer some of the best avenues to connect deeply with other human beings by allowing us to experience ourselves safely as a collective. Otherwise-jaded high schoolers will often sob with abandon after their theater production comes to a close. They are not sad about having to give up late nights, rehearsing lines, and rushing through homework; they miss the feeling of being part of something larger than themselves, something irreplaceable, something that lifts them out of their ordinary lives into ecstasy.

People with a history of abuse or trauma often suffer from a bad case of social anxiety, which makes it hard for them to become part of a collective and leads to isolation and feelings of abandonment. On the other hand the experience of safe and joyful connection is what helps people overcome their fears. If this inner conflict speaks to you at all, start small. Take a theater class or, better yet, a class in improvisational comedy, which consists mostly of games in which anything (within reason and safety) goes. Join a musical group or a choir. Play charades. If you are bold, maybe you could draw together a few friends in a band or singing group. You don't have to perform. You don't have to make money. Turn off the electronic media once a week and have talent night. Do it for the sake of joy, togetherness, and healing. Go outside your comfort zone bit by bit, and pretty soon you will find yourself uplifted in the wildly beating heart of ecstatically attuned humanity!

## ECSTATIC DANCE

Ecstatic dance has a long tradition throughout history and is found in nearly every culture. As legend goes, King David danced before the Ark of the Covenant. In the 1800s there was a saint in India who was so "mad for God" he would sometimes dance all day in front of his beloved Kali temple. Irresistibly attracted, his visitors and disciples would join in. As an eyewitness observer wrote, "Sri Ramakrishna was dancing in a circle. The devotees joined him. They all sang and danced. Their bliss was indescribable."[3]

In the United States there has been a rising tide of ecstatic dance from east to west. When I lived in Boston in the 1980s, a "Free Dance" held once a week across from Harvard University was an institution. Many people came, but often an old, slightly disheveled man could be seen letting his body and heart hang out while he twirled and danced. As it turns out, that old man was Morrie Schwartz, subject of the book *Tuesdays With Morrie*, a man many considered saintly towards the end of his life. Many cities still sponsor some form of the spontaneous free dancing he so loved for low or no cost.

During the same period, Gabrielle Roth developed her popular ecstatic- and trance-dance classes based on five rhythms of the body: flowing, staccato, chaotic, lyrical, and stillness. For three decades she has helped people shed their inhibitions and wake up the ecstasy in the body through movement, which she considers a form of meditation. Her videos can be found for free on YouTube.

On the West Coast, Debbie Rosas and Carlo AyaRosas gave birth to NIA at the same time Gabrielle was developing her program on the East Coast. NIA stands for neuromuscular integrated action, but it is so much more than exercise. NIA is described on its website (www.nianow.com) as "a sensory-based movement lifestyle that leads to health, wellness and fitness. It empowers people of all shapes and sizes by connecting the body, mind, emotions and spirit." Many people have been coming to NIA for help relaxing into their bodies and getting out of their heads to heal from PTSD as well as other conditions.

The great thing about ecstatic dance is that you can do it in a class or by yourself, in public or in your living room. There are

DVDs and websites that will give you the basics, and, after that, turn up the music, let your hair down, and just *move*!

## NATURE

If you want to experience ecstasy, plan a trip to a national park or even a local wilderness spot. When I reviewed numerous ecstatic experiences in my life to write this chapter, what kept coming up were scene after scene of extraordinary experiences in nature: sliding down a waterfall in King's Canyon National Park, looking into the magical pure-blue eye of Crater Lake, walking in an alpine meadow wildly abloom atop Mt. Shasta, seeing the Grand Canyon for the first time as dawn painted the canyon shades of purples and oranges, standing in the impossible majesty of the great old ones of the redwood forests in northern California, gazing at the heart-stopping Alps that dwarf humans into ants, contemplating the incomprehensible expanse of oceans, hiking up the Narrows Canyon in Zion National Park, and marveling at Yellowstone's impossible diversity and abundance of wildlife among the bubbling geysers.

We are blessed in this country to have some of the most beautiful preserved scenery on the entire planet. Every state has areas of beauty and wilderness, and visiting these places can be free or inexpensive. What a gift and resource! Placing oneself in the beauty of nature opens the mind and body to healing and bliss in a way few other experiences offer. When possible, get out into nature rather than just looking at it from a car, bus, or trailer. Immerse yourself in the oceans of Hawaii, sleep out under the stars in the parks, and wade in the rivers. Go out into your backyard and sit on the ground, a tree, or a large rock. Let your body absorb the abundant peaceful bliss of nature at the cellular level and heal!

# Darshan

Some remarkable human beings who exude an aura of bliss tangible to a large majority of people exist on our planet. Encountering such a being is called having *darshan*, Sanskrit for seeing into deep spiritual verity through another human being. We all know people in our lives who lift us up just by their presence; it can be anyone, our hairdresser, grocer, or teacher, but that presence largely depends on that person's mood and circumstance . . . or ours.

In darshan, the person we see emits the vibration of a powerful spiritual practice and connection. Sometimes people will weep with love, feel overcome with reverence, or go into a state of high joy just by being in the room with such a person, no matter the state they arrived in. These special people are not subject to moods, and their energy is seemingly inexhaustible. There are not many of them on the planet at any given time. Some of them have been available to large numbers of people for decades and travel widely. Having darshan with one provides an instant experience of bliss and provides deep healing within one's being.

Who are these people? Some of them are quite famous, but others are not. The Dalai Lama of Tibet is such a person. Despite the many adversities he has faced in losing his country and bearing the burden of terrible stories about his people, he bubbles over with an incomprehensible spiritual joy that is infectious to be around. Another such person is Mata Amritanandamayi, otherwise known as Amma or the Hugging Saint. Amma (amma.org) travels the world providing darshan to up to twenty thousand people in a single sitting, providing each with a grandmotherly hug and a special chant. Mother Meera in Germany is less well known and does not travel as much, but those who visit her come away extraordinarily uplifted and feel blessed by having been in her presence.

Braco (rhymes with matzo) was born in Croatia and he has the remarkable ability to confer healing through "gazing." He doesn't speak but gazes upon the audience for eight to ten minutes of powerful connection. Unlike other spiritual figures, he has no church and no dogma, and he does not speak publicly at all. He is well known in Europe, where thousands of people claim to have experienced healings from his presence. His life mission is to take this healing connection around the world, and he has started coming to the United States in the last few years. After a session, people are asked for testimonials. I heard one man stand up and volunteer that he was a veteran of the Vietnam War. Every night for forty years he had been plagued with nightmares and flashbacks of the war. This veteran claimed that after seeing Braco those dreams just stopped, and that he is a different man with an open heart who has healed from his extreme PTSD! Many such stories are heard from Braco's visitors. On his website, www.braco.net, you can find his latest touring information, as well as DVDs, which for some seem to have a remarkable healing effect.

If you know of such a special person, go for darshan. The cost of seeing these people ranges from nothing to a few dollars. Perhaps someone in your own community is quietly working in this way to uplift and heal humanity. We live in a unique time and place in human history that allows us the chance to find and travel to these radiant ones. Most people do not know that such people even exist. Making the effort to find darshan will reward you with an uplifting experience you will not forget, one that may help you to heal.

## DIVINE INNER BLISS

Diverse authors in different traditions have celebrated, instructed, and modeled the art of living in the divine presence of what is within us at all times: our own inner blissful nature. Thomas Merton, Father Bede Griffiths, Robert Thurman, Michael Bernard Beckwith, Eckhart Tolle, Maya Angelou, Swami Vivekenanda, Deepak Chopra, Jack Kornfield, Thich Nhat Hanh, Emerson, Thoreau, and hundreds more have shown us the way to an everyday bliss through stillness practices that lead us into the experience of our own divinity. Even while moving through the external world (maya), we can be still inside, fully present to the ecstasy and joy that is always within us, but that is extinguished like a flame on a windy day when we get into our reactions, opinions, and ego mind. Although I put meditation in the last chapter on wisdom, the goal and endpoint of advanced meditation practice is a permanent dwelling inside this bliss of presence. It can take lifetimes to achieve or just a moment of grace to descend.

Once we have tasted this bliss, the experience of suffering is changed forever. As the dancing saint Sri Ramakrishna put it, "Pain is mandatory; suffering is optional." With the awareness of bliss, sorrow is turned to poignancy and compassion; happiness is turned to gratitude; bitterness becomes appreciation, and anger becomes a momentary neurobiological event that Jill Bolte Taylor (the neuroscientist author with the famous "stroke of insight") claims can be disabled in less than thirty seconds.

If bliss seems beyond your reach, do not worry. Just know that ecstasy is there, in every moment, waiting for your head to turn and catch a glimpse. Anything can bring it: a dream, a waft of fragrance, a strain of music, a loving glance, a snuggle from your pet, or a fun activity. Live in the flow. Notice bliss. Invite ecstasy in. You will begin to live a life of healing beyond your wildest dreams.

*Be of good cheer. Do not think of today's failures,*
*but of the success that may come tomorrow.*
*You have set yourselves a difficult task,*
*but you will succeed if you persevere;*
*and you will find a joy in overcoming obstacles.*

—Helen Keller

# Tool 10

# Embracing Wholeness: The Motivation to Heal

---

YOUR TOOL KIT is now brimming with tools. Will you use them or let them gather dust in the closet? If you are like most people with traumatic stress, you are highly motivated in your healing when you feel poorly, but when you are doing better you tend to let your self-care practices slide. Or maybe you are the friend or the spouse of someone with traumatic stress, and you are tearing your hair out trying to get that person some kind of help, but he or she won't go. *Avoidance is part and parcel of the dis-ease of trauma and especially of PTSD, but, in the end, avoidance is an illusion. There is no neutral place to be with traumatic stress.* For this reason, traumatic stress is becoming the number one public health issue of our time.

When people present for psychotherapy or counseling, they rarely come wanting to be treated specifically for PTSD or traumatic stress. In every setting I have worked in, whether inpatient or outpatient, in my private office or in a medical center, even people with the most extreme amounts of abuse in their backgrounds have initially presented with these real-life peripheral complaints: premenstrual syndrome; difficulties with meditating; court-ordered treatment for an unrelated crime; drug abuse; various types of depression; general anxiety; social anxiety; desire to stop smoking; stress related to heart disease; morbid obesity; and even schizophrenia! In each of these cases, the clients and I didn't have to travel too far together to uncover some truly horrendous events that were still reverberating as traumatic stress in the patients' minds and bodies. They were all completely unaware that their presenting symptom was linked to trauma.

Why is it that people are walking around with huge amounts of undiagnosed, unacknowledged, and untreated trauma? The answer is quite simple. *PTSD is the only disorder for which one of the diagnostic criteria for the condition is avoidance of knowing about the condition itself.* By its very nature, PTSD is a hidden process. People diagnosed with PTSD have symptoms that fall into these categories:

1. Intrusiveness: Aspects of the event repeatedly intrude into one's consciousness. The intrusion can be through dreams, recollections, flashbacks, somatic experiences, and so on.

2. Avoidance: One is unwilling to expose oneself to stimuli in any way associated with the trauma(s), even to the extent of avoiding people or conversation topics related to the trauma. Avoidance behaviors can include substance abuse and other addictions.

3. Numbing: These symptoms are a different kind of avoidance. Avoidance is more of a conscious process, whereas numbing is often unconscious and automatic. Many of my clients were not

aware of numbing until I asked them about sensations in parts of their body. One patient reported being numb to sensation between her knees and throat, a sign of her intense abuse history.

When the victim is numbing and avoiding, the mind swerves away from trauma like a car careening around a deep, dark puddle. The traumatic "memory" is gone before it is even acknowledged. As mentioned in earlier chapters, it is important to understand that this avoidance is nobody's fault but is the very nature of trauma itself. Because of this largely unconscious mechanism, *it is easy for people to remain unaware of their traumas and the effect of those traumas for very long periods of time, sometimes decades.*

## THE EFFECTS OF UNTREATED TRAUMA

Although the mind may be able to evade the realization of trauma, the body cannot. Whether trauma is acknowledged or not, the effects of untreated trauma affect the body every waking moment of every day. *Over time the physiological effects of untreated trauma actually change the structures of the brain, nervous system, and endocrine (hormonal) systems.* Many of these changes are reversible with proper acknowledgment and treatment.

Science has made huge gains in understanding the mechanisms of trauma in the body over the last five years or so. Large strides continue to be made; new research on PTSD is emerging in the media every week.[1] Your primary care physician or even your therapist, however, may not be aware of recent research. Acquaint yourself with this information so that you can advocate for what you need medically and psychiatrically. In this era of fifteen-minute visits and overstressed health-care systems, we may need to connect the dots both for ourselves and for the professionals who want to help us get the care that we need.[2]

## Heart Disease

My husband, Peter Banitt, MD, is an interventional cardiologist and has been a source of referrals over the years. After the third or fourth cardiac patient referral in a row with serious trauma and heart disease, we both started wondering about the effect of trauma on the heart. We knew that heart attacks and extreme interventions could cause PTSD, but neither of us had given much thought to PTSD as a cause of cardiac issues. We started doing some research and found there is a huge body of recent evidence pointing to traumatic stress as a causative factor for heart disease, with risk factors right up there with obesity and cigarette smoking (both of which may also link back to trauma; stay tuned for upcoming research).

Three separate long-term studies of veterans conducted within the last five years show a clear connection between PTSD and the development of heart disease. A Harvard study shows that *the higher scores veterans showed on a test measuring PTSD symptoms, the more likely they were to have heart disease.*[3] The Geisinger Clinic also researched veterans and concluded that "early age heart disease may be an outcome after military service among PTSD-positive veterans."[4] A new study of 637 veterans was presented at the 2010 American Heart Association conference and published in July of 2011 in the prestigious *American Journal of Cardiology*. This landmark study showed that *the subjects with PTSD developed significantly more atherosclerosis and heart disease and were twice as likely to die over the forty-two-month course of the study from all causes* as those without the disorder.[5]

Unfortunately, these outcomes are not limited to veterans or even men. A study by the Harvard School of Public Health looked at over one thousand women over a fourteen-year period. *They found that women with five or more symptoms of PTSD were three times more likely to develop coronary heart disease compared to those with no symptoms.*[6] By contrast the well-known risk factor of smoking makes people two to four times more likely to develop heart disease than nonsmokers. These astonishing findings elevate PTSD to a major coronary artery disease risk, possibly on a par with diet and smoking.

## HPA Axis

In the last five years attention has turned to what is awkwardly termed the hypothalamic-pituitary-adrenal (HPA) axis. This long name refers to the *hypothalamus*, which nestles inside the core of the brain and has a prominent role in hormonal regulation via the *pituitary gland*, also a brain structure, and the *adrenal glands*, which sit like little almonds on top of the kidneys. Together they are responsible for many of the functions of the body: sleeping, energy levels, hunger, digestion, sexual arousal and activity, immune system functioning, and mood. The HPA axis facilitates interactions among all the glands of the body, including the all-important thyroid gland (important for metabolism). This system is extremely complex, and scientists are still working to understand all of its functions.

What we know for sure is that traumatic stress profoundly affects the physical functioning of the HPA axis and has consequences in each area of its regulatory activities. Many so-called medical complaints are looking more and more like effects of post-traumatic stress, including such common and hard-to-treat issues such as chronic fatigue, fibromyalgia, obesity, diabetes,[7] brain fog, chronic pain, allergies, low sexual desire or dysfunction, autoimmune diseases such as lupus and psoriasis, and gastrointestinal symptoms. Ironically, many of these are conditions that physicians have labeled over the years as psychosomatic. While that has not always been a friendly term, it is literally a true one. The brain is, of course, intimately connected with every physical function in the body. If the brain can be hurt by psychological causes and experiences, then it is only logical that the physical body can also be hurt by traumatic events via our brain. To paraphrase, the brain bone's connected to the . . . everything bone!

Many mental illnesses such as bipolar disorder, anxiety and depression, rage disorder, and schizophrenia also have their roots in HPA dysfunction. In 1997 a paper was presented by Bruce McEwen and Maria Magarinos of the Laboratory of Endocrinology in New York City that showed how prolonged stress actually damages and shrinks the hippocampus (a brain structure), leading to increased anxiety, impairment of short-term memory and the learning of spatial tasks, and impairment of the HPA axis.[8] Changes to the hippocampus are correlated with schizophrenia, recurrent depression, dementia, and even suicide.

It looks as if we will need to make significant changes in how we view physical and mental illness vis-à-vis traumatic events. In light of these new findings, the psychiatric disorder called somatization disorder is rapidly becoming obsolete. To be diagnosed with this disorder, one has to complain of dysfunction in a number of different bodily systems for which there is no physical cause. But hold on here! If the HPA axis is involved in all of these systems (and it is), then how can we claim ignorance any longer and say that this is all "in the patient's head" and not a physical effect? We can't, and I predict that within a decade or two (the wheels turn slowly in medicine) somatization disorder will be as defunct as the neurotic personality. Whatever is in our minds is in our brains, and whatever is in our brains is in our body. *To be traumatized is to be physically injured.* To conceive of PTSD as anything other than a very physical process is ignorant in the light of what we now know.

## The Epigenetics of Trauma

Hot off the research presses is the very recent idea that our environment actually alters our genetic code. Apparently the way cells express themselves in the body is far more malleable than once thought. *Epigenetics* is the study of how the environment permanently changes the expression of our genetic code, which then affects our children and our children's children down the line for several generations. Our genes have multiple potential expressions. How they express is a function of their environment. Another way to say this is that portions of our genetic material can turn on and off based on circumstances. To answer the age-old question, genetic expression is both nature and nurture.

In 2007 a group of scientists from the Traumatic Stress Studies Program at Mt. Sinai School of Medicine published a research study that looked at the cortisol (stress hormone) levels of *children* of people with PTSD. They mainly selected the adult children of Holocaust survivors but also looked at a few of the children of women who had been pregnant in New York City at the time of the 9/11 attacks.[9] They found that not only were these children more prone to develop PTSD themselves but they also had significantly lower amounts of cortisol than the general population. Low cortisol levels are associated with fatigue, decreased immunity, mood swings, and less resilience to stress overall. Apparently PTSD begets more PTSD as far as genetics are concerned. Ignoring PTSD does not make it go away, *even with succeeding generations.*

The scientists' conclusion: post-traumatic stress engenders profound changes in the physical body, not only in the victims but also in the victims' children and grandchildren, down to we-don't-know-how-many generations. The health problems that follow PTSD, both physical and emotional, affect our society in myriad ways: health-care costs; lost wages; lost productivity; crime; loss of intelligence (cognitive function); dysfunctional interactions that prevent problem resolution in marriages, businesses, and politics, etc. PTSD is a problem that snowballs with each succeeding generation. We have collectively had our heads in the sand about this issue. Now it is time to end the avoidance. PTSD hurts. PTSD kills. Untreated PTSD has the potential to unravel the very fabric of society.

## Relational Effects of PTSD

Friendly relations between people uphold our society. When people are suffering from extreme stress, they have less energy available to engage with friends, with their workplace, and with their family. If the pain is overwhelming as in active PTSD, those relationships can, at best, come to a screeching halt. At worst, permanent ruptures in relationships can occur through divorce, cut-off relationships, suicide, or homicide.

A state of permanent preoccupation with one's pain inhibits the flow of empathy and compassion between people that is so essential for a healthy society. It induces a kind of unchosen narcissism in which survival is the task of each hour of every day. It can warp how we view others and, by dampening our empathy, give rise to polarization and suspicion. We fail to see the other's perspective and come to reasonable solutions. The most extreme effects include bigotry, hatred, and paranoia.

Those who live with people with PTSD face the risk of becoming traumatized themselves through the process of vicarious traumatization. Navigating a relationship can become as difficult as threading a ship through a harbor filled with mines. You never know when you are going to hit a bomb and things will blow up. Under these conditions, happy and harmonious relationships are next to impossible, which puts people suffering post-traumatic stress between the proverbial rock and hard place. If they don't get the help they need, they will continue to be impaired in their relationships and ability to receive and give love, but getting help means facing their worst fears and experiences, something they may have been avoiding for years.

And, to add a horrible cherry on top, people are likely to unconsciously recreate the conditions of their traumas until those conditions are resolved, something we therapists call reenactment. The human mind wants to resolve conflict and grow. Just as a baby will keep getting up every time it falls in order to master the developmental task of walking, so will the mind keep trying to heal a past trauma. If it can't heal the original injury it will, unconsciously and automatically, create a similar condition to heal in present time. A common example would be that someone who was abused and abandoned in childhood picks an abusive, abandoning partner for a marriage and then is not able to leave because of a compulsive belief (in the face of all dangerous facts to the contrary) that the partner can and needs to be fixed. This powerful compulsion is the *unconscious* reenactment of trying to correct a childhood developmental lack with a present-day relationship. This behavior is not a personal failing; it is just how the mind works. The human mind is wired for mastery. It is both our greatest strength and our greatest weakness as humans. The antidote for reenactment is awareness, which will remain elusive if the original traumatic stresses are ignored and hidden.

## Societal Impacts of Untreated Trauma

Trauma throws a boulder into a pond. The ripples create concentric circles that continue to widen over time. First the effects are physical

259

and emotional, then relational, affecting our family, friends, and neighbors, and eventually they are economic, political, and global. Our prisons are full of people with the kind of untreated trauma that has the capacity to destroy any sense of attachment or moral regard for the other. Our traumatic response to the other not only fuels wars of aggression and terrorism but also exaggerates the need for defense.

Now, I am not suggesting that all criminals are victims, although many of them are. Of course, many who have had intense abuse histories are law-abiding, peaceful people. Much more research is needed to look deeply into why some folks with trauma are resilient while others are not, why some soar spiritually, becoming models for society, while others sink into moral decay, ruining the lives of others around them. Let us not make the mistake of thinking we have reached the endpoint of our knowledge (as society inevitably does until proven otherwise). We have not even begun to scratch the surface of how trauma has infected our society because we have not come to terms with the incidence of trauma in our communities. The denial that is part of the disease of trauma has entered our collective minds so that we do not see or acknowledge what is happening around us, right under our noses. If it were not for the work of Oprah Winfrey and Phil Donahue in the 1970s and '80s, we might still be ignorant that abuse in families and in our society even exists! There is a way out. We begin with telling, sharing our experiences safely, breaking the trauma sound barrier.

## WHY SHOULD I TALK ABOUT IT?
## THE RISKS AND BENEFITS OF DISCLOSING TRAUMA

New clients want to either tell me everything or tell me nothing about their traumatic past. Neither option works well. The very latest studies show that talking about what caused your traumatic stress benefits you in a number of ways as long as you do not become constantly overwhelmed or flooded with emotion.

But first, let's talk about why people don't disclose, and there are a very large number of people who *never* tell their story. If you understand why you don't, then you become free to reconsider and make a different, possibly healthier, decision.

## Talking Is Triggering

The very act of disclosure starts a cascade of hormones, especially adrenaline and cortisol, rushing through your body. Naturally, you want to avoid painful states, so you keep quiet. The truth is, the painful inability to tell your story stops you from getting help when you need it most. If your mother dies of old age, that is sad but not usually traumatizing. In your grief you can reach out to friends and get support. But, if your mother were to die in a car accident beside you, the act of grieving would become burdened with trauma. Talking about her might bring back a flood of memories and sensations from the accident that could interrupt your daily functioning for hours to days. Not only would you potentially be suffering more, but there would also be less chance of getting help from the people you couldn't talk with. Being in this situation is the very definition of being stuck between a rock and a hard place.

## People Can't Handle the Truth

You know what? You're right on this one—in most cases. The average people in your life might not be able to tolerate what you have to tell them. Even seasoned therapists struggle to cope with hearing difficult stories. At the end of the movie *Precious*, when the teen's horrifying story is finally told, she turns to her social worker and says, "I like you too, but you can't handle me. You can't handle none of this."[10] A therapist who specializes in trauma may be what you need if you are in a similar situation.

If your disclosure has to do with secretive bad behavior of someone people love, then the chances of them believing you and tolerating the information go from slim to none. I used to work at a child-abuse hotline. When acquaintances asked me what kind of work I did, it was a real conversation killer. They would avert their eyes, clear their throats, and change the subject. Nobody wanted to hear about or even think about child abuse. It was not because they weren't nice or compassionate individuals. People can be traumatized by hearing other people's stories. This vicarious traumatization can be likened to secondhand smoke for the nervous system.

## When You Tell Your Story, You Can't Be in Denial Anymore

Having your story out in the open makes it much harder to deny your reality inside of yourself. Sometimes people who have had a lot of childhood trauma have to be very dissociated and unfocused in order to make it through the day. When they do give some attention to their trauma, all hell can break loose in the physical and energy bodies and in the mind. Denial is not a failing; it is the circuit breaker being thrown. If you have a bad fuse and throw the switch, what happens? You either have another breakdown in the system or need to replace the fuse and/or wiring. In this case the fuse has to do with the meaning you make of your life and the wiring has to do with how your body processes this information. This situation is again paradoxical, another rock and hard place. In order to tell yourself, you need to tell others, and in order to tell others, you need to tell yourself. A good trauma therapist or friend can help you out of this dilemma.

## Disclosure Can Change Your World

Telling their true stories can and often will change people's lives profoundly. What if you have an incest secret you have never told? Telling will change your relationship and the entire family history permanently or, as commonly happens, may result in your being expelled from the family. What if as a soldier you witnessed an atrocity that will have grave legal consequences for all involved? Maybe you witnessed a violent crime you now have to testify about.

Telling your secret can feel like setting off a bomb in the middle of your life. But consider the alternatives. If you don't tell, you have to live with a terrible secret bottled inside you for the rest of your life, one that will probably make you ill. If you don't tell, other people might be unsafe that you could otherwise help. If you don't tell, victims might never get justice, and a perpetrator can keep on hurting other people. In the end what benefits one, benefits all. That's how the universe works because we are all interconnected. If it benefits you to tell, it will eventually benefit everybody. If it hurts others to keep your secret, it will also hurt you.

The entire field of psychotherapy is based on Freud's famous discovery of "the talking cure," the observation that patients who talked about their problems and conflicts not only felt better but also behaved better in their lives. The most up-to-date information on trauma supports the truth of the talking cure for discussing and disclosing traumatic incidents. There is a saying in the addiction field: "You are as sick as your secrets." Based on the emerging research, this appears to be literally true.

## Protection

People often feel a danger either real or imagined in telling about their hidden traumas. What they often fail to consider is the protection offered by disclosure, not only for themselves, *but for their children and their children's children.* An interesting body of research documents the effects of silence on the children of Holocaust survivors. The children knew their parents were in the camps, but never knew exactly happened because the parents could not talk about their experiences or chose not to. Not knowing the truth, for second and third generations, can lead to extra helpings of guilt and anxiety because the children fill in the blanks left by the parents with their own terrible fantasies. It is not unusual to see children of these survivors, or even grandchildren, in therapy, still working out the traumas of the original generation. We also see these dynamics in descendants of African slaves, Irish famine immigrants, Native Americans, and other oppressed groups. The more parents can work out their traumas, the less burden there is for succeeding generations.

**Physiological Effects**

Disclosure promotes physical health and well-being. It does not seem to matter whether the traumas are told in therapy, among friends, or in writing; what does make a difference is the telling. Some people find that telling over and over is necessary, and it can even become a second career. In his book *Touching The Void*, Joe Simpson documented the dramatically terrifying event of being left for dead on a mountain after a fall into a crevasse that shattered his leg.[11] He turned the trauma of his injury, abandonment, and ultimate escape into a tale of inspiration, courage, and awe that has touched thousands of people. After writing a book, making a movie, and becoming a highly sought-after motivational speaker, Joe has returned to climbing mountains, no small feat of healing after such a traumatic event. Telling the story of your trauma to others can heal, inspire, and uplift while providing you with many health benefits related to lower stress.

## Psychological Effects

Keeping secrets always hurts us in the long run. Human beings were not designed to be secret keepers. We are highly social beings. When we feel we need to withhold a story that is central to our experience of ourselves, we feel split into pieces. The pieces we don't tell about then feel exiled, abandoned, and angry. Sometimes they even act out in ways that are mystifying to us. If you've ever behaved badly and then wondered why you did that, an exiled part of yourself might hold the answer.

Look at it this way: there is good pain, and there is bad pain. A healing wound experiences pain, itching, and soreness. That is good pain. A wound that is not treated and is left to fester becomes swollen, inflamed, and full of pus. That is bad pain. Traumatic experiences are a lot like physical wounds. They either get better or they fester and make us worse. Telling hurts. Not telling can become so unbearable that people want to end their lives and sometimes the lives of others around them. The depression and anxiety secondary to not telling is a pain all its own, a pain that is alleviated immediately when you begin to tell your story and start to believe and integrate your realities.

## Disclosing Everything at Once

You remember that famous saying, "The spirit is willing, but the flesh is weak"? Some people come in and want to tell it all. They want to, and feel that they should, be done with their trauma work in twelve weeks or less. They think that healing means just reciting everything that ever happened to them, and they push forward glibly with incomplete processing of their emotion. These people are usually very disconnected from their bodies. In a very extreme circumstance, I have seen someone end up hospitalized when trying to process too much too soon.

I would like to take this opportunity to remind you that while you may have a very courageous and willing spirit, you still have a brain that is made of tissue, flesh, and blood. For the brain to heal (and the good news is that the brain is much more capable of healing than we originally thought), synapses have to be disconnected and reconnected. Structures within the brain may need to grow or shrink or move. While you can augment your healing process with holistic treatments, in the end *your body dictates how quickly or slowly you can heal*, just as with any other injury. We may want to be up and about on our broken leg in four weeks, but maybe it will take four years to get back to normal. And so it is when healing from trauma.

But healing can only begin with speaking our Truth. With an assurance born of years in the field and my own recovery from traumatic states, I urge you to tell. Speak. Write. Tweet. Sing it. Dance it. Express your secrets and heal safely, for yourself, your family, and all those whose lives you will one day touch.

## A New Vision for Healing

Once you have acknowledged you are suffering from traumatic stress, you can truly begin to heal. This book has shown how the human being can be conceptualized as having several layers around the deepest core (atman): the physical body, energy body, cognitive mind, wisdom mind, and bliss body. Trauma disrupts all these dimensions of the human being. Until recently the treatment of trauma in mainstream medicine has limited its interventions to the physical body and cognitive mind, even while many patients have sought alternative models of treatment. Now it is time for a more integrative model, and these models are appearing! As I was finishing this book, I stumbled serendipitously across two programs that exemplify multidimensional healing and incorporate a wide spectrum of healing modalities: Street Yoga and the Fort Bliss Restoration and Resilience Center.

## Street Yoga

Street Yoga (www.streetyoga.org) is headquartered in Portland, Oregon, and conducts teacher training for regional centers in several cities (New York, Seattle, Chicago, San Diego, Tucson) and even internationally. Its mission is to train practicing yoga teachers to conduct weekly yoga and mindful therapeutic classes for homeless youth, foster children, and other children who have been injured by abuse. Street Yoga partners with social service agencies, residential treatment centers, shelters, and other programs that are helping difficult-to-reach kids with a background of chronic and severe traumatic stress. These children are at great risk for juvenile delinquency, psychiatric disorders, substance abuse, and even death. The training for volunteers is thorough and gives teachers an in-depth education about PTSD and traumatic stress. It is highly rewarding for both teachers and participants. On her blog, Seattle yoga teacher Shelly Thorn describes her promising experience of teaching with Street Yoga:

> After a mere 35 minutes per week during the first quarter it was offered, the teens reported relief from backaches, shoulder pain, a bad knee, stress and anxiety. They reported being more awake in class after yoga (offered during the lunch hour) and more peaceful and relaxed. Counseling times were changed to occur just after yoga as the students were found to be more engaged and the counseling more effective when sessions occurred just after yoga

class. The counselor reported one student doing better in school and at home. I saw her come to be more engaged and exhibit increased confidence and joy in her practice. Another student was reported to have made a tremendous turnaround in her psychological recovery.[12]

Street Yoga also conducts programs for caregivers in their Mindful Parents and Caregivers training, which helps nonoffending caregivers come to terms with the abuse of loved ones and manage their own stress and gives them the necessary tools to help their children heal. Although they have not yet conducted peer-reviewed research, surveys are indicating a strongly positive reaction to the program from the teens participating in their Healing Child Sexual Abuse with Yoga program.[13] Street Yoga's model of healing from trauma is a living embodiment of many of the modalities outlined in this book, based on a thorough understanding of the multidimensional nature of traumatic injury and the power of yogic practices to heal minds and bodies with gentleness, respect, and compassion.

## Fort Bliss Restoration and Resilience Center

It may come as a surprise to some that the American military is a thought leader in the use of alternative treatments for PTSD, but one of the most integrative programs I have seen anywhere for treating traumatic stress is located in the ideally named Fort Bliss, Texas. The army, above all, is intensely pragmatic. It green-lighted this alternative model to improve the redeployment rates for highly trained personnel suffering from combat stress-injury (PTSD). Rates of redeployment of personnel with PTSD usually run from only 10 to 15 percent, but the Restoration and Resilience Center has an impressive figure of *61 percent redeployment rates* for those who complete treatment. This successful program has caught the eye of higher-ups. Over a ten-month period, the staff gave tours to over fifty VIPs including Defense Secretary Robert Gates, General George Casey, and Secretary of the Army Peter Geren, as well as several congressional representatives and general officers.

The founders of the program believe that every aspect of the human being needs healing in a caring environment to recover from war experiences. They have blended traditional modalities such as psychotherapy and medication with alternative treatments such as massage, biofeedback, art, and meditation. Their six-thousand-square-foot lodge-like facility is designed to have noisy and quiet spaces, therapy and alternative therapy rooms, and social areas such as a lounge and a recreation room. There is a strict daily schedule with no overnight stays, designed to facilitate a maximum level of healing. Participants stay in the program for six months with a four-week aftercare period. A typical week includes the following:

2/week: 1-hour individual psychotherapy sessions (1 primary, 1 secondary therapist) (*cognitive*)

4/week: 1½-hour psychotherapy groups (*cognitive*)

1/week: 1-hour Reiki session (*energy*)

1/week: 1-hour medical-massage session (*physical*)

1/week: 1-hour acupuncture session (*energy*)

4/week: 1-hour movement-therapy groups (*physical/bliss*)

4/week: 1-hour art-therapy groups (*cognitive/energy*)

4/week: ½-hour meditation groups (*wisdom/bliss*)

1/week: 1½-hour lifestyle-education group (*cognitive*)

5/week: ½-hour power walks (*physical*)

2/week: 2-hour water-polo sessions (*physical/bliss*)

4/week: 1½-hour physical-training sessions with NCOIC (*physical*)

1/week: 4-hour therapeutic outing (*bliss*)

1/week: 20-min. medical-management appt. every 2 weeks (*physical*)[14]

If you look carefully at this list you will notice that these treatments correspond perfectly to the koshas outlined in this book (*in italics*). At least one treatment for each level of the human being is represented here, an impressively effective holistic model.

## CHANGING YOUR OWN OUTCOME

So what does this mean for you, the reader? Many of you will not have the opportunity to participate in a holistic program. If you can, great! Go for it! Many of you will not want to or be able to afford medical treatments or find a specialist for your PTSD. The field of mental health is on the brink of precipitous change from old pathological models to compassionate holistic care such as the programs listed above. Honestly, right now there are not enough PTSD specialists to go around in either model. And, yet, there is so much that *you can do*.

I recommend that you make your own residential treatment plan. Go through each chapter and each kosha. Find the treatments that resonate with you the most (at least one per chapter), and write them down. Make an action plan for yourself and your healing. Ideally you will have therapeutic activities for yourself penciled in every single day. If you have a supportive friend, spouse, or family member, get that person involved supporting you in a positive and friendly way. If you don't have anybody like that in your immediate circle, go online. We have this wonderful blessing of the Internet now, a place where you can easily find other like-minded people working on their own healing. There are even online support groups for PTSD! Check in regularly with yourself and your treatment plans. Make time for doing so, and put it in your appointment book. I call these CEO days, time set aside for you to be the CEO of your own life. Healing from traumatic stress is arduous and requires time. There is no way to cut short on time and heal fully. You gotta do the dirt time!

With wisdom, patience, openness, and practice, all effects of trauma can be healed. We have the tools. Healing from trauma is a task we did not request. No one would wish for this kind of suffering. It is agony. And yet out of the dark seeds of trauma can emerge a healing fountain of wisdom, compassion, resilience, and strength. In the multidimensional healing of ourselves, we rise to the highest levels of our potentials as human beings and become a shining beacon of light for others and for the world.

# Acknowledgments

FIRST, I WOULD LIKE to thank my wonderfully supportive spouse and children for putting up with a dirtier house, missed appointments, later dinners, weekend days gone writing, and a generally more scattered brain during the considerable time it took to write this book. You guys rock!

I had many readers for this book, and I appreciate each and every one of you for your encouragement and good eyes: Peter Banitt, MD; Michael Berletich, MAcOM, LAc.; Marna Harrington; Scott Shephard, D.C.; Mark Lilly; Farah Damji; Elizabeth Lyon; and Lauri Grossman, D.C. Thanks also to my editors, Richard Smoley, Sharron Dorr and, especially, the eagle-eyed Will Marsh at Quest Books.

The universe has sent a stellar cadre of teachers, supporters, and guides over the years. Without you, this book could not have been birthed: Babaji Bob Kindler; Father Bob VerEecke, S.J.; Shannon Kelly; Ainslie MacLeod (and guides); Bessell Van Der Kolk, MD;

the Kripalu Center; Brian Weiss, M.D.; Karen Binder, LICSW; Stephen O'Neill, LICSW; Susan Weinstein-Winter, LICSW; Margot Mariana; Jean Houston; Elizabeth Lyons; and my agents, Jeff and Deborah Herman.

Other angels and synchronistic messengers include Rachel Sample; Julie Fast; the Willamette Writers Conference; Susan Hare, LMT; Molly Hottle of the *Oregonian*; Monique Gallagher; Jacob Teitelbaum, MD; Dickson Thom, DDS, ND; Jerry Vest, LISW, ACSW; Briant Nierstedt, LCSW; Danielle Cossette, LISW; and Peter Menice. You have helped and inspired me to have the courage to bring this book into being.

And last of all, a therapist is nothing without her clients. Obviously, you shall remain unnamed, but you all have taught me so much through the years. Know that your hard work on yourselves and patience with me and our process together has contributed to the information found in this book and will go out to help many others. Thank you!

# Notes

## INTRODUCTION

1. A Sanskrit word, *adhara* (pronounced aad-haar) means "substratum," "prop," or even "container." It describes the multidimensional human vehicle for universal consciousness (in other words, the human being) and was first put forward in writing by the Advaitan sage Adi Shankara (AD 788–820). His writings were translated, compiled, and published in 1921 in the small but potent book *Vivekacudamani* (Crest jewel of discrimination), which codified teachings that went back hundreds or maybe thousands of years in oral transmission from sage to student.

2. Most states have trained dispatchers and emergency teams that can evaluate emergency psychiatric conditions through their local counties. To find this information, go to the front of your local yellow pages. You could also call 211 for this information if it is available in your area.

## Tool 2

1. Some controversy has arisen about certain kava supplements causing a negative physical reaction to the liver in formulas that were not

275

traditionally prepared. Please check with a physician about the product you are using if you have any questions about its safety.

## TOOL 3

1. Daniel J. Siegel, *Mindsight* (New York: Bantam, 2010), 5.

2. Mark W. Smith, CAPT, CHC, USN, "Spirituality and Combat," (lecture, Atlanta, November 7, 2009).

3. These faiths all trace their origins back to a single man called Abraham.

4. Table is from Smith, "Spirituality and Combat." The "Indigenous" column is author's construction.

## TOOL 4

1. Jay Kogen and Wallace Wolodarsky, "Last Exit to Springfield," *The Simpsons*, (television program, March 11, 1993).

2. Arie Uittenbogaard, "Meaning and Etymology of the Name YHWH," Abarim Publications. Accessed May 3, 2011, www.abarim-publications.com/Meaning/YHWH.html.

3. Conventional Western scholarship would place the date closer, but according to oral history and ancient teachings many Indians would trace their lineage back many more thousands of years. Nobody really knows for sure. It could conceivably go back much further.

4. Long before Einstein, the rishis had their own theory of relativity. Theirs was not mathematical but an observation of the impermanence of all objects in the space-time continuum. They saw that in falsely identifying with three-dimensional reality through the ego/mind instead of with the immutable Brahman through the Atman, suffering occurs.

5. Some esoteric Christians believe that Jesus was referring to the third eye in this mysterious passage: "The lamp of the body is the eye. It follows that if your eye is clear, your whole body will be filled with light. But if your eye is diseased, your whole body will be filled with darkness. If then, the light inside you is darkened, what darkness there will be!" (Lk 11:34–35). All Bible quotations are from *New Jerusalem Bible*.

6. Jesus challenged everyone around him with this declaration of oneness: "In all truth I tell you, before Abraham ever was, I am" (John 8:58).

7. Perhaps this is why Jesus said, "In truth I tell you, anyone who does not welcome the kingdom of God like a little child will never enter it" (Mark 10:15–16).

8. Eckhart Tolle, *The Power of Now: A Guide to Spiritual Enlightenment* (Novato, CA: New World Library, 2004), 52.

9. Swami Madhavananda, *Sri Sankaracarya's Vivekacudamani* (Kolkata: Advaita Ashrama, 2003), 80.

## Tool 5

1. The website www.omega-research.com has dozens of links to research articles on the beneficial effects of omega-3 fatty acids.

2. J. D. Amsterdam, L. Yimei, I. Soeller, et al., "A Randomized, Double-Blind, Placebo-Controlled Trial of Oral Matricaria Recutita (Chamomile) Extract Therapy for Generalized Anxiety Disorder," *Journal of Clinical Psychopharmacology* 29, no. 4 (August 2009): 378–82.

3. E. G. Peniston and P. J. Kulkosky, "Alpha-Theta Brainwave Neurofeedback Therapy for Vietnam Veterans with Combat-Related Posttraumatic Stress Disorder," *Medical Psychotherapy: An International Journal*, 4 (1991): 47–60.

4. Steven M. Silver and John P. Wilson, "Native American Healing and Purification Rituals for War Stress," in *Human Adaptation to Extreme Stress: From the Holocaust to Vietnam*, ed. John P. Wilson, Zev Harel, and Boaz Kahana (New York: Plenum Press, 1988).

## Tool 6

1. One can get confused by the many different English spellings and capitalizations of these Chinese words. You will see tai chi also listed as taiji, t'ai-chi, or tai chi chuan. Likewise, qigong can be chi kung.

2. M. Enserink, "Luc Montagnier, French Nobelist Escapes 'Intellectual Terror' to Pursue Radical Ideas in China," *Science* 330, no. 6012 (Dec. 2010): 1732.

3. "Ley-lines," Ancient-wisdom: Online Prehistory, accessed September 9, 2011, http://www.ancient-wisdom.co.uk/leylines.htm

4. Mauro Emoto, *The True Power of Water* (Hillsboro, OR: Beyond Words Publishing, 2005), 145.

5. N. K. Subbalakshmi et al., "Immediate Effect of 'Nadi-Shodhana Pranayama' on Some Selected Parameters of Cardiovascular, Pulmonary, and Higher Functions of Brain," *Thai Journal of Physiological Sciences* 18 (2005): 10–16.

6. Swami Nikhilananda, trans., *The Gospel of The Holy Mother Sri Sarada Devi* (Madras: Sri Ramakrishna Math, 1984), 158.

## TOOL 7

1. According to the website of the National Center for Victims of Crime, one in four girls and one in six boys will be sexually assaulted before age eighteen. Studies have shown that up to 20 percent of the offenders of these children are fathers; for girls that statistic ranges from 30–50 percent (National Center for Victims of Crime, http://www.ncvc.org/ncvc/main.aspx).

2. Antoine Lutz et al., "Long-Term Meditators Self-Induce High-Amplitude Gamma Synchrony during Mental Practice," *Proceedings of the National Academy of Sciences of the United States of America* 101, no. 46 (2004): 16369–73.

## TOOL 8

1. "Michael Jordan/Public Enemy," *Saturday Night Live* (September 28, 1991).

2. In the 1990s there was a highly visible debate in the media about the validity of repressed memories. This debate in cognitive psychology has been resolved over the last decade, largely due to the research of Jennifer Freyd, PhD, at the University of Oregon, who has confirmed in numerous studies the existence and mechanisms of repressed memories.

3. "Purification" does not mean our minds are dirty, but rather refers to the need to clean up the confusion, misidentification, neurotic

tendencies, ignorance, and damage in the deep mind that we all carry from this and other lifetimes.

## TOOL 9

1. Rivers of Recovery, "Medical Research Study Summary," Univ. of Utah, Salt Lake City VA, Univ. of Southern Maine, 2009, www. riversofrecovery.org/what/medical_study.php.

2. Flash mobs are groups of people that assemble at public locations for entertainment and consciousness raising. They often involve dancing or singing. To the onlooker they seem spontaneous. YouTube has a number of flash-mob events one can view.

3. M. Gupta, *The Gospel of Sri Ramakrishna*, trans. Swami Nikhilananda (New York: Ramakrishna-Vivekenanda Center, 2000).

## TOOL 10

1. If you are interested in staying up to date on the latest treatments and research, you can set an alert word such as "PTSD" in your Google settings to have media results sent to your email inbox.

2. This frustrating reality can itself be triggering of the trauma of feeling helpless and uncared for. Many people bring a spouse, friend, or advocate along to doctors' visits to help keep track of information and keep them grounded in case a triggering situation in the doctor's office blocks their ability to remember details.

3. Laura D. Kubzansky et al., "Prospective Study of Posttraumatic Stress Disorder Symptoms and Coronary Heart Disease in the Normative Aging Study," *Archives of General Psychiatry* 64 (2007): 109–16.

4. Joseph A. Boscarino, "A Prospective Study of PTSD and Early-Age Heart Disease Mortality Among Vietnam Veterans: Implications for Surveillance and Prevention," *Psychosomatic Medicine* 70 (2008): 668–76.

5. Ahmadi Naser et al., "Post-Traumatic Stress Disorder, Coronary Atherosclerosis and Mortality," *American Journal of Cardiology* 108 (2011): 29–33

6. Laura D. Kubzansky et al., "A Prospective Study of Posttraumatic Stress Disorder Symptoms and Coronary Heart Disease in Women," *Health Psychology* 28 (2009): 125–30

7. B. Nowotny, M. Cavka, and C. Herder, "Effects of Acute Psychological Stress on Glucose Metabolism and Subclinical Inflammation in Patients with Posttraumatic Disorder," *Hormone and Metabolic Research* 42 (2010): 746–53.

8. M. Magarinos and B. McEwen, "Stress Effects on Morphology and Function of the Hippocamupus," *Annals of the New York Academy of Sciences*, June 1997: 271–84.

9. R. Bierer and L. Yehuda, "Transgenerational Transmission of Cortisol and PTSD Risk," *Progress in Brain Research* (2007): 121–35.

10. Geoffrey Fletcher, *Precious* (based on the novel *Push* by Sapphire), directed by Lee Daniels (Santa Monica, CA: Lion's Gate, 2009).

11. Joe Simpson, *Touching the Void* (New York: Harper Perennial, 1998).

12. Shelly Thorn, "Street Yoga Stories," *8 Limbs Yoga Blog and Information*, October 13, 2010, http://www.8limbsyoga.com/blog/index.php?s=street+yoga&submit=Go (accessed February 17, 2011).

13. Mark Lilly and Jaime Hedlund, RYT, "Healing Child Sex Abuse with Yoga," *International Journal of Yoga Therapy* 20 (2010): 120–130.

14. Fort Bliss Restoration and Resilience Center, http://www.tricare.mil/twr/downloads/RRCENTER.pdf (accessed February 17, 2011).

# Bibliography and Recommended Reading

Ahmadi, Naser et al. "Post-traumatic Stress Disorder, Coronary Atherosclerosis and Mortality." *American Journal of Cardiology* 108 (2011): 29–33.

American Psychiatric Association. *DSM-IV.* Washington, DC: American Psychiatric Association, 1994.

Amritasvarupananda, Swami. *Awaken, Children! Dialogues With Sri Sri Mata Amritanandamayi.* Vol. 6. San Ramon, CA: Mata Amritanandamayi Center, 1994.

Andrews, Ted. *Animal-Wise: The Spirit Language and Signs of Nature.* Jackson, TN: Dragonhawk Publishing, 1999.

Avdibegovic, E., A. Delic, K. Hadzibeganovic, and Z. Selimbasic. "Somatic Diseases in Patients with Posttraumatic Stress Disorder." *Medicinski Arhiv* 64, no. 3 (2010): 154–57.

Beckwith, Michael Bernard. *Spiritual Liberation: Fulfilling Your Soul's Potential.* New York/Hillsboro: Atria Books/Beyond Words, 2008.

Blome, Gotz. *Advanced Bach Flower Therapy.* Rochester, VT: Healing Arts Press, 1992.

Bonheim, Jalaja. *The Hunger for Ecstasy: Fulfilling the Soul's Need for Passion and Intimacy.* Emmaus, PA: Rodale Books, 2001.

Boscarino, Joseph A., "A Prospective Study of PTSD and Early-Age Heart Disease Mortality Among Vietnam Veterans: Implications for Surveillance and Prevention," *Psychosomatic Medicine* 70 (2008): 668–76.

Boscarino, J. A., C. W. Forsberg, and J. Goldberg. "A Twin Study of the Association between PTSD Symptoms and Rheumatoid Arthritis." *Psychosomatic Medicine* 72, no. 5 (June 2010): 481–86.

Bowman, Carol. *Children's Past Lives: How Past Life Memories Affect Your Child.* New York: Bantam, 1998.

Boyd, Doug. *Rolling Thunder.* New York: Dell, 1974.

Brennan, Barbara Ann. *Hands of Light: A Guide to Healing through the Human Energy Field.* New York: Bantam, 1987.

———. *Light Emerging: The Journey of Personal Healing.* New York: Bantam, 1993.

Brenner, Charles. *An Elementary Textbook of Psychoanalysis.* New York: Doubleday, 1974.

Brown, Daniel, Alan W. Scheflin, and D. Corydon Hammond. *Memory, Trauma, Treatment, and the Law.* New York: W. W. Norton, 1997.

Brown, Tom. *Grandfather.* New York: Berkley, 1993.

Chödrön, Pema. *No Time to Lose: A Timely Guide to the Way of the Bodhisattva.* Boston: Shambhala, 2005.

———. *When Things Fall Apart: Heart Advice for Difficult Times* Boston: Shambhala, 1997.

Chopra, Deepak. *Reinventing the Body, Resurrecting the Soul: How to Create a New You.* New York: Harmony Books, 2009.

Cori, Jasmin Lee. *Healing from Trauma: A Survivor's Guide to Understanding Your Symptoms and Reclaiming Your Life.* Cambridge: DaCapo Press, 2008.

Cousens, Gabriel. *Spiritual Nutrition.* Berkeley, CA: North Atlantic Books, 1986.

Csikszentmihalyi, Mihali. *Flow: The Psychology of Optimal Experience.* New York: Harper Collins, 1990.

Dalai Lama, The, and Howard C. Cutler. *The Art of Happiness.* New York: Riverhead Books, 1998.

Del Mastro, M. L., trans. *Revelations of Divine Love: Juliana of Norwich.* New York: Image Books, 1977.

DeWitt, Bryce, and Neill Graham, eds. *The Many-Worlds Interpretation of Quantum Mechanics.* Princeton: Princeton University Press, 1973.

Dobson, John, and Dr. Ruth Ballard. *Beyond Space and Time.* Hollywood, CA: Temple Universal Publishing, 1979.

Eckberg, Maryanna. *Victims of Cruelty: Somatic Psychotherapy in the Treatment of Posttraumatic Stress Disorder.* Berkeley, CA: North Atlantic Books, 2000.

Emoto, Masaru. *The Hidden Messages in Water.* Hillsboro, OR: Beyond Words, 2004.

———. *The True Power of Water.* Hillsboro, OR: Beyond Words, 2005.

Figley, Charles R., and Wiliam P. Nash. *Combat Stress Injury.* New York: Routledge, 2007.

Fort Bliss Restoration and Resilience Center, http://www.tricare.mil/twr/downloads/RRCENTER.pdf (accessed February 17, 2011).

Foster, Steven, and Christopher Hobbs. *Western Medicinal Plants and Herbs.* New York: Houghton Mifflin, 2002.

Freud, Sigmund. *The Ego and the Id.* New York: W. W. Norton, 1960.

Freyd, Jennifer. *Betrayal Trauma: The Logic of Forgetting Childhood Abuse.* Cambridge, MA: Harvard University Press, 1996.

Gill, J., M. Vythilingam, and G. G. Page. "Low Cortisol, High DHEA, and High Levels of Stimulated TNF-Alpha, and IL-6 in Women with PTSD." *Journal of Traumatic Stress* 21, no. 6 (December 2008): 530–39.

Gokulananda, S. *How to Overcome Mental Tension.* Kolkata: Ramakrishna Mission Institute of Culture, 1997.

Goleman, Daniel. *Destructive Emotions: A Scientific Dialog with the Dalai Lama.* New York: Bantam, 2004.

———. *Emotional Intelligence: Why It Can Matter More than IQ.* New York: Bantam, 1995.

Griggs, Barbara. *Green Pharmacy: The History and Evolution of Western Herbal Medicine.* Rochester, VT: Healing Arts Press, 1981.

Handwerger, K., and L. M. Shin. Is Posttraumatic Stress Disorder a Stress Induced Circuitry Disorder? *Journal of Traumatic Stress* 22 (2009): 5, 409–15.

Hay, Louise L. *Heal Your Body*. Carlsbad, CA: Hay House, 1982.

Heider, John. *The Tao of Leadership: Leadership Strategies for a New Age*. New York: Bantam, 1985.

Horner, Althea. *Object Relations and the Developing Ego in Therapy*. Lanham, MD: Rowman & Littlefield, 1984.

Houston, Jean. *Jump Time: Shaping Your Future in a World of Radical Change*. Boulder, CO: First Sentient Publications, 2004.

Ingerman, Sandra. *Soul Retrieval: Mending the Fragmented Self*. San Francisco: HarperCollins, 1991.

Ingram, Julia. *The Lost Sisterhood: The Return of Mary Magdalene, the Mother Mary, and Other Holy Women*. Fort Collins, CO: DreamSpeaker Creations, 2004.

Iyengar, B. K. S. *Light on the Yoga Sutras of Patanjali*. London: Thorsons, 1996.

Jensen, Derrick. *A Language Older Than Words*. White River Junction, VT: Chelsea Green, 2004.

Judith, Anodea. *Wheels of Light*. St. Paul: Llewellyn Publications, 1987.

Jung, C. G. *Memories, Dreams and Reflections*. New York: Random House, 1989.

———. *Synchronicity: An Acasual Connecting Principle*. Translated by R. F. C. Hull. Princeton: Princeton University Press, 1960.

Kabat-Zinn, Jon. *Full Catastrophe Living: Using the Wisdom of Your Body and Mind to Face Stress, Pain and Illness*. New York: Delacorte Press, 1990.

Kaplan, Gary B., Jennifer J. Vasterling, and Priyanka C. Vedak. "Brain-Derived Neurotrophic Factor in Traumatic Brain Injury, Posttraumatic Stress Disorder, and Their Comorbid Conditions: Role in Pathogenesis and Treatment." *Behavioural Pharmacology* 21, no. 5–6 (September 2010): 427–37.

Kaptchuk, Ted J. *The Web That Has No Weaver: Understanding Chinese Medicine*. Chicago: Congdon & Weed, 1983.

Katie, Byron, and Stephen Mitchell. *A Thousand Names for Joy: Living in Harmony with the Way Things Are.* New York: Random House, 2007.

Kaufman, Barry Neil. *Son-Rise: The Miracle Continues.* Tiburon, CA: H. J. Kramer Inc., 1994.

Kelly, Shannon. "Healing the Wounded Angels . . . The Foundation of Spiritual Magick: A Shaman's Perspective." Draft, 2005.

————. *Initiation: The Foundation of Belief.* Portland, OR: Soul Truth, 2008.

Kibler, J. L. "Posttraumatic Sress and Cardiovascular Disease Risk." *Journal of Trauma & Dissociation,* 10, no. 2, (2009): 135–50.

Kingsolver, Barbara. *Animal, Vegetable, Miracle: A Year of Food Life.* New York: HarperCollins, 2007.

Kluft, Richard P. *Childhood Antecedents of Multiple Personality.* Washington: American Psychiatric Press, 1985.

Kluger, Jeffrey. "Genetic Scars of the Holocaust: Children Suffer Too." *Time,* September 9, 2010: 9.

Kohanov, Linda. *Riding Between Worlds: Expanding Our Potential Through the Way of the Horse.* Novato, CA: New World Library, 2003.

Kubzansky, Laura D., Karestan C. Koenen, Avron Spiro III, Pantel S. Vokonas, and David Sparrow. "Prospective Study of Posttraumatic Stress Disorder Symptoms and Coronary Heart Disease in the Normative Aging Study." *Archives of General Psychiatry* 64 (2007): 109–16

Kubzansky, Laura D., Karestan C. Koenen, Cynthia Jones, and William W. Eaton. "A Prospective Study of Posttraumatic Stress Disorder Symptoms and Coronary Heart Disease in Women." *Health Psychology* 28 (2009): 125–30

Lambrough, Peter, and George Pratt. *Instant Emotional Healing.* New York: Random House, 2000.

Lazar, Sara W., Catherine E. Kerr, Rachel H. Wasserman, Jeremy R. Gray, et al. "Meditation Experience Is Associated with Increased Cortical Thickness." *NeuroReport.* 16, no. 17 (2005):1893–97.

Lerner, Mark D., and Raymond D. Shelton. *Comprehensive Acute Atraumatic Stress Management.* Commack, NY: American Academy of Experts in Traumatic Stress, 2005.

LeShan, Lawrence. *How to Meditate*. Boston: Little, Brown, 1986.

Levine, Peter A. *Waking the Tiger: Healing Trauma: The Innate Capacity to Transform Overwhelming Experiences*. Berkeley: North Atlantic Books, 1997.

Levine, Peter A., and Maggie Kline. *Trauma Through a Child's Eyes*. Berkeley: North Atlantic Books, 2007.

Lewis, Thomas, F. Amini, and R. Lannon. *A General Theory of Love*. New York: Random House, 2000.

Lilly, Mark, and Jaime Hedlund, LYT. "Healing Child Sex Abuse with Yoga." *International Journal of Yoga Therapy* 20 (2010): 120–30.

Loyd, Alex, and Ben Johnson. *The Healing Code*. Peoria, IL: Intermedia Publishing Group, 2010.

Lutz, Antoine, Lawrence L. Greischar, Nancy B. Rawlings, Matthieu Ricard, Richard J. Davidson. "Long-Term Meditators Self-Induce High-Amplitude Gamma Synchrony during Mental Practice." *Proceedings of the National Academy of Sciences of the United States of America* 101, no. 46 (2004): 16369–73.

MacLeod, Ainslie. *The Instruction*. Boulder, CO: Sounds True, 2009.

McCourt, Frank. *Angela's Ashes*. New York: Simon & Schuster, 1996.

Millman, Dan. *The Way of the Peaceful Warrior*. Tiburon, CA: H. J. Kramer, 1980.

Morehouse, David. *Psychic Warrior: Inside the CIA's Stargate Program: The True Story of a Soldier's Espionage and Awakening*. New York: St. Martin's, 1996.

Morgan, Marlo. *Mutant Message Down Under*. New York: Harper Collins, 1994.

Mortensen, Greg, and David Oliver Relin. *Three Cups of Tea*. New York: Viking Penguin, 2006.

Muni, Swami Rajarshi. *Awakening Life Force: The Philosophy and Psychology of "Spontaneous Yoga."* St. Paul, MN: Llewellyn Publications, 2004.

Nachman-Hunt Nancy. "The Spirituality of Feeling: An Interview With Michael Jawer." *Advances in Mind-Body Medicine* 24, no. 4 (Winter 2009–2010): 24–28.

Nan, Huai-Chin. *Tao and Longevity: Mind-Body Transformation*. Boston: Red Wheel/Weiser, 1984.

Narby, Jeremy. *Shamans through Time: 500 Years on the Path to Knowledge*. New York: Penguin, 2004.

Nhat Hanh, Thich. *Anger: Wisdom for Cooling the Flames*. New York: Riverhead, 2002.

————. *The Miracle of Mindfulness*. Boston: Beacon Press, 1976.

Nicolson, N. A., M. C. Davis, D. Kruszewski, and A. J. Zautra. "Childhood Maltreatment and Diurnal Cortisol Patterns in Women with Chronic Pain." *Psychosomatic Medicine* 72, no. 5 (June 2010): 471–80.

Nikhilananda, Swami, transl. *The Gospel of the Holy Mother Sri Sarada Devi*. Madras: Sri Ramakrishna Math, 1984.

Nityaswarupananda, Swami. *Astavakra Samhita*. Kolkata: Advaita Ashrama, 1996.

Nordqvist, Christian. "Post Traumatic Stress Disorder Doubles Premature Death Risk in Veterans." November 18, 2010. www.medicalnewstoday. com/articles/208518.php.

Nowotny, B., et al. "Effects of Acute Psychological Stress on Glucose Metabolism andSubclinical Inflammation in Patients with Posttraumatic Stress Disorder." *Hormone and Metabolic Research* 42, no. 10 (September 2010): 746–53.

Ogden, P., K. Minton, and C. Pain. *Trauma and the Body: A Sensorimotor Approach to Psychotherapy*. New York: W.W. Norton, 2006.

Orloff, Judith. *Dr. Judith Orloff's Guide to Intuitive Healing: 5 Steps to Physical, Emotional, and Sexual Wellness*. New York: Bantam, 2000.

Ornstein, Robert E. *The Psychology of Conciousness*. San Francisco: W. H. Freeman, 1972.

O'Toole, B. I., and S. V. Catts. "Trauma, PTSD, and Physical Health: An Epidemiological Study of Australian Vietnam Veterans." *Journal of Psychosomatic Research* 64, no. 1 (January 2008): 33–40.

Peniston, E. G. & P. J. Kulkosky. "Alpha-Theta Brainwave Neurofeedback Therapy for Vietnam Veterans with Combat-Related Post-traumatic Stress Disorder." *Medical Psychotherapy: An International Journal* 4 (1991): 47–60.

Perkonigg, A., T. Owashi, M. B. Stein, C. Kirschbaum, and H. U. Wittchen. "Posttraumatic Stress Disorder and Obesity: Evidence for a Risk Association." *American Journal of Preventive Medicine* 36, no. 1 (2009): 1–8.

Pert, Candace B. *Molecules of Emotion: Why You Feel the Way You Feel.* New York: Scribner, 1997.

Prabhavananda, Swami, and F. Manchester, trans. *The Upanishads: Breath of Eternal.* Hollywood: Vedanta Press, 1983.

Prior, Stephen. *Object Relations in Severe Trauma.* Lanham, MD: Rowman & Littlefield, 1996.

Radin, Dean *The Conscious Universe: The Scientific Truth of Psychic Phenomena.* New York: Harper Collins, 1997.

Ruiz, Don Miguel. *The Four Agreements: A Practical Guide to Personal Freedom.* San Rafael, CA: Amber-Allen Publishing, 1997.

Rasmusson, Ann M., Paula P. Schnurr, Zofla Zukowska, Erica Scioli, and Daniel E. Forman. "Adaptation to Extreme Stress: Post-traumatic Stress Disorder, Neuropeptide Y and Metabolic Syndrome." *Experimental Biology Medicine* 235, no. 10 (October 2010): 1150–62.

Salzberg, Sharon. *Lovingkindness: The Revolutionary Art of Happiness.* Boston: Shambhala, 2008.

Sams, Jamie. *Dancing the Dream: The Seven Sacred Paths of Human Transformation.* San Francisco: HarperCollins, 1998.

Sams, Jamie, and David Carson. *Medicine Cards: The Discovery of Power Through the Ways of Animals.* New York: St. Martin's, 1999.

Sanford, Linda T. *Strong at the Broken Places: Overcoming the Trauma of Childhood Abuse.* New York: Avon Books, 1990.

Sankaracarya, Sri. *Vivekacudamani.* Translated by Swami Madhavananda. Kolkata: Advaita Ashrama, India, 2003.

Schemmerer, Richard. *Reconnection with the Power of Love: Co-Creation with the Intelligence of the Heart.* Bloomington, IN: AuthorHouse, 2004.

Schiraldi, Glenn R. *The Post-Traumatic Stress Disorder Sourcebook: A Guide to Healing Recovery, and Growth.* New York: McGraw-Hill, 2000.

Schwartz, Richard C. *Internal Family Systems Therapy.* New York: The Guilford Press, 1995.

Scott-Tilly, Donna, Abigail Tilton, and Mark Sandel. "Biologic Correlates to the Development of Posttraumatic Stress Disorder in Female Victims of Intimate Partner Violence: Implications for Practice." *Perspectives in Psychiatric Care* 46, no. 1 (January 2010): 26–36.

Seng, Julia S. "Posttraumatic Oxytocin Dysregulation: Is It a Link Among Posttraumatic Self Disorders, Posttraumatic Stress Disorder, and Pelvic Visceral Dysregulation Conditions in Women?" *Journal of Trauma & Dissociation* 11, no. 4 (2010): 387–406.

Shapiro, Francine. *Eye Movement Desensitization and Reprocessing.* 2nd ed. New York: The Guilford Press, 2001.

Shapiro, Francine and Margo Silk Forrest. *Eye Movement Desensitization & Reprogramming: The Breakthrough "Eye Movement" Therapy for Overcoming Anxiety, Stress, and Trauma.* New York: Basic Books, 1997.

Siegel, Daniel J. *The Mindful Therapist.* New York: W. W. Norton, 2010.

———. *Mindsight: The New Science of Personal Transformation.* New York: Bantam, 2010.

Simmons, Robert and Ahsian Naisha. *The Book of Stones: Who They Are and What They Teach.* Berkeley: North Atlantic Books, 2007.

Simpson, Joe. *Touching the Void* (New York: Harper Perennial, 1998).

Solomon, M. and Siegel, D. J., eds. *Healing Trauma: Attachment, Mind, Body, and Brain.* New York: W. W. Norton, 2003.

Spitzer, C., S. Barnow, H. Volzke, B. Lowe, and H. J. Grabe. "Association of Posttraumatic Stress Disorder with Low Grade C-Reactive Protein: Evidence from the General Population." *Journal of Psychiatric Research* 44, no. 1 (2010): 15–21.

Sturgess, Stephen. *The Yoga Book.* Rockport, MA: Element Books, 1997.

Subbalakshmi, N. K., et al. "Immediate Effect of 'Nadi-Shodhana Pranayama' on Some Selected Parameters of Cardiovascular, Pulmonary, and Higher Functions of Brain." *Thai Journal of Physiological Sciences* 18, no. 2 (2005): 10–16.

Sullivan, Kathleen. *Unshackled: A Survivor's Story of Mind Control.* Tempe, AZ: Dandelion Books, 2003.

Taylor, Jill Bolte, *My Stroke of Insight: A Brain Scientist's Personal Journey.* New York: Viking, 2008.

Terr, Lenore. *Too Scared to Cry*. New York: Basic Books, 1990.

Thorn, Shelly, *8 Limbs Yoga Blog and Information*. October 13, 2010. http://www.8limbsyoga.com/blog/index.php?s=street+yoga&submit=Go.

Tolle, Eckhart. *A New Earth: Awakening to Your Life's Purpose*. New York: Dutton, 2005.

———. *The Power of Now: A Guide to Spiritual Enlightenment*. Novato, CA: New World Library, 2004.

Turk, Jon. *The Raven's Gift: A Scientist, a Shaman, and Their Remarkable Journey Through the Siberian Wilderness*. New York: St. Martin's, 2009.

van Dernoot Lipsky, Laura, and Connie Burk. *Trauma Stewardship: An Everyday Guide to Caring for Self While Caring for Others*. San Francisco: Berrett-Koehler Publishers, 2007

Venkatesananda, Swami. *Vasistha's Yoga*. Albany, NY: State University of New York Press, 1993.

Vivekenanda, Swami. *The Complete Works of Swami Vivekenanda*. (Vols. 1, 3, 4). Kolkata: Advaita Ashrama, 1989.

Walker, Evan Harris. *The Physics of Consciousness: Quantum Minds and the Meaning of Life*. Cambridge, MA: Perseus Publishing, 2000.

Wansbrough, Henry, ed. *The New Jerusalem Bible*. New York: Doubleday, 1990.

Wauters, Ambika. *Chakras and Their Archetypes: Uniting Energy, Awareness, and Spiritual Growth*. Berkeley, CA: The Crossing Press, 1997.

Weiss, Brian. *Many Lifetimes, Many Masters: The True Story of a Prominent Psychiatrist, His Young Patient, and the Past-Life Therapy That Changed Both Their Lives*. New York: Simon & Schuster, 1988.

———. *Messages From the Masters*. New York: Warner Books, 2000.

Whitecliff, Angelika. *21 Days with Braco*. Kealakekua, HI: Awakening Within, 2009.

Wilson, James, and Jonathon Wright. *Adrenal Fatigue: The 21st Century Stress Syndrome*. Petaluma, CA: Smart Publications, 2001.

Wingenfeld, K., D. Wagner, I. Schmidt, G. Meinischmidt, D. H. Hellhammer, and C. Heim. "The Low Dose Dexamethasone Suppression Test in Fibromyalgia." *Journal of Psychosomatic Research* 62, no. 1 (January 2007): 85–91.

Whitaker, Kay Cordell. *The Reluctant Shaman: A Woman's First Encounter with the Unseen Spirits of the Earth.* San Francisco: HarperCollins, 1991.

Wilson, John P., Zev Harel, and Boaz Kahana, eds. *Human Adaptation to Extreme Stress: From the Holocaust to Vietnam.* New York: Plenum Press.

Wolf, Fred Alan. *The Yoga of Time Travel: How the Mind Can Defeat Time.* Wheaton, IL: Quest Books, 2004.

Woolger, Roger. *Healing Your Past Lives: Exploring the Many Lives of the Soul.* Boulder, CO: Sounds True, 2004.

Yogananda, Paramahansa. *Autobiography of a Yogi.* Los Angeles: Self-Realization Fellowship, 2009.

# Index

**Quest Books**
encourages open-minded inquiry into
world religions, philosophy, science, and the arts
in order to understand the wisdom of the ages,
respect the unity of all life, and help people explore
individual spiritual self-transformation.

Its publications are generously supported by
The Kern Foundation,
a trust committed to Theosophical education.

Quest Books is the imprint of
the Theosophical Publishing House,
a division of the Theosophical Society in America.
For information about programs, literature,
on-line study, membership benefits, and international centers,
see www.theosophical.org
or call 800-669-1571 or (outside the U.S.) 630-668-1571.

**Related Titles**

*Breathe Into Being*, by Dennis Lewis

*Drawing from the Heart*, by Barbara Ganim

*Feng Shui for the Body*, by Daniel Santos

*The Meditative Path*, by John Cianciosi

*Spiritual Healing*, by Dora van Gelder Kunz

*War and the Soul: Healing Our Nation's Veterans
from Post-traumatic Stress Disorder*, by Edward Tick

*Yoga for Your Spiritual Muscles*, by Rachel Schaeffer

To order books or a complete Quest catalog,
call 800-669-9425 or (outside the U.S.) 630-665-0130.